D1631616

Gordon Brown

Gordon Brown

The First Year in Power

Hugh Pym and Nick Kochan

BLOOMSBURY

First Published 1998
Bloomsbury Publishing Plc 38 Soho Square London, W1V 5DF

Copyright © 1998 by Hugh Pym and Nick Kochan

The moral right of the authors has been asserted

PICTURE CREDITS

Alpha: page 1 *top* (Andrew Knutek), page 2 *top* (Steve Finn), page 5 *bottom*
(Marco Deidda), page 6 *top*
Camera Press: page 7 *top* (Andrew Hasson)
Express Newspapers Plc: page 4 *top right*, page 7 *bottom left*
Independent Picture Syndication: page 8 *bottom*
Network: page 3 *top* (Andrew Ward)
PA News: page 1 *bottom* (Rebecca Naden), page 2 *bottom* (Lucy Husband), page 3
bottom (Stefan Rousseau), page 4 *bottom* (Adam Butler), page 5 *top* (Ben Curtis),
page 6 *bottom* (Sean Dempsey), page 7 *bottom right*
Rex Features, London: page 4 *top left* (Richard Young)
Scottish Television Enterprises: page 8 *top*

A CIP catalogue record for this book is available from the British Library

ISBN 0 7475 3701 1

10 9 8 7 6 5 4 3 2 1

Typeset by Hewer Text Ltd, Edinburgh
Printed in Great Britain by Clays Ltd, St Ives plc

This book is dedicated to Julius Kochan,
and Andrew, Jonathan and Kirsty Pym

Contents

Acknowledgements

Many busy people, both in and out of government, have given freely of their time to help us. Most wish to remain anonymous; we thank them all.

We would also like to thank our agent and patient friend David O'Leary for his sane counsel. Keith Grey has provided tireless support with administration; and Lawrence Joffe has transcribed uncomplainingly and with unusual flourish.

Susan Pym and Laura Lehman-Kochan have given us all their support and we cannot thank them enough; Caroline Pym has minded grandchildren way beyond the call of duty.

Finally we would like to thank everybody at Bloomsbury Publishing for the dedication and speed they have applied to a project which called on all our resources.

London, 9 June 1998

Introduction

It was another rabbit out of Gordon Brown's hat. Just as he had caught the City – and the country – on the hop when he gave the Bank of England independence to set interest rates when he first came to power, so thirteen months later he conjured up another surprise. This time he was throwing out the old conventions on public finances, declaring to the House of Commons that the traditional annual haggle over departmental spending was to be abolished in favour of a fixed three-year plan. This set the seal on the first burst of reforms he had pioneered for the New Labour Government.

Here, in June 1998, was a Chancellor who was in his element. He was capturing the headlines, not just with his economic policies but also with a high-profile visit to Paris to see Scotland play in the World Cup. His usually stiff-set features were relaxed as he gave a television interview about his love for football. To cap it all, he was interviewed on prime-time television by the glamourous presenter Ulrika Johnsen.

Gordon Brown has been a dominant figure in the New Labour Government, and is shaping up to be one of the most powerful post-war Chancellors. He has commanded widespread support, but has by no means satisfied everyone. There have been mutterings about how he threw his weight around in Whitehall, and some members to the Left of the

Party have set him up as the bogeyman. Only the day before Brown's dramatic Commons statement the MP Ken Livingstone attacked him in an article in the *Independent*, calling him, in as many words, power-crazed, myopic and reactionary in the extreme. Livingstone alleged that Tony Blair had given Brown unprecedented powers for a Chancellor in return for Brown's agreement to stand aside from the 1994 leadership contest.

The unusual nature of Gordon Brown's relationship with the Prime Minister poses a teaser for those who watch the political stage. In some fields of policy, Brown seems at least as powerful and decisive as Tony Blair himself. The history of their relationship, dating back to the moment Blair took power as leader of the Labour Party, is shrouded in mystery. Brown's extraordinary access to the ultimate power at Number 10 has bred suspicion and jealousy – particularly among other ministers.

Brown's critics decry him as a tight-fisted Chancellor, but there are many dimensions to his character. He has contrived so far to appear as both a radical romantic who draws on his religious and Scottish roots for inspiration and idealism and a ferocious pragmatist who will exercise power single-mindedly. Whether or not the burdens of office will allow him to continue doing so is one of the question marks over his future in power.

Brown's personal life is no less intriguing. The common belief that Brown is a one-dimensional workaholic and political addict is being disabused by the emergence of a relationship – with public relations executive Sarah Macaulay – to absorb the very few spare hours between waking and sleeping open to the Chancellor. But the uncertain outcome of that relationship (at the time of writing) is destined to keep the public guessing.

The essence of Brown's personality is equally opaque. Friends talk about his charm, wit and 'cuddliness', while colleagues complain about the dour Presbyterian Scot surrounded by his aggressive lieutenants and scowling in the corner at Cabinet meetings.

His political qualities are beyond question – a fact that was recognized with his designation as the *Spectator* Parliamentarian of the Year in 1997. But Chancellors always argue that they should be judged only over the longer term, and this has certainly been the case with Brown, for whom long-termism has become nothing short of a mantra. So, early judgements are prone to error and this book does not attempt to give a definitive verdict.

However, Brown's first year has been a fascinating lesson in how one man and his colleagues can devise an agenda in opposition and implement it in power. In many ways it is also indicative of the inside story of Labour back in office after eighteen years in the wilderness.

Chapter One: The First Days in Office

Gordon Brown had never known a moment like it. Hundreds of Civil Service staff, from the top mandarins to the shift-working cleaners, were cheering him. They had lined the hallway, the stairs and the balcony, overlooked by the imposing bust of Charles James Fox, as Brown entered the Treasury. It was 4 o'clock on the afternoon of 2 May 1997. He had just been appointed Chancellor of the Exchequer and the Treasury staff had turned out to see in the new man, who would provide Labour's first pair of hands on the economic levers of power in eighteen years. Not since Ramsay MacDonald and his Labour colleagues arrived in Downing Street in 1924 had the great offices of state been taken up by politicians with no experience of government. As Brown climbed the elegant staircase the civil servants had spontaneously burst into applause. Exhausted but exhilarated in the aftermath of victory, he was taken aback. It was, he told his advisers, the best experience of his political career.

But he quickly regained his composure as he moved into the Treasury's first-floor corridor. There was to be no time for sentiment or reflection on Labour's astonishing election landslide. Brown had an agenda carefully mapped out. Alongside him was his trusted quartet of advisers who had slogged with him through the last exhausting years of opposition: Ed Balls, the bespectacled thirty-year-old economics adviser; Sue Nye, Brown's tall, blonde personal assistant who had endured the agonies of defeat in 1992 in Neil Kinnock's private office; Charlie Whelan, chain-smoking, tough-talking press adviser; and Ed Miliband, his youthful, lanky political adviser.

Escorted by Sir Terence Burns, the Treasury's chief civil servant, they marched along the drab corridors which could have passed for those of a pre-war hospital. Sir Terry showed them into the Chancellor's office, a long, high-ceilinged meeting-room with a large mahogany table and eighteen chairs in the centre, a desk at one end and a set of armchairs at the other.

'Well, Chancellor, where shall we start? Perhaps I could talk you through the briefs for incoming ministers which my staff have drawn up,' said the Treasury Permanent Secretary. He was expecting that after a short meeting the new Chancellor would want to depart with his red boxes for a weekend of reading and rest.

'There is something important we must discuss,' said Brown. Whelan, Nye and Miliband took this as their cue to leave the room to start inspecting the other offices.

'Read this,' said Brown as he handed Sir Terry an envelope. The Treasury man took out two pages of A4 paper and raised his eyebrows in astonishment. It was a draft letter from Brown to the Governor of the Bank of England, Eddie George, indicating that the new Chancellor wanted to hand over his powers in the setting of interest rates. It was effectively giving the Bank of England independence, the most radical shift in monetary policy in half a century. 'And I want to do it on Tuesday,' said Brown, 'which will mean working all weekend, so let's start now.'

The crowds were still milling around the bottom end of Whitehall, savouring the extraordinary atmosphere following Blair's arrival in Downing Street. They were pressed up against the Downing Street gates, hoping for a glimpse of one of the new Cabinet ministers leaving Number 10. Paper Union Jacks were littering the pavements. It was 6 o'clock in the evening and Charlie Whelan had sneaked out of the Treasury for a drink at the Red Lion pub immediately opposite. Whelan had never pretended to be an economist and he was happy to make excuses while the 'pointy heads', as he liked to call them, got down to business. It was more than thirty-six hours since he had last slept but Whelan was in his element. Always gregarious, convivial and a lover of the political gossip mill, he lapped up the congratulations from lobby journalists eager to hear the inside story of Labour's dramatic night of victory. He had no intention of revealing that fifty yards away his colleagues had already got down to work on a bold and hitherto unexpected political manouevre. Whelan was beginning to wonder about the danger of a leak over the Bank Holiday weekend. He was a master of the art of timing information flow to the media; it had been his role in the long build-up to the election. But Whelan knew it was fatal to lie to journalists – if found out it would destroy his credibility. Better by far to be evasive with the truth and to wriggle free before telling an outright untruth. But suppose a journalist asked directly, 'Are you giving the Bank control over monetary policy?' It was a possibility which would haunt Whelan for the whole of that weekend.

Sir Terence Burns and the Treasury mandarins may have been shocked, but this first dramatic initiative of the New Labour Chancellor, indeed the first initiative of the New Labour Government, can be traced back five years. Ed Balls, as a young journalist on the *Financial Times*, had written a pamphlet setting out the case for Bank of England independence. At the time Labour policy was to reform the Bank and its secretive management board, the so-called 'Court', but no one in the Party was advocating handing over control of interest rate policy. After joining Gordon Brown's team in 1994, Balls dusted down his paper and discussed it with the Shadow Chancellor. Reworked but unchanged in essence, it reappeared in the spring of 1995 as a paper submitted at an election strategy meeting.

At the meeting were Tony Blair, Gordon Brown, Ed Balls, Philip Gould, Blair's polling guru, and others from the leader's staff. Economics were not high on the agenda, the talk was more of focus groups and the packaging of policy. But Brown and Blair were sensitive to the charge that Labour had no economic policy, that for all the talk of Welfare to Work and skills there was no economic 'big picture' in place. Balls's paper might at least head-off that criticism. It talked of a policy framework for a

Labour government, the need for stability after the rollercoaster ride under the Tories. It laid down building blocks such as the aim of borrowing only for investment, not current spending. And it spelled out that this was a model which would pave the way for an independent Bank of England.

In May 1995 both Tony Blair and Gordon Brown made important economic policy speeches. Blair gave the annual Mais lecture, an event attended by the great and the good in the City. For most of the financiers present it was a first glimpse of the new Labour leader and a first opportunity to assess the substance of the man apparently on the march to Downing Street. The core of the speech reflected the Balls document. It proclaimed Labour's adherence to tough rules on public spending and commitment to reform of the Bank of England. Brown's speech at a Westminster conference put more flesh on the bones but specifically stopped short of advocating immediate independence for the Bank. Structural reforms, yes – for example setting up a monetary policy committee with outside experts to assist the Governor and the Bank's own staff. But the Shadow Chancellor said that moving further would only be contemplated if the Bank had built up a good track record of advice.

The words used amounted to a carefully crafted formula designed to steer Labour through until the election. At the time Kenneth Clarke, the Chancellor, seemed to be in open warfare with Eddie George. Clarke was very publicly defying the advice of the Bank and refusing to put up interest rates. It was a smart political judgement, Clarke in the end being proved correct with his assessment that the economy was not sufficiently strong to need higher interest rates. But whatever the rights and wrongs, Brown did not want to get trapped into taking sides. If he had announced then that he favoured more autonomy for the Bank it would have been interpreted as 'Labour backs George against Clarke' and 'Labour backs high interest rates'.

So Brown and Balls proposed that Labour look at reform and the case for Bank of England control over interest rates, but stressed that they were not committed to it. To blur their position even further, Brown and Balls did not use the word 'independence'. Allowing the Bank 'operational responsibility for setting interest rates' was the goal which Labour laid down but only, of course, after the Bank had proved itself with a 'good track-record of advice'.

So it was with a holding position on the Bank of England that Labour went into the 1997 election campaign. Brown and Blair could talk extensively of the need to reform decision-making at the Bank, the need for openness and greater accountability. That played well with the Party and, they hoped, with former Tory voters. Where they were vulnerable was from attacks by the Liberal Democrats, who had for some time advocated full independence for the Bank of England. Malcolm Bruce, the Lib Dem Treasury spokesman, would taunt Labour for the vagueness of their policy; it would offer the worst of both worlds, he argued, with control over interest rate policy falling awkwardly between Whitehall and Threadneedle Street. But Bruce's attacks did not create waves. Much to Charlie Whelan's relief, Gordon Brown got through fifty interviews and press conferences during the campaign without being seriously questioned over his plans for the Bank of England.

In fact it was not until the last days of the campaign that Brown decided that if elected his first act as a Labour Chancellor would be to hand over control of interest rates to the Bank. On a visit to the United States in March he had met Alan Greenspan and been impressed again by the arguments for an independent central bank on the American model. He remarked to Balls how extraordinary it was that interest rates in the US were never discussed as a political issue, in stark contrast to the controversy surrounding Ken Clarke's handling of monetary policy. On the flight home he told Balls and Whelan that he had made up his mind on the issue. Back at Westminster he phoned Tony Blair who agreed in principle and left it to Brown to decide the timing.

On the Tuesday night before polling day, meeting with his advisers as they so often did at Labour MP Geoffrey Robinson's flat above the Grosvenor House Hotel, Brown announced that he wanted to move on Bank of England independence immediately upon taking office. Whelan was delighted. Economic arguments aside, he believed it would be a 'monster story' and a political masterstroke. Geoffrey Robinson was not so sure and needed some persuading. After all, he had experienced the last Labour government and had reservations about losing control of monetary policy.

The following day, while Brown chaired Labour's final election press conference, Balls and Robinson stayed at the flat working on a draft letter to Eddie George. Balls dug into the files on his laptop computer and extracted his 1995 document on the Bank of England. With some deft cutting and pasting they pulled out and polished the central passages. Balls remembers that writing this 'Dear Governor' letter seemed a weird and amazing thing to do while so many friends and colleagues were out making their final push against the Tories. Brown later suggested minor changes and another draft was produced. Forty-eight hours later it would be presented to Sir Terence Burns and his Treasury colleagues. Thus was created the most radical monetary policy initiative since 1945.

There was an important strategic consideration underpinning Brown's decision to take this radical step. Once in office he knew he would find it nigh impossible to resist pressure for an increase in interest rates. For months Ken Clarke had opted to hold rates steady despite ever-increasing demands from the City for a tightening of policy. Eddie George made little attempt to conceal his view that rates would rise steadily whoever won at the polls. So, Brown and his team asked themselves, did they really want the history books to record that their first act in power within a week of Labour's landslide victory was to set in train an increase in mortgage rates? Announcing independence for the Bank of England on the day of the election victory would grab the attention – whatever decision was made on an interest rate increase. And with all this Brown's gut instinct was that if they did not move instantly on reform of the Bank of England the initiative might become bogged-down and blocked by opponents within the Treasury.

And so while new Labour ministers and MPs were still relishing the moment of triumph, and while traffic built up on the main routes out of London ahead of the May Bank Holiday weekend, there was a buzz of activity at the heart of the Treasury.

Nick McPherson had been Kenneth Clarke's Principal Private Secretary for three years, the Treasury civil servant who was effectively the Chancellor's personal assistant. It was a punishing role which involved many late nights and weekends in the office. McPherson had done more than the usual stint and was looking forward to a transfer to another post in the Treasury in December 1996. But after some persuasion he reluctantly agreed to remain until after the election. By the morning of 2 May he was exhausted but delighted still to be serving in the Chancellor's office. With the rest of the country he had stayed up late to see his new political masters sweep into power. Early the following morning he had helped Ken Clarke shift his belongings out of Number 11 Downing Street. There had been precious little time; the Blairs, anxious to move their family into the flat at Number 11, had signalled that they wanted to get on with it. When Brown arrived that afternoon McPherson remembers an 'amazing sense of enthusiasm, excitement and new purpose' which contrasted with the dying days of the minority Tory administration. And from that moment on there were perpetual meetings right through the weekend. 'It was an extraordinary scene,' he recalls, 'as we tried to choreograph wall-to-wall meetings and inflow and outflow of officials.'

Once Brown had fired the gun for the changes to the Bank of England, the leading Treasury civil servants responded in the finest Civil Service tradition. Sir Terry Burns remembers a 'whirlwind . . . things got off at a cracking pace'. In the last week of the campaign he and his colleagues had done the groundwork for legislation to set up an independent central bank but only to bring Britain into line with European rules should the new government decide to join the single currency. Burns had anticipated an informal arrangement allowing the Bank of England some autonomy. But Brown's draft letter and desire to move immediately to Bank independence had come out of the blue. 'It was a considerable surprise that they were prepared to legislate,' he said later.

So the preliminary Treasury work had not been in vain. The five civil servants who had toiled for long hours in the last days before the election on an outline Bank of England Bill now began working furiously to the tight timetable set by the new Chancellor. They worked solidly through Friday, Saturday and Sunday nights. Only a handful of staff was involved in the exercise, on a strictly 'need to know' basis. They were all impressed by the detailed homework which Brown and his advisers had obviously done. As one Treasury official remarked later, 'We weren't exactly expecting them to arrive in government with precise ideas on reform of the court of the Bank of England.' And civil servants like nothing better than a clearly focused brief from their politicians. 'Once the instructions were received, people welcomed the opportunity, there was a great feeling of excitement,' recalled Nick McPherson. By 10 o'clock on the Saturday morning they had produced a draft for discussion with Brown and Balls. Some minor changes to the letter were proposed and a pile of supporting briefs had been drawn up.

While the Treasury crackled with the electricity generated by the new Chancellor – outline plans for the first Budget as well as for the Bank of England were being chewed over in numerous different meetings – Brown's ministerial team was arriving. The names had all been agreed with Tony Blair well before polling day. One Treasury insider remembers it thus: 'The ministers were appointed at curious times of the day, often in the middle of meetings. Geoffrey Robinson and Dawn Primarolo suddenly walked in immediately after being appointed.' Helen Liddell and Alistair Darling completed the team, the latter as expected becoming Treasury Chief Secretary, the controller of the purse-strings.

Darling had flown down from his Edinburgh constituency at his own expense, still a 'member of the public' until he had made his appearance at Number 10 Downing Street to be appointed by Tony Blair. 'That day was very curious. I went straight to a meeting with Gordon, then there was this unwelcome intrusion when we had to go to the Cabinet Office to be rehearsed through being made privy counsellors.' Brown was one of the few new Labour ministers already a member of the Privy Council. Darling and the other newcomers were rehearsed six at a time by a Whitehall mandarin with a sketch on the floor to illustrate the elaborate series of movements for the swearing in and kissing of hands. For new Labour ministers with no previous experience of government this ceremony must have seemed absurd, while at the same time providing a daunting reminder of the realities of taking office. At 6 o'clock they were shipped in a convoy of Rovers to Buckingham Palace for the ceremony in the presence of the Queen. That evening Darling stayed with friends at their farmhouse in Essex. Over a glass of Pimm's he savoured the lovely May evening. 'They said, what does it feel like to be a member of the Cabinet . . . it was the first time I had thought about it like that.' But he was back at the Treasury at 8 on the Sunday morning.

Throughout that first Sunday in office meeting followed meeting as Brown's dramatic new initiative was honed and polished. He slipped out of the Treasury late in the afternoon and was driven in his new ministerial Rover through Trafalgar Square and across Oxford Street, unnoticed by the crowds of tourists. His destination was Islington and an address he had visited on countless occasions – 1 Richmond Crescent, home of Tony and Cherie Blair. Here the then leader and Shadow Chancellor had plotted strategy and policy changes while in opposition. There had been frequent Sunday evening meetings over mugs of coffee, the two men lounging in armchairs, papers strewn around them, sometimes joined by Alastair Campbell and Ed Balls or party strategists like Margaret McDonagh.

This was to be Brown's last visit to Richmond Crescent. The new Prime Minister and his family were busy packing boxes with toys, books and clothes ready for the removal lorries to transport them all to Downing Street the following morning. By agreement they were to move into the spacious flat above the Chancellor's official residence at Number 11 Downing Street. Brown was happy to settle for the pokier attic apartment next door; it would, after all, mean he had made it to Number 10.

This time Brown's mission was simple. He pulled out the draft letter to the Bank of England Governor and showed it to Blair. They had briefly discussed it in Downing Street on the Friday afternoon but Brown was now confirming his intention to press ahead with the plan on Tuesday morning; Tony Blair readily and enthusiastically agreed. He could see the strategic advantages in moving swiftly and surprising the financial markets. And he was pleased that after all the slog of reforming Labour's economic policy Gordon Brown would be heading the first initiative of the new government. He asked Brown to contact and inform his Cabinet colleagues, starting with John Prescott and Robin Cook.

Brown and Blair discussed another matter as they sat among the crates and boxes. The junior ministerial ranks of government were now being filled and the new Prime Minister ran through his choices, most of which had been decided well before 1 May. A key appointment was the Europe Minister at the Foreign Office. Brown had earlier pressed the claims of Doug Henderson, an old ally and someone who was in step with the Chancellor over the single currency. In opposition Henderson had held a Home Affairs brief and had never been part of the Shadow Foreign Affairs team. He was not the first choice of Robin Cook, who would have preferred the left-winger Peter Hain or the incumbent from the Shadow team, Joyce Quin. To Brown's satisfaction Blair confirmed that Henderson was to have the job. It came as a shock to the affable Scotsman who was resting at home in his Newcastle North constituency. He took a call from Blair that Sunday afternoon. The message was, 'I want you to be Minister of State at the Foreign Office, get the first plane down'. Within hours Henderson was at Blair's home in Islington. After a short briefing he was dispatched to Brussels for a Council of Ministers meeting the following day. Henderson was to become Labour's first envoy to Europe, with authority to signal a historic break with the Conservative years by confirming that Britain would sign up to the Social Charter.

By the morning of the May Bank Holiday Brown was ready to bring the Bank of England into his confidence and inform the Governor of his new powers. Nick McPherson phoned Eddie George at his South London home and asked him to come into the Treasury. George replied that he and the Deputy Governor were shortly to leave for a meeting in Frankfurt. McPherson stressed that the Chancellor personally wanted to meet the Governor that day, so in due course Eddie George and Gordon Brown were sitting facing one another across the long table in the Chancellor's office. It was a fascinating encounter, a new Labour Chancellor confronting the pivotal figure in the financial establishment, and a Conservative-appointed one to boot. As far as the press and the outside world knew, it was a meeting scheduled to take place the following Wednesday. Enquiring journalists had been told that was the day for Brown's first session with the Governor. As the television cameras and journalists camped around Whitehall focused on the removal lorry in Downing Street and a track-suited Cherie Blair hurrying in and out of her new residence, the Chancellor got down to business.

Brown handed his draft letter to George and outlined his plan for a nine-strong monetary committee to be headed by the Governor. A second Deputy Governor was to be appointed and the two deputies would sit on the committee alongside Mr George. The Chancellor would appoint four outside members, the Governor two more from inside the Bank. The committee would be vested with the power to decide the level of interest rates and the Chancellor would only be free to overrule them at a time of a national emergency. George was astonished but delighted. He left asking for time to consult his colleagues at the Bank. But the Chancellor's line as they communicated later by phone was, 'You've got twenty-four hours, take it or leave it; we have to get legislation into our first Queen's Speech and if you say no you won't get another chance for at least a year and a half.' George then indicated his approval.

Later that day Brown and his advisers strolled along Whitehall past the crowds at the foot of Downing Street and up to Number 11, official home for generations of Chancellors of the Excheq-uer. It was a relief getting away from the frenetic atmosphere at the Treasury and they managed to relax a little as they explored the draughty, high-ceilinged rooms. Brown himself had never been inside Number 11 before. Here they discussed how they would unveil the Bank of England announcement the following day. Whelan drew up a presentation strategy for Jill Rutter, the head of the Treasury Press Office. Reuters were to be informed just before the markets opened at 8 in the morning and leading political editors were to be tipped off. They were to be told of the Chancellor's meeting with the Governor and of a later press conference allowing them to assume that interest rates would rise. However, crucially, there was to be no mention of the moves towards independence for the Bank of England. That, Brown and Whelan had decided, must be held back and sprung on the media and the markets later on the Tuesday morning.

Whelan, fresh from the presentational triumphs of the Labour election campaign, envisaged a presidential-style press conference, to be screened live on Sky TV and viewed by dealers around the City. He wanted Brown on a podium carrying the sign 'HM Treasury' with the famous government crest 'Dieu et mon Droit', well lit and projecting the image of authority and control. Treasury staff, accustomed to off-camera briefings only, were bemused. As one insider put it, 'we tried to avoid holding press conferences with Ken Clarke as we didn't want them hijacked by questions about Tory splits on Europe.' And there was no question of a ready-made Treasury backdrop or podium. Whelan contacted the Labour Party's favourite set designers and gave them the brief to deliver early the following morning.

There was a momentary panic for Whelan on the Monday night. Robert Peston of the *Financial Times* called him to enquire whether the Chancellor was bringing forward his meeting with the Governor. His spin doctor's guile tested to the limit, Whelan bluffed his way through the call and threw Peston off the scent. But through the Tuesday morning the strategy turned to reality, exactly as planned. As radio and television bulletins speculated about an interest rate rise, the Gordon and Eddie show was playing for the first and last time inside the Treasury. On the advice of the Governor of the Bank of England the Chancellor decided to raise interest rates by one-quarter per cent to 6.25 per cent. In future, Brown noted, it would be George and his new committee who would make such decisions. That news was conveyed to economics correspondents who were kept under guard with briefing notes inside the Treasury until the press conference got underway. There was just time for Brown to put in courtesy calls to former Chancellors of the Exchequer to inform them of his plan for the Bank of England. The Tories Howe, Lawson and Lamont all supported the move. Denis Healey, the last Labour Chancellor, did not. Brown's immediate predecessor Kenneth Clarke was not contactable: messages were left but not answered. The new Chancellor also spoke to Alan

Greenspan, the American Central Bank chief, who passed on his congratulations.

As planned, Brown's announcement surprised and pleased financial analysts and pundits. It completely overshadowed the rise in interest rates. Indeed, as Brown and his team noted later, long-term interest rates in the markets fell with the perception that the Bank of England would make a better job of monetary policy than the politicians. The stock market certainly seemed to ignore the higher cost of lending as shares surged to a record level. The secret had held, there had been no leaks, and the press coverage could not have been rosier. 'Flash Gordon gets off to a flying start' was the *Independent*'s comment, the *Daily Mail* referred to Brown's 'dramatic double coup'. To Brown's particular satisfaction it was the lead story in the *Washington Post*, the *New York Times* and the *Wall Street Journal*. On a trip to a youth-training scheme in South London the following day Brown was preparing to push out new lines to the press. But Whelan blocked it. The Chancellor, he reasoned, could hardly improve on that morning's coverage, so better to quit while ahead.

Reflecting two months later, Gordon Brown was in no doubt that he had got the timing right: 'It was the only time you could have done it without there being huge allegations about political manipulation . . . if you had done it at two months people would have said, "He's got a problem here, hasn't he, he's trying to get out of it."' To Brown the over-riding issue was credibility and the need to convince the financial markets that the Labour government was not in the business of making decisions in its party political interest.

Buoyed by the near universal praise for his pre-emptive strike – which most commentators concluded was the most significant shake-up at the Bank of England in its 300-year history – Brown finished his first week in office in high spirits. He threw a party for new MPs at Number 11 Downing Street on the Thursday and another for lobby journalists on the Friday, the drinks paid for out of his own pocket. He cracked jokes about the Blair family in the flat above and whether Jack Straw would impose a curfew on them. There was an impromptu speech of thanks from the chairman of the parliamentary press gallery, Michael White;

and sprinkled among the guests from the economics and political media were staff from Labour's Millbank Tower. Brown was keen to extend his generosity to the foot-soldiers of the Party as much as the glittering stars of the campaign team.

For Gordon Brown and his new ministerial colleagues an extraordinary week in British politics was ending on a high note. It seemed like an age since the election victory. The City of London establishment, so often the scourge of Labour governments, could not heap sufficient praise on the new political masters. The newspapers were fawning and unwavering in their enthusiasm. Brown, rather than Blair, had taken the limelight in this first act of the New Labour administration.

Blair was familiar to every household because of his pre-eminence in the election campaign, but now his relatively unknown right-hand man, the Chancellor, was stealing the show. People wanted to know more about the dark, brooding Brown.

Chapter Two: Thane of All He Surveys

Twenty years ago Gordon Brown was a legend in his native Scotland, a phenomenon among free thinkers and political activists the country over. His long hair reaching down to his shoulders, his plastic-bagfuls of papers, his absolute prohibition on luxury and his chaotic lifestyle were testimonies of a man who was determined never to belong to the status quo. His seemingly endless store of inventive ideas aimed at shaking up his university, his country and his Party ensured he was in the vanguard of all radical thinking in Scotland. His ferocious will, idealism and drive attracted crowds of admiring fans and political sympathizers.

When Labour won the election in 1997, Brown's image had changed to fit the times. The long hair had long gone, the plastic bags had been replaced with shiny briefcases and red ministerial boxes, and a middle-class girlfriend from London was eradicating the neglect of creature comforts. But the man himself had hardly changed. He had the same nervous energy, lack of pretension and irreverence, the same 'Howya doing! Did ya see the match last night? Good, ah! Pity about the ref. Now, about this policy we're doing . . .' sort of informality as always. Meanwhile, Brown's television performances continued to show the old Scots ruggedness.

The same continuity was not obvious in Brown's politics,

however. The son of the manse had won friends through his idealism and ability to challenge the establishment. But now he was preaching what many perceived to be right-wing economics for pragmatic political purposes. Brown's challenge now is to keep those who know the Old Brown loyal while continuing to forge ahead with the New Labour politics which he has nurtured with Tony Blair.

Brown's rugged politics were made in two places: his local church and Edinburgh University. As a young child Brown used to hear his father, a Presbyterian minister, railing against the ills of society. Reminiscing, he says: 'You cannot be brought up going to church twice a day on Sundays for most of your first fifteen years without it having a big effect on you!' That took him into the Labour Party, and as early as the age of twelve he was canvassing in elections. He was delighted when he heard that Sir Alec Douglas Home had been ousted as Prime Minister. It was a victory for the plain folk, of which the Browns counted themselves honourable members.

The pulpit is the one place in which Presbyterians give vent to passion and Brown's speaking techniques betray these roots. English ears may just hear rousing oratory; but Scottish listeners discern something else – in the same way that African–Americans brought up in the Southern Baptist tradition responded when they heard Martin Luther King, or react when they hear Jesse Jackson today. An old friend of Brown's, the Scottish geriatrician Colin Currie, says, 'Gordon has a kind of triple-rhythm thing, with a distinctive rising Presbyterian accentuation: "I will say this bit in this tone of voice, then go up half a tone, and then again." But you know he cannot go up forever, so it is a bit like *Bolero*! If Rory Bremner listened a little more carefully, he could do Brown even more effectively than he does!'

Hard and unselfish labour was a theme regularly propounded in his father's sermons. On one Sunday, for example, Gordon heard his father say: 'Men and woman perhaps never had more leisure time than today; the working week was for many never shorter, and yet the common reply for some called to service is: "We have no time, we are so very busy." Is it true that people are as busy as they make themselves out to be? Or is it just an absence of discipline or systematic method?' Gordon would have to follow his father's injunction and work harder than anyone else.

These paternal and church influences stressing the simple ethical principle that work is good for you has made Brown a model for Cabinet colleagues, his constituents and also for his family. When his younger brother Andrew was feeling low some years ago, Gordon reminded him of Ramsay Macdonald's solution to the grief he was feeling after the death of his wife: work, work and work. Andrew's more relaxed approach to life (albeit he is still a successful television editor) may explain why Gordon told a newspaper reporter that he thought his brother was 'spoilt', apparently forgetting that Andrew was at his side when he was in shock at the time of John Smith's death.

Brown's family background gives some clues as to the way he is split between social revolutionary and economist. His father's family were tenant farmers who lived modest lives. His mother's family, on the other hand, came from thriving commercial stock, and at twenty-one she was a director of the well-established family building firm, John Souter of Aberdeenshire. Children of business people typically go into professions but the junior Browns were swayed by their father's social conscience to enter politics, and each of the three boys now has some political involvement.

Moral virtues like service and commitment appear with almost the same degree of repetition in Gordon Brown's academic and personal writings as do long-termism and fairness in his political writings. They are also evident in the deep furrows on his brow and the swept-back dark curls of hair when he is wrapped up in work. Brown shares with his mentor and late friend, the former Labour Party leader John Smith, the view that we are not sent to this earth to enjoy ourselves, but to carry out a practical purpose – to develop our talents to serve others. But whereas Smith had a love of wine, women (his wife and three daughters) and song, Gordon Brown takes it all very seriously. Carol Craig, an old friend from college, says, 'I have never met anyone as focused as Gordon on getting on and doing what was of interest to him, at great personal expense. You don't do what Gordon has done without missing out on most of what life has to offer.'

At a young age Gordon was already developing a social conscience. When he accompanied his father to visit the poor fisherfolk of Kirkcaldy after the sea wall had burst and the coastal area was ruinously flooded in the 1950s, he saw the meaning of a loss of income. When he read about the Holocaust he instinctively felt for its victims. As a schoolboy aged twelve, Gordon Brown wrote eloquently against Nazi persecution of the Jews in a newspaper article, and identified with the unemployed and the underprivileged. Later, his sense of human dignity and an identification with suffering brought him close to the problems of the Third World and real poverty. Brown's compassion for the genuinely dispossessed is tempered by his contempt for the work-shy in the prosperous First World.

At Edinburgh University, Brown learned the science of politics. He became the second student rector and impressed the fellow-students with the power of his political nous as well as his innovative ideas. Says Craig: 'Gordon was very charismatic, he was very unusual, he had a lot of confidence, he was very intellectual, and he was definitely very attractive to people because he had that sense of a young man that was going places, and people used to say that he was a future leader of the Labour Party.' This was a time when many of his radical university colleagues were moving into far left and anarchist organizations, such as Bill Campbell, Brown's contemporary and later his publisher, but Brown stuck by the Labour Party.

While at Edinburgh, Brown began work on a PhD on the Scottish Labour Party. This would eventually lead to his writing a book on James Maxton, the Scottish independent socialist. Maxton was one of Brown's Socialist heroes, but the biography does not pull its punches in criticizing him for putting ideological purity before political pragmatism. It was a mistake Brown himself would aim to avoid at all costs, and on 2 May 1997 Brown moved into power, whereas his hero never did. Professor Ben Pimlott, a political historian, stresses the importance of Brown's intellectual background: 'Unlike most members of the Cabinet, he has roots in the movement, some understanding of the origins of old Labour, its Socialist origins. Although he takes a hard line, he is driven by a mission.'

Brown expresses his commitment to the Party with a passionate enthusiasm which will not be thwarted or contradicted. He believes he is part of a great mission based on ideas which will bring real and long-lasting change and he is unstoppable. Colin Currie says: 'Working with Brown is a real intellectual adventure. The man is fascinated by ideas. I often remember these weekend "seminars", where we would wrestle through an idea and I would go away, only to come back to Gordon and wrestle with it a bit more!' Colleagues talk about Brown's sponge-like ability to suck up ideas and splurge them out at a great rate of knots if they will advance the New Labour cause.

His capacity for systematic work is sometimes questioned by civil servants. They suggest Brown gets fixed on a single policy or strategy to the detriment of other matters which require his attention at the same time, like the red boxes and the dull administration integral to the Chancellor's job. But it would be a brave civil servant who dared complain to Brown, as he has a quite ferocious temper.

Helping him sort out his writing and clarify his thoughts is a small group of friends, led by Colin Currie, that includes a number of MPs and Treasury colleagues. They turn his outpouring of thoughts into sentences, and support him when he is under pressure. These intimates see a quite different side to his personality from the public; they talk about his vulnerability, charm and charisma laced with little private jokes and ironic asides that are lost on the intrusive media. Carol Craig says, 'Gordon attracted people who wanted to give up time and energy to service – doing research, writing speeches, giving him ideas. He had a whole team of people who always did that.'

Brown pushes himself to the limit, punishing all around him with his dedication to bring his ideas to reality. He can type through until early in the morning on speeches to perfect them, and drives himself and others to distraction as he demands their involvement in the process. If the speech is not finished, he will go home, sleep a few hours and rise early to start again. By the time he returns to the office he is worn to a shred, haggard and drawn; his neck is barely able to support his head, his nails are bitten down even further – to the point where those around him feel an almost sympathetic pain. The nail-biting is disturbing and looks deeply neurotic, leading to concern that Brown brings too much pressure on himself for his own good.

Old friends say that Gordon Brown is never happier than when he is slinking into a bookshop or a library, or scribbling out his immediate thoughts and then bouncing them off his mates. 'He is his own best researcher,' Currie says. Brown is on record as saying that more than anything else he hated being called an academic, and much preferred the description of ideologue. Yet some feel that the intellect overwhelms the personality, making Brown almost too scholarly, too dry to achieve his goal of being the supreme politician.

Brown's passion for perfectionism has made him a very powerful political opponent, one at whose hands many have suffered. Opponents in the former Conservative government say he was alone in giving them the sort of dusting they rarely received at the hands of Labour politicians. Journalist Anthony Howard saw Michael Heseltine shortly after John Smith died. 'Michael asked, "Who will be the next leader of the Labour Party?" I said, "No doubt at all, Tony Blair." He said, "You must be joking, that boy's never laid a glove on me. Now you take Gordon Brown, he's hit me twice and he hit me hard." Michael recognized him as a serious heavyweight. Remember that Commons speech about Heseltine and the tigerskin? In this game, when you are hit, you know you are hit!'

On the platform Brown can be relaxed even when regaling an audience off the top of his head rather than from a prepared script when necessary. He says that when he arrived at the Labour Friends of Israel meeting at the 1997 Labour Party Conference he had not expected to have to give a speech. Fifteen minutes later he was on his feet, discoursing on his father's early interest in Israel (Brown senior was chairman of the Church of Scotland's Israel Committee) and then using learned scholarly quotes to praise the Jewish principle of family support for each of its members. His carefully written and targeted address to the Conference, designed to warn public sector unions against demanding excessive pay rises, paled in comparison. Brown revels in his ability to think on his feet, once confiding that he had lost a page of a speech on Welfare to Work, but 'I knew enough about the subject to fill up the gaps. It didn't show, did it?'

Brown never misses a trick on detail, as Nigel Lawson has discovered. On one occasion Brown was preparing a speech to attack Lawson on the topic of 'teenage scribblers' and he was determined to land a hard punch. He went to endless lengths to find details to ensure he got it absolutely right, even to the point of sending a researcher away to dig up Lawson's writing when he had been the *Sunday Telegraph*'s City editor decades earlier. In due course, the researcher discovered a contradictory statement from an old article, which had the former Chancellor reeling in a Commons debate. Brown is a perfectionist with all his work, and cannot lay down a speech if there is a word or paragraph out of place. He wants every gap in his defences covered, there must be no Achilles heel, and no missed opportunity to land a blow and maximise his adversary's pain to greatest effect. He was still playing around with paragraphs in his March Budget the day before it was due to be printed. The script had clumps of text in brackets, just in case he wanted to insert it and remove another part. Stories of Brown's perfectionism are legion. He once spotted a phrase in a press release which had the tone of old Labour, and he insisted the entire print-run be pulped and reprinted.

Brown's high-speed lifestyle and single-minded dedication come at the price of a minimal private life. This suggests eccentricity to the many who have a traditional image of a politician. While Brown enjoys considerable public affluence as a minister, he lives in a private squalor. The aggressive troublemaker of Kirkcaldy is overwhelmed by the minutiae of everyday living. So shopping and domestic tidiness get neglected. Friends say it is doubtful whether he has made half a dozen trips to the supermarket in his life, and he is unlikely to know the price of a pint of milk. Tales abound of his lack of familiarity with the commercial world. On one occasion he sent out an aide to buy his standard suit from Marks and Spencer – he is not a great experimenter with clothes – but the shop had run out. The aide, working against a tight deadline, had to find something for his man to wear that night. He rushed to a tailor who had to produce something quickly and expensively.

He thought Brown might be less than happy but to his surprise Gordon was delighted and wanted three more.

Then there is Brown's vagueness. On one occasion he was so immersed in a conversation about political tactics that he opened a car door into on-coming traffic and saw the door smashed and swept away in an instant.

Brown's domestic chaos is legendary. During his university days, visitors would find him with just a couple of tins of baked beans in the cupboard and papers and books everywhere. Such was his devotion to work that for days he would eat no more than the bare essentials. Home is now a substantial turn-of-the-century detached villa in North Queensferry near Edinburgh. Guests can roam around a sitting-room where the curtains are drawn but a Scalextric set is still set up – left over from his nephews' visit months before. Whether the Chancellor watches the cars go round in an occasional idle moment between pamphlets can only be guessed at.

In the hall the wallpaper has peeled off the wall and the sitting-room furniture comprises no more than fragile garden chairs and a rickety table. The curtains hang precariously on their railings. The kitchen has been modernized, but only at the behest of Brown's girlfriend, Sarah Macaulay, who insisted that it needed a revamp when she started spending time at the house. (She arranged it, because she knew her partner would never get round to it.) To the outsider, this house seems strangely bleak for a holder of high office. But to the puritan Brown this is home as he likes it.

Brown's passion for football puts him in the respectable company of many great politicians, but the fanaticism with which he pursues it is slightly eccentric. He is quite capable of watching three games a day on the television perched over his desk. He will bust a gut to get to a match where he will fling his arms around with the best of the fans. Even when he goes to America on holiday he searches out bars with satellite televisions running games back home.

The gusto and simple energy that he used to display when he sold programmes at Raith Rovers have stayed with him into adulthood. The Treasury Minister, Helen Liddell, recalls one occasion in the office. 'We were up to our ears, just a few weeks into government, my press officer who's Scottish suddenly remembered she wanted away early that day because she was going to watch the Scottish Cup Final – you could see the envy in Gordon's face. He said, "I wish I was going to that." I said, "You're the Chancellor, I'm sure we could get you tickets." But he wouldn't allow that. He wouldn't abuse his position.' Brown's football addiction is shared by many of the people with whom he has surrounded himself, like Ed Balls, Charlie Whelan and Geoffrey Robinson.

Brown's fierce drive to win makes him an uncompromising ally. Colleagues know before they join the team that he has a ferocious temper. He flies off the handle easily when challenged or obstructed, sending opponents into cold sweats and friends into embarrassed silences. Brown's own silences are so awesome that colleagues know when not to speak out of turn. Peter Mandelson and other colleagues in opposition and government have felt the lash of his tongue. Brown has often warned colleagues that so and so 'wants to do us in', as if politics was Gorbals gang warfare with Brown a gang leader taking a rival honcho behind the flats for a beating.

His skills at planning and political tactics are greatly admired Although he is not so ruthless, his immediate colleagues are notorious for their aggression and turf-watching. Observers speak of him having a group of ministers and friends watching Brown's back. Friends and gang members like Nick Brown (Chief Whip), Dougie Henderson (Minister for Europe) and Nigel Griffiths (Minister of Consumer Affairs) quietly watch Brown's patch and try to fend off the Blairites.

TUC General Secretary John Monks is not one of Brown's closest friends, but he respects him nonetheless: 'He's very far-sighted, in political fighting terms. He's got a base, he's got a network, and when the government was formed you saw the power of the network. Prescott's got a network, but he didn't have as many people and they didn't go as far. This is a clan of people who owe their first loyalty to Gordon Brown. Then he has the strong and loyal Private Office who are combative, bright and courageous; Charlie Whelan is highly imaginative and effective.

'In Scotland more than anywhere else, Brown is building a

network of people. Dewar stands between Blair and Brown. Certainly Gordon wouldn't have had Cook in Scotland, he would much rather have had him as Foreign Secretary. Brown is very combative. He has considerable gifts of charm, and the political gift of schmoozing.'

Brown enjoys the political dust-up, the chance to make a good speech and get the applause. A gentle smile plays around his lips and he juts his neck forward as he lands blows on his opponents. When the words are flowing, Brown has great rhetorical flourish, reminiscent of Michael Foot in his prime. Lord Healey, Labour's last Chancellor, recounts that when he saw Brown giving a speech in his first campaign for the Dunfermline East seat, he marked him down as a future Prime Minister. But later, when he saw him on television, he crossed him off the list as a Labour leader. 'Brown's performances fall so far short of Blair's that there was no contest when the Party had to choose a leader,' says Healey. 'He did very well in the Commons, but not on television. There he tends to talk like a zombie. He has a bad eye and a very slack lower jaw. He looks humourless but, if you know him, he is full of humour, and has one of the most charming and genuine smiles I know when he is amused. He also has great ability. Immense. As Chancellor you have to have a brain. But he is not an intellectual in the sense of letting his mind play over the whole of life.'

The former Chancellor and Foreign Secretary says that Brown might have made a successful eighteenth-century Prime Minister, but now the Labour political powers that be need someone to capture an audience of Middle Englanders who demand a smooth TV appeal and a promise of a soft, comfortable, middle-class life to come. The Scotsman's tense body language, diffident smile and gaucheness are not ideal for mass public consumption, working against Brown's chances for the premiership. Brown may yet believe he can attain the ultimate prize for his personal sacrifice as the leader of his Party; he may also be prepared to wait as long as it takes to be summoned. But his friends fear that he will waste away his life and opportunities hankering after something for which he is not well suited. They say that the man with the social conscience may lack the egotistical ruthlessness necessary for leadership. Some claim that the extent of his hunger for the job was tested when a friend phoned him after the news of the death of John Smith to ask him what he was doing to rally his cause. 'I'm thinking, I'm thinking,' was the response. He was also reportedly writing John Smith's obituary at the same time as the Blair camp was mustering its forces. Feelings had welled up that overwhelmed his capacity to undertake the rational scheming necessary to lead a campaign for Labour's top job. He wanted to be left alone by the world, to retreat into his Scottish eyrie; the Party and loyal supporters were calling for his leadership and he was not there.

Carol Craig, now an expert on personnel management, gives an insight into Brown's failure to seize the opportunity: 'Gordon was not cut out for the cut and thrust of politics, for the intrigue, for the double-dealing . . . he always hated it, and it gave him a lot of personal angst. Conniving doesn't come naturally to him, it goes against the grain. He doesn't shuffle off easily things that are emotionally challenging.' But she thinks he may be changing to accommodate to power and influence. 'He has had to toughen himself up and do it very deliberately, because by nature he is very sensitive and he wants everyone to like him. He doesn't cope well with people disliking him. He feels he is an honourable guy and he finds it very difficult to deal with people stabbing him in the back. It is a fundamental part of him.'

Brown's disappointment has seeped into the public domain, but he has still got down to the duties of government with the enthusiasm that infused his years in opposition. There are fewer live football matches in his diary and he has more meetings to attend and official documents to read. He says he misses the time in the open air that he could take when in opposition, as now his main activity has to be thinking about policy and planning speeches. He spends long nights in the Treasury attacking his word processor, banging the keys with a vengeance until sweat pours off his brow.

He still also passes his wealth of thoughts on to his team of writers led by Colin Currie. And his colleagues still gather, as they always have, in his study (newly renovated by his nephew, to his great delight) overlooking the Firth of Forth, where they absorb a romantic view over to Edinburgh Castle, Arthur's Seat and the Forth Bridge. Brown can mull ideas over as he surveys the vastness of the water and the endless grey sky, listens to CDs, dips into one of the books on his well-stocked shelves and watches soccer. There, he is the thane of all he surveys, cut off from the outside world, the world of unplastered walls and unfurnished rooms, the world of Westminster and of bitter politics. The relief for a man who feels the uncomprehending world rests on his shoulders is almost tangible.

His comfort was having at the end of a phone- or fax-line the constant advice of some of new Labour's brightest and best. One in particular had been a friend in adversity and was now a pillar in power.

Chapter Three: Ed Balls – Youthpower

Anthony Powell would have revelled in it: Ed Balls's wedding to Yvette Cooper may yet be the source for a Cool Britannia novelist to write trilogies on the self-conscious enjoyment of new power. This was New Labour on show. The guest-list for the happy event at the Cavendish Hotel in Eastbourne in January 1998 contained the cream of the country's trendy media, the people who were making the image: Will Hutton and Andrew Marr, top brass from the *Financial Times* like the acting editor Andrew Gowers and economist Martin Wolf, and a number of young New Labour MPs with their children.

This was not just New Labour, it was also New Treasury; spin-doctors like Charlie Whelan and fellow adviser Ed Miliband were there too. Multi-millionaire businessman and minister Geoffrey Robinson with his glamorous wife promenaded on Eastbourne beach alongside the Chancellor, who made a rare and carefully choreographed public appearance with his girlfriend Sarah Macaulay especially for Ed's do.

Three hundred or so guests crowded into the lobby of the splendid hotel to listen to the wedding speeches. (Children played in the crèche thoughtfully provided elsewhere in accord with best New Labour principles.) The speakers' microphone was situated in a balcony on the first floor overlooking the guests below; the scene had shades of the triumphalist election rally of eight months before. The two best men and two best women charted at length the short but brilliant careers of Ed and Yvette – something, one guest commented bitchily, that seemed to interest the speakers more than their friendship with the happy couple.

A bitter-sweet laugh was raised by an allusion to 'neoclassical endogenous growth theory', the highfallutin piece of economics which Balls had written into a speech for Gordon Brown and which Michael Heseltine picked on, saying it was 'not Brown's but Balls's'. That was a *faux pas* made before the New Labour administration had even taken power, but the Eastbourne in-crowd tittered at the way their nuptial host had stolen some unwelcome limelight from his boss. Then Ed and Yvette addressed the crowd below: one tall, broad and bespectacled, the other only slightly shorter and pretty enough to be regarded as one of the belles of the new intake.

Ed Balls and his new wife live in the New Labour heartland of London's Canonbury and are bright and shining stars of the Party. Both had become prominent at Westminster since the last election. Yvette, MP for Pontefract and Castleford, is the granddaughter of a Cumbrian miner (as she would remind those who dared to doubt her socialist credentials) and a former writer for the *Independent*. She is one of the youngest MPs of the new intake, a protégé of Gordon Brown's confidently expected to rise through the ranks.

Ed Balls had achieved one of the most powerful positions in the land. He was closer to the Chancellor than any minister except Tony Blair. He was making economic policy, he had the highest civil servants at his beck and call, and had become a media star. To have achieved this by the tender age of thirty has taken some doing. Ed's brains are the stuff of media legend and his capacity for spotting trends in economics is beyond question, though whether he is quite the most remarkable outsider in the Treasury since John Maynard Keynes, as some suggest, has yet to be proved.

His ability to develop a relationship with Gordon Brown, where so many have failed, is as remarkable as his ability to pass exams. In fact the two men complement each other well. Where Brown is diffident and ill at ease with the people that run the Civil Service and great institutions of State, Balls is confident and breezy. He might as easily have had a high-flying career in a major company, the World Bank or the Civil Service itself as in politics, and some say he might still do so.

Balls's facility with economics is stimulating and useful, but Brown is unquestionably the master and decisive in determining policy. Where the younger man comes in useful is as a foil for flak from ministerial colleagues, the Treasury and the media, and his reputation for intellectual brilliance reflects well on economic policies so long as they keep working. If the policies come unstuck Balls's star could dim as quickly as it rose, and the press won't miss a chance to kick him where it hurts.

Born in Norwich in 1967, Ed Balls grew up in Nottingham where, like former Chancellor Ken Clarke, he attended Nottingham High School. Ed's father, a zoologist who works in the field of animal testing (he edits a learned periodical on the subject to which Ed Balls has contributed articles on animals, morality and the law), was the Labour Party's chairman of the local ward and that was how Ed got into the Labour Party. There was no great ideology involved. His dad wanted to pack the meetings with loyal supporters and Ed was willing to play ball. 'Dad got me to join because he needed some votes. I was always a Labour Party member and became education officer for my ward.'

In fact Ed, or Eddie as he was known by his friends, was not that interested in Labour politics at university, and when he went to Keble College, Oxford, to read Politics, Philosophy and Economics he joined all the main parties' political societies after reading a novel by Geoffrey Trease in which one of the characters does the same thing. It was basically a way of meeting people, especially politicians, and Ed got known at Oxford for being gregarious.

In his second year he was persuaded to stand for President of the Junior Common Room, the college student union that arranges social life and provides student representatives for the college bodies. He was a likeable sort of chap and got elected, but no one at the time could have envisaged that Ed's presidency would cause a furore that old colleagues still remember.

As President of the JCR, Ed had the job of leading negotiations on behalf of the students with the college authorities to decide that year's rent rise. In most years, the radical students put in for an unrealistically low rise, leading to conflict, threats of strikes and bad feeling. So Ed thought: be different, be moderate. He proposed a small rent rise that the authorities might just accept. Left-wing students fought him bitterly; they sent him hate letters, they voted him down in a vote of no confidence, they caused havoc at the college. Meetings that were usually ignored by apathetic students were packed out, and Ed became an object of speculation. He kept his position by winning a referendum and now claims he won a tactical victory on the rents by applying the principle he later pressed on the Chancellor, namely, 'Be radical, but only when it is credible.' That enabled Balls to embarrass the Principal of the college who wanted to show his University colleagues how tough he could be with bolshie students.

It was here, in the college union, that Eddy acquired his New Labour credentials, says his economics tutor Tim Jenkinson. 'He was by taste a New Labour sort of person before New Labour existed. I got the impression that he had middle-of-the-road tendencies. He was quite happy with neoclassical economic theory, arguing with it on constructive grounds, but not dismissing it as a discipline.'

Bashing the 'Trots' was good fun, and Ed's name became known around the university, not just in college. But he also wanted to become known in the real world beyond the ivory tower of Oxford. That meant giving his academic work, his economics and his philosophy the intense concentration he had been devoting to his politicking. The matter was pressing because the tutors who pick the brightest undergraduates and give them scholarships to help pay their way to success were threatening to remove the award Ed had received at the beginning of his second year. Balls had to persuade them he was just as clever as they had thought he was. He succeeded and kept the scholarship.

For six months he ditched his student politics and social life and went at his course hammer and tongs. What most people do in two years, he did in six months. The intense burst of activity left normally hardbitten dons' jaws dropping in admiration. Tim Jenkinson taught him in his third year. 'It was certainly very impressive to see how he became incredibly organized, and went in single-minded pursuit of a first-class degree.'

Balls was awarded his first-class honours. He did not get the top mark in the University, but fourth was not bad for somebody who had left the work until the last moment. Later the media talked about Balls having a brain the size of the planet. 'Clever, yes,' says Tim Jenkinson, 'brilliant maybe, but he's no Einstein. It amuses me how newspaper articles talk about Ed having a brain the size of the planet . . . I am sure Ed does not push this particular line. There is this mythical image of the most brilliant person, but journalists are trying to push him into being something he isn't. It's not as if he got a congratulatory first, ten miles ahead of the field. He got a good first-class degree, but did not come top of his year.'

More important for Balls's future, however, than the quality of the degree, was his developing interest in policy. He was no ivory-tower academic, although he could pass their tests with ease. Rather, he was thinking practically about markets, power and politics. Keble philosopher Jim Griffin, who taught him for his three years at Oxford, says 'He had an unusual combination of a very practical bent and a very independent, intellectual approach to things. He was an intellectual with his feet on the ground, not a detached ivory-tower sort of person.' And Tim Jenkinson found him 'fascinated by the ways in which markets might not work, and how governments might correct those deficiencies'. Balls is now able to turn the philosophy he learnt at Oxford to the purpose of power. For example he looks to the Philosophy of Mind course for interpretations of the word 'intention' as in 'intention to join the Exchange Rate Mechanism'.

The *Financial Times*'s chief economics leader writer Martin Wolf says: 'When he left Oxford Balls was still a Keynsian interventionist. I think that's what most people who came out of Oxford were. His exposure to the ideas that underpinned New Democratic thinking was pretty direct after that.' In fact Balls was anticipating New Labour thinking, and indeed the Harvard New Democratic economics that he was about to imbibe with the assistance of a Kennedy Memorial Scholarship. He was helped in this direction by his Keble tutors who saw not just his talent but his inclination and ambition.

Harvard was the place for Balls, not only because of its reputation for academic excellence, but also because it had on its staff two of the leading architects of Democrat-style New Economics. They were Lawrence Summers, later to become President Clinton's deputy finance secretary, and Robert Reich, a future secretary for Labour. Balls sat at the feet of these two gurus and lapped up their interpretation of the labour market, of the Welfare system, of growth theory. Gordon Brown would meet both men through Balls, who would be a key intermediary in the transfer of ideas between the US and the UK governments.

After a year on the standard course for a master's degree in public administration, Balls researched regional unemployment in Britain – a topic that was also exercising Brown at the time. Balls took his thoughts to his tutor Larry Summers, but Summers criticized the paper for a lack of data and sent Balls away. Ed arranged to work at the UK Treasury that summer, and he spent the entire time rooting around for data to support his thesis. When he got back to Harvard in the fall of 1989, for his second year, he gave Summers the data. 'I opened this bag, I dumped all this stuff on his desk, regional house prices, regional vacancies, regional unemployment.' Summers realized he had a serious student on his hands. The American academic arranged for the young English scholar to receive funding for a year's reading and research at the National Bureau for Economic Research in Cambridge, part of the Harvard campus.

Summers opened doors to Balls. One of these was at the American Department of Labour where he met the leading labour statistician Larry Katz, another Harvard academic. The three men went to work on the British regional unemployment problem, all the time wondering how Balls would use the findings, but impressed by his determination to achieve an intellectually satisfying conclusion. Balls trawled the unemployment registers of northern England for his statistics, but they came to life in Cambridge, Massachusetts.

The study of regional unemployment and house prices in Britain in due course became a paper entitled 'Britain divided, regional unemployment, a hysteresis of Britain'. Balls lost interest in the research and the paper was never published, but what he discovered was the foundation for the Harvard-style solutions he would bring to Gordon Brown and the British Treasury. It would also provide the ballast for Gordon Brown's assault on the Conservatives' 'failure to attack regional economic inequalities' – one of the 'four great industrial evils of our time' Brown identified at the Labour Party Conference of 1991. In fact, Balls says that Summers was keen to take him on at the World Bank, when he moved there as head economist, but Balls had by this time decided his destiny was in Britain. The search for the British movers and shakers who would help him build his career had begun.

The passport to power was the *Financial Times*, which Balls joined as a leader writer in 1990. The raw recruit knew a lot about economics – and clearly dazzled the editor Richard Lambert – but little about writing. This deficiency was solved by an old hand at the paper, and its finest economist, Martin Wolf. The two sparred at editorial conferences in front of their admiring colleagues, Wolf taking the rightist position, Balls the left-leaning one. Some journalists suspected that Balls was a huckster whose arguments contained more show than substance. But his pugnacious, clipped delivery, together with an unabashed enthusiasm for economics, made him very hard to argue with. Over four years, Wolf knocked Balls's writing into some sort of shape, and he progressed from leader writer to columnist in the paper's 'Economic Notebook'. This skill was recognized with the award of the Wincott Prize for Best Young Business Journalist of the Year in 1992.

In fact Ed might have stayed at the *FT* had two events not occurred. The first was a rare setback. He had become passionately keen about Africa, and in particular about the World Bank schemes to alleviate African countries' debt problems. He desperately wanted to become the paper's Africa editor in Nairobi but the editor demurred. Balls was not used to rebuffs and was 'pretty gutted'. His interest in Africa's economic problems would later be shared by Gordon Brown and a number of his personal team.

The second development was that Ed Balls, as he liked to

be known by now (rather than Eddie), had struck up a rapport with Gordon Brown, to whom he had been introduced by the former Demos think-tanker Geoff Mulgan in mid-1992. Balls started brain-storming with Brown at 9 a.m. meetings at 1 Parliament Street, where Brown had an office, before going on to *FT* editorial meetings at 10.30.

In December 1992, three months after the meetings with Brown began, Balls published a Fabian pamphlet entitled *Euromonetarism* which lambasted the Exchange Rate Mechanism and called for an independent Central Bank. This document anticipated much of the New Labour economic programme – 'a quite brilliant synthesis', said one economist – and, given the eventual outcome to ERM, was highly prophetic. Gordon Brown was impressed. With hindsight Brown may have actually approved of the pamphlet's tone, although he was a member of John Smith's Shadow Cabinet, which supported staying in the mechanism. Later on, Balls was able to provide the economic rationale for other elements in Gordon Brown's New Labour economic thinking, such as the minimum wage and Bank of England independence.

More pamphlets on the Central Bank, labour economics and employment followed – mostly, Balls admits, based on material he was recycling from his newspaper articles – and Balls put down his marker as an ambitious Party economist who had Brown's ear. By early 1993, Balls appears to have allayed Brown's initial suspicions that he was 'too-clever-by-half', and Brown offered him a job as his economic adviser. But to the shock of Brown and those around him Balls declined. It looked as though the blue-eyed boy of modern economics was playing games. Could he elude them?

But for Balls, this matter – like almost everything else in his career – needed extensive, exhaustive calculation. He greatly admired Gordon Brown, but was not sure that the Labour Party was yet fully committed to the middle-of-the-road economics he espoused. Then there were his friends at the *FT*, in particular Martin Wolf, warning him against hitching his colours too closely to someone else's political mast. Wolf says the role of political adviser was a 'poisoned chalice' for the young man he considered to be an intellectual with a quite exceptionally enquiring and open mind. It seemed to Wolf that the political adviser in the British sense – a job that has been imported from the United States where its role is quite different – has neither the freedom to adhere to his principles nor the opportunity to exercise pure power. Another deciding factor may have been Balls's active romantic life with an *FT* journalist. In fact, according to inside sources, he had 'cut a swathe' through the fragile female hearts at the newspaper.

The *FT* top brass wanted Balls to stay and in 1993 even gave him his own regular column with a small photo at the top. But he was swinging against journalism. He had never liked reporting, but more importantly he was frustrated by seeing politicians exercising power and responsibility when he wanted to do it himself. This had become evident to him as he travelled round Africa, Asia and America for the *FT*'s foreign surveys and met the top people there. Despite his strong views and insights, which one may assume he shared with his interviewees, he was unable to have any impact beyond that available through his article.

While Ed was on the verge of leaving the *Financial Times*, his younger brother Andrew was just beginning to make his mark. Andrew Balls has followed a career uncannily similar to that of his older brother – economics at Oxford and Harvard followed by journalism. His tutors talk of Balls junior being more academic and reserved. Ed says Andrew is more gifted in journalism than he. 'He writes much better, he is more sceptical and trouble-making than I am. I didn't like reporting; he likes reporting and making mischief.' It may not be long before the media are talking of the Balls brothers, and not just for after-hours drinks.

For Ed, Brown's blandishments, and those of the Labour Treasury team, won through and eventually he took the job in Brown's office in January 1994, at the same time as Charlie Whelan, and the team of economist and spin-doctor began preparing for the forthcoming election. They worked in tandem from the start and formed a formidable two-pronged attack: both aggressive, both believers in their man, both pretty cynical about the press and confident of their ability to swing the media. The only difference was that Whelan understood the media and thought he could pass muster on economics. Balls understood economics and thought he understood the media. The road to Number 11 was being planned stage by stage.

Soon after he moved in with Brown, Ed Balls arranged a number of visits to the United States in 1994 and 1995. As the two men shared long journeys over the Atlantic, they discussed economic theory, political strategy and of course their frustrations with some colleagues who could not see what they were on about. And when the intellectual ardour wore off as jet-lag set in, the conversation turned to football. Balls is a keen footballer and a supporter of the Canaries, Norwich City, while Brown, a devoted follower of the game, supports Raith Rovers.

Balls took Brown round his old stomping grounds to meet his teachers. They went on to Washington, where Balls had arranged meetings with Robert Reich, Larry Summers and Alan Greenspan at the Federal Reserve to brainstorm the British economy. They also observed the market economy around them, and Brown was repeatedly struck by the way the independent Federal Reserve Bank had taken the controversy out of interest rate levels. It confirmed something he had been planning for the UK for a long time, and something to which Balls was committed.

The South of France was another venue for early brainstorming. In the three years prior to the election, Brown, Whelan and Balls retreated several times to a very comfortable flat overlooking the sea in Cannes, owned by Geoffrey Robinson. Brown and Balls talked policy and tactics, with occasional breaks for tennis and the local cuisine. Some of these trips were no more than long weekends, others were longer, but the bonding grew more intense. Neither Balls nor Brown was yet ready to commit to their new female partners, so these were 'boys together' occasions, and all the stronger for it.

Balls was now at the heart of the opposition think-tank and policy creation and it was very exciting. But he also found the resistance he was encountering from some in the New Labour stable galling. He could not understand why the labour and Welfare theories he had imbibed in the United States, which so appealed to Gordon Brown, were not going down so well with everybody in Tony Blair's office, especially Derek Scott, Blair's economics adviser.

Ed repeatedly came over to the *FT* for lunch to moan, even talking about throwing in the towel. (According to former *FT* colleagues on whose shoulders he cried) Blair's office seemed to him an 'ideas-free zone' in those early days, and he gave the impression that he was struggling with the practice of power, even if he enjoyed the theory of it. Balls now denies he made such a statement. One *FT* staffer said, 'Ed had a pretty awful time when he first went to Brown. He was really down. When he was here, he was politically naïve, he didn't understand that politics was a rough trade. He thought it was about ideas.'

Balls also had to deal with flak when he served as secretary of the committee overseeing Labour's economic changes. Outlining his programme in tawdry Labour Party committee rooms to left-wing MPs who did not respond to his cool scientific detachment was a far cry from high-flying intellectual argument at Harvard or the *FT*. His view of the economy as a series of models and processes rather than people and values set some heads shaking. In the research paper in which he devised 'a model which would get you to independence of the Bank of England', he concluded that the accountability of the newly liberated Bank of England would be attractive to the Labour Party Conference; but he left his own conviction unclear. No one was in any doubt that he could think and talk, but did he believe in anything? The Labour MPs were puzzled.

Balls's 'muscular' mind (in the words of one tutor) was what appealed to the hard-driven and determined Brown, and the two bounced ideas off each other to great effect. Martin Wolf says, 'I didn't realize how close the relationship would be. It has worked for Gordon and Ed to an extraordinary degree.' The Shadow Chancellor's confidence in his younger protégé and, to an extent, guide, became more important as the 1997 election loomed. Labour's position in the polls looked as though the Party would stay supreme, and civil servants wanted to find out more about Brown and his policies. They sought access to Brown, but he handed them over to Ed.

In 1996, Balls began a series of meetings with Sir Terence Burns, the Permanent Secretary at the Treasury and one of the country's leading economists. An architect of Tory monetarism, Burns was a leading scholar at the London Business School before joining the Treasury in 1980. During the election campaign Balls was also having meetings with groups of civil servants about Labour's budgetary principles. After the election Balls also had a one-to-one meeting as Brown's spokesman with Eddie George to discuss the Chancellor's plans for monetary policy.

The meetings with the Treasury insiders were quite unusual in constitutional terms, as the senior servants would usually only talk about exceedingly sensitive topics such as the mechanics for the hand-over of power and general economic principles with the politician himself. But Balls and Burns said that they needed to discuss these heady matters as part of the process of devising an agenda for Burns's first meeting with Brown. Burns was in no doubt that he was talking to the key member of the Brown team, and was impressed by Balls's optimism and confidence. 'What was striking about Ed, quite early on in the election campaign, was that he spent all his time thinking about government rather than the election. He moved on to thinking about the next battle rather than the one they were engaged in.'

The relationship between Balls and Burns seemed to advance, and in the course of 1996 there were a number of meetings where Balls ranged over the full gamut of New Labour economic theory, while staying clear of detailed policy. Although Burns met Brown in January 1997 and on one other occasion, Balls remained the key Treasury contact. The two met during the election campaign, and again on the day after Labour was elected to office for the first time in eighteen years. 'The bit when Tony went into Downing Street I saw from Terry Burns's office. Me and Terry Burns sat and watched Tony on TV, and then I stayed and I saw Gordon going from there.'

Burns installed Balls with the paraphernalia of office that every new government receives after an election. Balls finds it hard to express the heady exuberance of those early days in power. 'I was given a waiting room round the corner, and an amazing experience, stuck in this room completely bare, with all these briefs, "the incoming government" – completely mindblowing. Then I gave them back, saw

Gordon a bit for lunch, came back here to carry on reading them.'

Balls was quickly ensconced in a substantial office round the corner from the Chancellor's, and Whitehall realized he was no usual political adviser. Rather, he was the Chancellor's *alter ego*, the bluff, confident counterpart to his shyer and more reserved master. Balls, as one member of the Brown camp puts it, is the Chancellor's gatekeeper, and no one passes without his say so.

Balls established the power balance with Terry Burns right from the start. The civil servant realized that Balls had the Chancellor's ear and therefore took him seriously. Despite his relative youthfulness he could not be patronized. He knew what his minister wanted and, in the eyes of the Civil Service, had the power to get it.

Balls began to exercise his powerful position over Burns. One of the civil servant's key projects under the Conservative government was to redevelop part of the Treasury building through a public finance initiative. This would require the Treasury to move temporarily to Vauxhall. Brown and Balls did not like the idea, and they relished the opportunity to show Burns who was boss. A source at the *Financial Times* recalls Balls telling Brown over lunch, 'This is the thing that Terry Burns has been working on for the last three years of his life, and we scuppered it.' It can have come as no surprise that relations between Balls and Burns would sour so dramatically and publicly in the course of the year. Senior sources in the Treasury with less respect than many for Balls describe him as a 'marketer and packager' of economic policy rather than its creator.

The speed with which Balls acquired hard-nosed cynicism came as a shock to those who had known the open-minded intellectual at the *FT*. A thicker skin would be reasonable given the particularly brutal world of politics, but this had gone too far. 'A certain amount of steel has entered his soul. There is a streak of braggadocio, of swaggering, which sits ill with his previously sensitive soul,' said one source. That was also the impression created for many of Whelan as well as Balls by the fly-on-the-wall television documentary *We*

Are the Treasury in which Balls figured prominently at the Chancellor's side.

Critics have been too quick to make a judgment, however. A measure of immaturity from a thirty-year-old with no political experience must have been expected. Power, as one MP put it, is a 'tremendous rush' and it would be surprising if it did not initially go to the heads of those who have studied it for so long but never exercised it.

Balls, as everyone knows, is the apple of the Chancellor's eye. But there is a view shared by some Labour MPs that this may not be healthy. Is the Chancellor so besotted with Balls that he is incapable of checking his wilder excesses? For the moment he is enjoying himself enormously, says his former mentor Martin Wolf. 'The job he's got is terrific fun, very powerful, but what does he do afterwards?' Observers speculate that there is no route for Balls other than a parliamentary career alongside his spouse and his current boss.

Balls and Brown have tied their fates together. As they listen to each other's ideas and thoughts late into the night in the murky Treasury offices, the tall, broad-shouldered man, with utilitarian spectacles and a wave of short mousy hair, and the stocky, dark Chancellor, each knows that he is in the advance guard of New Labour. Their ability to blend Washington and Westminster, Harvard and the House of Commons will in the long-run set the new government's economic and social agenda, and sign its political fate. It will also determine whether Balls and Brown are personally identified with triumph or failure.

Ed Balls's marriage to Yvette was more than just a social occasion. It was a political statement of the confidence of the New Treasury, and a call to its friends to celebrate, and stay loyal.

Balls could now revel in the euphoria of New Labour, and enjoy at last the economic triumphs that he had engineered.

Chapter Four:
Where the Budget Billions Came From

The crowds streaming out of Westminster Underground station on the morning of 2 May were hoping for a glimpse of New Labour taking power. A glimpse of Tony Blair going into Downing Street if they were lucky or maybe a new minister milking the moment and the applause. They did not stop to watch two men, haggard from lack of sleep, talking earnestly beside the newspaper stand opposite Big Ben. Yet this was a highly significant moment for the new government. Ed Balls, after a night driving down from Pontefract to the Festival Hall and then three hours' sleep, was making a pre-arranged rendezvous at 10 o'clock with a City accountant, Chris Wales. As planned, he collected a stack of brown envelopes packed with documents. This was Labour's economic secret weapon, ready for delivery. Project Autumn was complete. As Balls remembered later, 'That day was the most bizarre of my life.'

The foundations for Labour's first Budget were laid more than a year before the election. The architects were Geoffrey Robinson and Ed Balls. For the final months of opposition, when every other Labour politician and spin-doctor was focusing on winning the election and refusing to tempt fate by looking further ahead, Robinson and Balls were planning for power in the Treasury. Sue Nye and Charlie Whelan, having seen so many near-misses for Labour, were almost superstitious in their refusal to talk about government. Nye even rebuked Balls for his obsession with a phantom Labour Budget which could, at the whim of the electorate, evaporate into the ether. But Gordon Brown's economic troubleshooters knew their priorities. Working in great secrecy, Balls and Robinson crafted line by line tax proposals and draft parliamentary bills. Traditionally Labour economic policy had been cobbled together in an endless series of sub-committees. The work of Balls and Robinson was swiftly endorsed by Labour's Economic Policy Committee. For the first time Labour called on some of the finest technical brains in the City of London to help draft policy. The result was the pile of brown envelopes which Balls collected at Westminster Underground station the morning after polling day. The detail and thoroughness of this work astounded Treasury civil servants when the documents dropped on their desks later that day.

At the heart of this work was the windfall tax. It was to provide the funds for Labour's most ambitious commitment, getting a quarter of a million unemployed young people back into work. All other tax-and-spend options had been closed down by Brown and Blair. The levy, as Labour liked to call it to avoid use of the T-word, was to be imposed on what were deemed to be excess profits made by utility companies privatized under the Conservatives. From the moment he became Shadow Chancellor in 1992, Gordon Brown had sounded-off against the bosses of these businesses, the privatized industry fat cats as he called them. Water, gas and electricity company annual reports had been pored over by Brown's researchers. They had charted the inexorable rise in profits and pay packets since the businesses were privatized. Gleefully, Brown had brandished this research at press conferences. He had promised to make the utilities pay through a one-off levy. Brown realized he would have billions to play with. The scourge of youth unemployment had long nagged at his socialist soul. He was appalled that many households had no one in work and that in some there were two generations who had never known employment. The windfall billions, he decided, could make a start on righting that wrong. But the success of a first term at the Treasury would hang on the windfall tax raising money quickly without legal challenge. Every dot and comma would have to be scrupulously planned and checked-out.

Secrecy was of paramount importance. Leaks, even before the election, would compromise Brown's room to manoeuvre once he was in office. Worse still, if the windfall tax proposals were passed to the Tories they would be open to a barrage of criticism both from Labour's political opponents and the utilities facing the tax. There had to be deniability. If work by barristers and accountants fell into the wrong hands, the line would have been, 'Lots of people are doing their own research on the windfall tax, what do we know about it?' Robinson and Balls collected no documents so there was nothing to be lost on the back seats of taxis or in wine bars. All paperwork was kept under lock and key in the offices of the accountants and other finance houses which were covertly assisting Labour. Meetings were held discreetly in Geoffrey Robinson's penthouse apartment above the Grosvenor House. Dispatch riders would ferry drafts and outlines between the City and Westminster but only rarely to the Commons – 'too risky', in Balls's view.

So who were Labour's allies in this clandestine operation, code-named Project Autumn because it was supposed to be ready before the end of 1996 in case there was a snap election? Step forward Chris Wales from one of the 'big six' accountancy partnerships. Wales's company had reservations about working on the windfall tax because their client-list included some of the very utilities who were targeted. The upshot was that they agreed to do the work 'pro bono', in other words without a fee. Like Labour, they had every reason for keeping the work under wraps and 'non-attributable'. Wales's brief was to run the numbers coming from Balls and Robinson through financial models, testing the impact of the tax on the different companies' profitability and balance-sheets. He gathered a team of six accountants who worked almost full-time from the summer of 1996 onwards. It was painstakingly detailed research, a significant contribution from the City firm and critical to the success of Labour's economic policy. The windfall tax, after all, was expected to raise billions to pay for the New Deal for jobless youngsters.

Alongside the accountants were the lawyers. Leading barrister Michael Beloff QC and a junior, Rabinder Singh; made themselves available at a discounted fee. They started from first principles on how the windfall tax would work and steadily drafted a complete bill. Balls and Robinson were determined to achieve a legally watertight scheme, capable of standing up to the sort of High Court challenge which the privatized industry bosses were already threatening. Legal opinions piled up, the financial projections swelled and multiplied. Different sizes of windfall tax were tested and run through the accountants' computer models. Nothing was left to chance. A former parliamentary draftsman was brought back from retirement in France for a day a week, his task to fine-tune the bill until it was ready to be slotted into Labour's legislative programme. It had to be a bill which would not waver under the scrutiny and natural scepticism of the Treasury.

While Wales and Beloff beavered away at the windfall tax, further cohorts of financial experts were enlisted by Brown's team. Another accountancy partnership, Cooper and Lybrand, again working 'pro bono', produced a study of assets held by public-sector authorities like local councils. This was to be the basis of Labour's call for an audit of national assets and for every government department to produce a register of what they owned. There was a clandestine deal with another accountancy firm to second a member of staff to Labour for nine months. A visiting research position was set up at the London School of Economics. The accountant holding this paper title got to grips with the computer modelling facilities and then, following instructions from Balls, produced tax and benefit simulations based on Labour's plans. The LSE title was a cover allowing Brown instant deniability if any of this financial groundwork leaked. As Balls put it, 'You always had to be able to say it never had anything to do with us.'

With a personal tax expert working on pensions and savings, other accountants picking over capital gains and environmental taxes, and management consultants pulling together studies on the private finance initiative in schools and hospitals, Balls and Robinson controlled a web of commercial research activity. 'Here are the principles, here's what we want to achieve in this timetable, go away and have a look' was the brief for each adviser. Balls and Robinson would shuttle backward and forward between smart City office complexes and Robinson's flat. They would regularly kick ideas around with the Shadow Chancellor and check with Brown that they were pointing in the right direction.

Inevitably the Treasury started sniffing around the secret plans for the windfall tax. While the Tories limped through the final months in office, trying with little success to puncture the armour of Labour's economic policy, senior Treasury mandarins were poring over blueprints supplied by Balls. But he did not give them the nitty-gritty of the windfall tax, i.e. which utilities would pay and how much. Sir Terence Burns was anxious to get his hands on the final draft and to begin detailed preparation inside the Treasury. He suggested that one Treasury civil servant and a senior tax official from the Inland Revenue should start wading through the forest of documents. It was a request refused by Brown's team – the need for absolute leakproof security again the reason.

The 'need to know' basis of this groundwork on the windfall tax did not even extend to the Shadow Cabinet. Labour's most senior politicians knew the outlines of the plan, of course, but they were not privy to decisions about which companies would pay and which would be exempt. What about BT, for example? It was a running source of press speculation that BT would be exempt as it was not a classic privatized utility like water, gas and electricity. The lawyers warned Brown and his advisers that BT could not be excluded in principle. Yet they played along with the suggestion that no decisions had been made, even with the Shadow Cabinet. They could not allow anything said in opposition to be used against them in a court-case after the election, for example a claim by another utility that there had been unfair discrimination.

Two other central pillars of Brown's first Budget were pieced together in these last months of opposition. First there were the changes to corporate taxation. From January 1997 onwards, again with the help of carefully briefed teams of accountants, Balls and Robinson conceived and hammered-out a plan to transform the way companies pay their tax. The existing system tended to encourage businesses to pay out dividends rather than invest profits. This was because the tax deducted from dividends paid to shareholders could be written-off against a company's final corporation tax bill. It was known as Advanced Corporation Tax (ACT). Labour's plan was to abolish ACT and spread companies' tax payments more evenly. This would affect business cash-flow but Balls and Robinson had prepared a sweetener in the shape of a cut in the rate of corporation tax. Reducing business taxes would look like a new departure for Labour and fit snugly with the Party's carefully nurtured image as a friend of industry. Controversially, they also planned to abolish the tax credit given to pension funds, a move which would provoke squawks of protest on Budget Day itself.

The second focus for Balls and Robinson was on the other side of the budgetary equation. On 20 January 1997 Gordon Brown made one of the crucial moves of the phoney election campaign by promising not to raise income tax rates and announcing that he would stick to the spending targets already outlined by Kenneth Clarke. That transformed the terrain of the party political economic debate. On the one hand it was harder for the Tories to tar Labour with a high-tax, high-spend brush. On the other it had become near impossible for Labour to offer any spending commitments. The Iron Chancellor had control of the purse-strings; no senior colleague could promise higher expenditure unless it was funded from savings elsewhere, hence the paucity of policies with price-tags attached. The pledge to cut school class-sizes was one of the few because it was a spending commitment funded by a cut, namely the abolition of the assisted place scheme. So Labour moved into the final stages of the campaign better equipped to face down Conservative claims of a hidden tax bombshell but at the same time vulnerable to the jibe that the cash-strapped public services would be no better off under a Labour government. The formula for public consumption was, 'We are sticking to the Tories' spending targets'. In private Brown's economic advisers were cooking up something rather different.

In the middle of December 1996 Balls had visited the Treasury for one of his clandestine pre-election meetings. Until then his conversations had been with Sir Terence Burns and they had ranged around very broad outlines. This time Burns brought with him Paul Gray, the Treasury's budget director. After being introduced to Balls, Gray got down to the nitty-gritty. How, he asked, would a Labour government organize a spending round in the year after the election? This touched a nerve with Balls. The question of how to deal with new Cabinet ministers demanding resources was one which had troubled Brown and his colleagues. They knew a Labour government would have to keep spending tight. The last thing they wanted was a scrap with the big departments like Health and Education within months of the election. Brown wanted to put in place long-term spending reviews. He did not need short-term battles with the rest of the Cabinet, the like of which were annual events under the Tories with their Star Chamber system of resolving competing demands. Balls's reply to Gray was simple: 'How can we avoid a spending round in the first year?' The Treasury mandarins scratched their heads and pointed out that the new government might want to look at the £5 billion contingency reserve, the money set aside each year 'for a rainy day' or an emergency demand on the Exchequer. A New Labour Treasury might, they argued, opt to rattle the contingency piggy bank and push some of the cash towards the spending ministries. That sowed the seed of an idea in Balls's mind which would lead to a vital piece of the Budget jigsaw falling into place.

Balls returned to the Shadow Chancellor's office that December afternoon and reported back on his meeting. He told Brown he thought he had worked out how to do the spending reviews. The gist of his argument was that Labour should announce that they would adhere to the Conservative government's planned spending totals but at the same time secretly pre-allocate some of the cash in the reserve. The second part of that equation would be kept under wraps with the Shadow Cabinet, let alone the Tories or the electorate unaware of the embryo spending plan. Gordon Brown liked what he heard and decided provisionally that the first Labour Budget would target an extra £1.2 billion at the Health Service and £1 billion at schools, the funds to come from the reserve. That was most definitely not made public in his headline-grabbing 20 January speech when he promised to stick with already announced totals. Beyond Brown's immediate circle only Tony Blair knew of the hidden billions ready to be plucked out of the air for hospitals and schools. And as Labour marched on towards the election, front-benchers loyally repeated the mantra that not a penny extra could be found above what the Tories had planned, because it was they who had 'messed up' the public finances. In doing so they had to brazen out taunts from the Liberal Democrats who claimed that only their Party was being straight with the voters about the need for higher spending on services and infrastructure.

The conjuring up of the hidden £2.2 billion in the first Labour Budget was intended to do more than generate gushing headlines. Making a big symbolic commitment to the two priority areas of health and education would enable Brown to reaffirm that there would be no spending round that autumn. He could stress that he was not relaxing the overall departmental totals set by the Conservatives. But he could reassure Labour MPs and pressure groups, not to mention fellow-ministers, that extra resources were being targeted at public services in the government's first year. Balls presented the plan to the Treasury top brass during the election campaign. Previous meetings had been with Burns and Gray but this time the young economics adviser found himself up before the full mandarinate. John Gieve, secretary of the key Cabinet spending committee known as PX, was amongst the group who questioned Balls about a Labour government's expenditure plans. While Balls's Labour friends and colleagues pounded the doorsteps and churned out the press releases, the thirty-year-old found himself being put through his paces by the Whitehall establishment. The bureaucrats had their doubts about Labour's spending masterplan. 'You wait and see' was their line, 'the spending ministers will not accept it.' Sceptically, they predicted that even New Labour would not be able to break free from the traditional autumn haggle of the spending round.

As Election Day came and went, as Brown and his advisers moved from opposition to power, the handout remained a closely guarded secret. The amount would later be boosted by more than £1 billion from the windfall tax. Only Brown's and Blair's immediate circles were in the know. The figures were not fed into the Treasury machine until days before the Budget. Until then gaps were left in draft documents and the Budget bible, the Treasury Red Book. David Blunkett and Frank Dobson at Education and Health respectively were not told of the windfalls which would come their way. On the basis of 'need to know',

John Prescott was briefed only a week before the Budget. The new Chancellor was determined that the news would not leak. If it had come out, his carefully nurtured reputation for fiscal caution would have been tarnished as commentators concluded that Labour had gone soft on spending before the first Budget had been delivered. Blunkett and Dobson were not let into the secret until forty-eight hours before the Budget. They were handed draft press releases and warned of dire consequences if news of the surprise spending increase leaked. There was an implicit threat to withdraw the cash if news got out. Brown's people knew, though, that this was an empty threat because by that stage the Budget papers were complete and printed up.

From the moment Brown had inflicted a humiliating defeat on Kenneth Clarke over VAT on domestic gas and electricity in December 1994 it had been a Labour commitment that the tax would be further reduced if they took office. With no intention of raising pensions, Brown could hail a reduction in the fuel tax as doing Labour's bit for the elderly. Cutting VAT on domestic energy to 5 per cent became one of Labour's well-publicized election pledges. But there was always a technical risk that such a move would fall foul of European rules. Anxious to implement the reduction in the first Labour Budget, Brown needed to know where he stood with Europe on this issue. The Treasury advised him that technically the European Commission might have a case but in practice the Brussels bureaucrats would be unlikely to treat it as a point of principle.

Gordon Brown wanted his first foray into Europe to be rather more than a low-key 'get-to-know' session with his EU counterparts. He was determined to make an impact and serve notice from the outset that he was not to be taken for granted or pushed around by Europe's finance ministers. The new Chancellor and his advisers decided they could use the VAT issue to their advantage by setting up what would look like a showdown with Europe. A plan of action was devised around the margins of the media drinks party at Number 11 Downing Street at the end of Labour's first week in power. Brown was due to fly to Brussels for his first meeting of European finance ministers on Monday 11 May. He would be ready, so the pre-determined line went, for a spat with Europe over VAT on

WHERE THE BUDGET BILLIONS CAME FROM   53

domestic fuel. Selected journalists were briefed for front-page stories on the Monday morning; a television news team would travel on the plane to Brussels on the Sunday evening.

On the Sunday afternoon while political correspondents prepared their 'Brown set for clash with Brussels' story, the Chancellor himself was focused on football rather than on finance ministers. Geoffrey Robinson had resigned his directorship but was still a major shareholder in Coventry City. That afternoon Coventry were in London for a crucial relegation clash with Tottenham Hotspur. Brown, Balls and Whelan joined Robinson in the directors' box at Spurs. Over the half-time drinks the owner of Spurs, the brash, bearded multi-millionaire Alan Sugar, was introduced to the Chancellor. Sugar, a paid-up Tory supporter during the 1980s, was keen to find favour with New Labour. He had worked out a possible role for himself as a business evangelist, touring schools and explaining the secrets of his rags-to-riches career. Brown readily accepted. The kick-off had been delayed because a surge of latecomers had arrived at the turnstiles. So by the end of the match Brown's entourage had precious little time to get to the airport for the Brussels flight. The driver managed the journey in forty-five minutes and got them on to the tarmac in time to board the Sabena flight minutes before take-off.

The hard line in Europe strategy paid off handsomely for Brown. Initially the Commission made it clear they were unhappy with the British VAT proposal and asked for time to consider it. Brown retorted that that was not good enough and that they had had plenty of time to deliberate. Eventually the Commission, backed by the finance ministers, anxious to ingratiate themselves with the newest member, drafted a statement confirming there was no legal obstacle. Having teed-off the day predicting Brown's dust-up with Europe, broadcasters and papers concluded that he had won an important battle. Treasury insiders were surprised that such a meal had been made of the issue. They knew that the Europeans were most unlikely to try to block a reduction in VAT. They admitted to being impressed with the way Whelan had worked up the story and generated favourable headlines on two successive days.

The Brown team decided that on every visit to Brussels there must be an initiative which the British government could take credit for. Better that, they reasoned, than being rolled over by the European ministers with their own alliances and agendas. So they served notice that they would introduce a jobs initiative at the next meeting. Brown had also learned something about how to watch his back in these European conclaves. Monsieur Arthuis, the French Finance Minister, had aired the idea of an informal stability pact of member states which joined the single currency, those outside to be excluded. Brown's recollection was, 'They put up this proposal and tried to bounce me at the first meeting . . . I stopped it.' Certainly by the end of the day it looked like Round One to Gordon Brown.

As they flew back to London speculation was already building up about the Budget. The date 10 June, less than a month away, was being floated in the press, apparently well-sourced to the Treasury. And at that stage the Chancellor's aides were tempted by the idea. They had always wanted to unveil Labour's first Budget within six to ten weeks of the election. Their aim was to underline the momentum of the new regime and demonstrate to the country that there was no slacking over the delivery of manifesto commitments. The date 10 June was particularly tempting as it was exactly the same number of days after the election as Geoffrey Howe's first Budget in 1979. Leaving it any later would box-in the new Chancellor as there were summit meetings at Amsterdam and Denver to come. The next alternative was 2 July, which would allow Brown to say that he was delivering within two months of coming to power (but only just!). Brown himself could not decide. As one source put it, 'Originally in opposition Gordon wanted to go quickly, then he decided we needed more time, then it was quickly again.' As a result the Treasury was in overdrive for the first weeks after the election, frantically pulling together the policies in case the new masters wanted to go to the Commons in June. It wasn't until 1 June, with just ten days to spare, that Brown finally opted for the July date. In retrospect it would have been better to go early as Treasury insiders admitted later. Yes, they had more time to prepare, but on 10 June there were no warning signals about consumer spending getting out of control. Going then would have meant an easier ride from the City.

Although they never knew it, a small group of south Londoners played a part in the preparation of the Budget. In opposition Brown had learned the secrets of focus-group opinion research as Labour honed and tailored its policies to be voter-friendly. Small, carefully chosen groups of floating voters in marginal seats were assembled in a relaxed and convivial atmosphere. Policies and propositions were dangled in front of the group and individuals gave their impressions and opinions. Used properly, focus groups were a valuable tool not for deciding policy but working out how to present it. Why not, Brown reasoned, do the same with economic policies, to investigate which measures played best with a sample of voters and which, if any, needed better explanation? Schooled in the traditions of Budget secrecy, Treasury officials were distinctly nervous about the idea of revealing anything to a focus group. The exercise was eventually given clearance, with strict caveats from on high. Ed Miliband and a leading political market researcher who had worked with Labour in opposition were put in charge of the first pre-Budget focus group.

With a brief to be ultra-discreet, the market researchers assembled a focus group of typically varied voters at an anonymous suburban house in Norwood, south London. The group was told simply that a media organization wanted to test reaction to hypothetical measures. The real policies would be mixed up with invented policy ideas. Miliband slipped out of the Treasury, armed with sheaves of documents. Travelling down to Norwood, he felt as he if he was part of a cloak-and-dagger operation. He cold only hope that there was no sharp-witted Labour supporter present who might associate him with the Chancellor.

The exercise served its purpose and the secret was not rumbled. Miliband returned to the Treasury relieved and able to brief Brown with some interesting conclusions. The group had been impressed with the idea of new funds for hospitals and schools. They warmed to the figures expressed as thousands of pounds per school rather than the overall total in billions. It certainly gave some valuable fat for the Chancellor to chew on in the final run-in to his Budget.

News of the financial shot in the arm for the Health Service and Education may not have leaked but other possible Budget initiatives did. The thorny problem of tax relief on mortgages had troubled Conservative Chancellors and after Gordon Brown took office he found it in his in-tray. For years the Treasury had pressed for the tax relief, known as Mortgage Interest Relief at Source (or MIRAS), to be scrapped. It was a throwback to an era when house-price inflation was non-existent and encouraging home ownership was considered to be a worthy policy aim. Once the roaring housing market boom of the 1980s took off and Chancellors began throwing cold water at the economy, MIRAS began to look like a government incentive for home-owners to line their pockets. Economists, both in the Treasury and further afield, agreed it looked outdated. However, no politician with a feel for the Middle England vote wanted to be the one to remove this homebuyer's perk. With a new government and a new Chancellor, the Treasury dusted down the MIRAS file and revived its argument for abolition. Brown, given his revulsion and oft-stated opposition to the boom-and-bust years of Chancellors Lawson and Lamont, was sympathetic.

What to do about MIRAS evolved into one of the few areas of disagreement between Gordon Brown and Tony Blair as they discussed Labour's first Budget. Blair, always with an eye to the voters who had flocked from the Tories to New Labour, bridled at the idea of phasing out MIRAS. Was it right, he asked, that a Labour government elected on a promise to hold income tax rates should within months of taking office be tightening the tax burden on the middle classes? Killing off MIRAS would, so the argument went, allow opponents to claim that Labour was showing its old anti-property, anti-enterprise colours. Brown argued for the economic case for MIRAS to be consigned to history but he relented when the Prime Minister put his foot down. MIRAS would not be abolished, and Brown conveyed his thinking to senior figures in the government.

Within days of that meeting the *Sunday Times* ran a front-page story claiming that MIRAS would survive Labour's first Budget unscathed. Brown was furious. An important and highly sensitive policy decision appeared to have leaked and he suspected one of those present was responsible. Whelan suspected that Peter Mandelson, anxious to leave no room for debate on the future of MIRAS, had wanted to get the latest official thinking into the public domain. The Chancellor, however, considered that no final decision had been made. He came to the view that a scaling-down of MIRAS was required, in line with a steady reduction announced by previous Chancellors and justifiable in the light of accelerating consumer spending and house prices. So in a change of tack Brown decided that MIRAS should be trimmed from 15 per cent to 10 per cent. He advised the Prime Minister that he felt strongly that this was the correct course of action. Blair endorsed it. Government advisers allowed newspapers to speculate that MIRAS would be scrapped. With the media prepared for the total abolition of the tax relief a cut from 15 per cent to 10 per cent would not look so punitive. Now it was Mandelson's turn to be angry. In a stand-up row on the Monday before the Budget after a presentation meeting in Downing Street, he accused Whelan of 'spinning' the Budget to the Sunday papers. Blair needed to be reassured by Brown that there had not been authorized leaks.

Alleged leaks would threaten to overshadow Brown's speech on Budget Day itself. But in the week leading up to 2 July he had other more basic concerns – like getting enough sleep, for example. Inconvenient though it was, he was obliged as Chancellor to join Blair in travelling to Denver, Colorado for the summit of seven leading industrialized nations known as the G7. All through the weekend before his first Budget, while Blair paraded the international stage with Bill Clinton and other world leaders, Brown fretted about getting home. The Concorde chartered to carry the Prime Minister's and Chancellor's entourage was due on the return leg to stop off in New York on the Sunday. The personal rapport between President and Prime Minister was plain for all to see and Blair had been invited by Clinton to stay on for twenty-four hours after the G7 summit. Brown insisted on pressing on home to put the finishing touches to his Budget and to get at least one night's jet-lag-free sleep. After frantic calls to airlines and amidst some friction between the Downing Street and Treasury staffs in Denver, Brown was booked on a scheduled flight from New York to London on the Sunday evening.

Back at the Treasury on the Monday there was the unlikely

sight of the Chancellor snoozing on a sofa just forty-eight hours before a Budget. Even the workaholic, politically driven Brown needed to catch up on his sleep after the punishing ordeal of Denver. A lifetime of devotion to politics and dedication to the Labour Party was leading to this first chance to exercise real power with the Budget box. And Brown wanted to be fresh for the final hours of refining the speech which would give him a place in Labour's history books.

Chapter Five: Budget Day

A morning photo-call with the Chancellor is as traditional a part of Budget Day ritual as the battered red box itself. Gordon Brown was to break with tradition on both counts. It was New Labour, New Budget box, Brown having commissioned apprentices from the Rosyth naval dockyard in his constituency to create the leather-bound, gilt-engraved metal box. And where his predecessors had opted for the 'walk in the park' with the ducks of St James Park and a crowd of photographers, the new Chancellor brought the cameras in to witness a working breakfast.

The Treasury ministers were assembled at 8 o'clock at Number 10 Downing Street and photographers and television crews were ushered upstairs for a rare glimpse of the flat. Brown himself was the last to arrive, having overslept for the first time in years. Whelan encouraged pictures of the team eating breakfast in shirt-sleeves, with the Chancellor bizarrely frying up eggs and bacon. After weeks of giving the orders in the preparation of the Budget this was supposed to depict the Chancellor as a team-player. But the platters of fried food were left to go cold as the ministers, anxious to look healthy, toyed with muesli and orange juice. An even more bizarre Budget Day spectacle had been promised with a plan for the Chancellor to pose for the cameras on his exercise bike. At the last minute that idea was vetoed by Whelan.

While the camera shutters clicked and the eggs and bacon sizzled in the Downing Street flat, the morning news bulletins were reporting that Brown's Budget had leaked, the most damaging possible allegation for any Chancellor to face on Budget Day. Whelan quickly found himself in a fire-fighting operation, first with the BBC. The economics correspondent Anthony Brown had reported on air that tax relief on private health-care would be abolished. This had been a long-standing Labour commitment, made plain by Party spokesmen long before the election although it was not in the manifesto. The Treasury press office confirmed it to the BBC and that was enough for the story to be dressed-up as an exclusive. More damaging, though, was a *Financial Times* story. Robert Peston, the paper's political editor, reported that share prices had soared the previous day on rumours that the plan to abolish tax credits on dividends was to be shelved. A source described as 'a senior member of the government' was quoted as saying, 'The markets are bonkers,' which was taken as a veiled hint that they were wrong in their assumption about a change of heart by the government. The story was also apparently well-informed on the Chancellor's plan to reduce the government's financial deficit over a five-year period.

Peston had already been a thorn in the side of the Treasury. Four weeks before the Budget he had raised fears of a leak, again on the question of abolishing tax credits. The sleek and wiry Peston, the son of a renowned economist who as a peer sat on the Labour benches in the Lords, had covered the City before joining the parliamentary lobby. He had taken interest in the tax credits issue when Tory Treasury ministers had toyed with the same idea some years previously. Testing and probing a range of sources, he had felt confident enough to predict that Labour would go further than the Conservatives had dared and scrap what had become a tax incentive for big companies to pay dividends rather than invest in plant and machinery. No other newspaper picked up the story and ran with it, concluding that it was a technical financial measure best left to the pink pages of the *Financial Times*. But Peston's story looked to experienced

Treasury hands too well-sourced to be dismissed. In opposition Ed Balls, anxious to up Brown's profile in the City, had tipped Peston off about speeches and policy announcements from the Chancellor. Suspicious eyes in the Treasury wondered again about the link.

The Tories scented blood, seeing an unexpected opportunity to embarrass the new government on this day of days. Their own final Budget the previous November had been upstaged when the *Mirror* newspaper was offered a sheaf of stolen press releases outlining Ken Clarke's measures. Here was a chance for revenge and, what's more, it looked like a genuine leak from inside the Treasury. The Shadow Chancellor Peter Lilley was determined to exploit it. He tabled a private notice question, a device to force a ministerial statement in the Commons which would have to take precedence over other business including the Budget. It was a potential spanner in the works for the new Government.

Apart from agreeing the words and tone of the ministerial response to Peter Lilley, which was to be delivered by the Leader of the House, Ann Taylor, there was little left for the new Chancellor to do as the minutes and hours ticked away. With scores of technical measures to unveil there is not much scope to change or tinker with a Budget speech at the eleventh hour. The press releases have been printed and bundled up ready for distribution the moment the Chancellor sits down at the end of his speech. The hard work has been done and there is nothing the speech-maker can do to improvise or ad lib. So Brown's next task was the Budget Day broadcast, the traditional pre-recorded address for transmission that night. His predecessors had opted for a straightforward across-the-desk presentation in the Chancellor's study at Number 11 Downing Street. Brown and Whelan had kicked around the idea of recording the broadcast in a school to underline the importance of education. That proved impossible to organize so they opted for the garden at Number 10.

Next in this choreographed Budget routine, Gordon Brown was to walk from Downing Street to the Commons accompanied by the Rosyth trainees. The image to be conveyed was that this was a Budget for young people and employment opportunity and something very different from the immediate precedents of the Conservative years. It was another part of Whelan's grand media strategy for the Budget; after all Tony Blair had set the tone with his unexpected stroll to the Commons on the day of the Queen's Speech and now this was to be the Chancellor's turn. But the idea was shelved at the last minute. Brown had already recorded the broadcast which opened with the words 'Earlier today I walked to the Commons with the Budget box . . .' Some hurried re-cutting was required. As planned, the Chancellor welcomed the trainees inside Number 11 and was presented with his new Budget box. He put them at their ease as they posed for a photo-call in the entrance hall. As young Scots from the Dunfermline area they were Brown's people and he could relate to them in a way he could not to City financiers or Treasury top brass.

Soon after 2 o'clock Brown prepared to leave Number 11. Every newspaper picture editor and television producer expected the classic pose on the threshold with the Budget box held at shoulder-height and the manufactured grin. Tory Chancellors from Clarke back to Howe had faced the cameras with their wives alongside. Charlie Whelan and Sue Nye realized they had a problem. They did not want to see a picture of a solitary Brown – they feared it would generate headlines about the unmarried Chancellor. They intended that he should appear before the banks of cameras surrounded by the Rosyth apprentices. Whelan's last words to his boss were, 'Whatever they shout, don't step forward on your own.' He was not disappointed. The people behind the cameras were. Repeated shouts of 'Sir, sir, one on your own, sir' failed to pull Brown forward with his box. And as he boarded the official Rover accompanied by Sue Nye there was a chorus of boos and whistles from the media crowd on the other side of Downing Street. However unpopular the move, every newspaper carried pictures of Brown with his young visitors, with one exception: the *Guardian* had mysteriously captured Brown on his own holding the Budget box. Or had they? Experienced eyes detected the use of an airbrush and the removal of heads and shoulders, rather in the way Soviet politicians had been purged from group photographs when they fell from favour. It seemed an unlikely

trick for the *Guardian* to play. When Whelan called the editor
Alan Rushbridger to complain he got a mumbled apology and the
explanation that it had been a mistake by the picture desk.

At 3.27 p.m. Tony Blair was getting to the end of a robust series
of exchanges at Prime Minister's Questions. William Hague had
taunted him over the reports of Budget leaks. Blair had parried
by referring the Tories to the statement which the Leader of
the House was to make. The Chancellor of the Exchequer
appeared behind the Speaker's chair. He had a brief word
with the Northern Ireland minister and Scottish MP Adam
Ingram. The attendant, taken by surprise, cleared a crowd of
MPs from the gangways, and the Chancellor edged his way
along the front bench. There was a resounding cheer from
the Labour benches as Brown squeezed himself in between
Blair and Jack Straw. Next to them was Ann Taylor, by now
facing up to the prepared attack by Peter Lilley. Blair muttered
words of sympathy to Brown about the Tory wrecking tactics.
Brown's response was simple: 'We've waited eighteen years for
this, we can wait another eighteen minutes.'

And so at thirteen minutes to four Brown got to his feet to
deliver his first Budget. In the officials' box at the back of the
Chamber, those who had planned and drafted the words for so
long were opening up their thick wads of Budget papers ready
to follow the speech. Balls, who had devoted so much energy
to these measures and policies in opposition, looked white and
exhausted. At times he had his head in his hands. Alongside him
were Ed Miliband and Doug Alexander, diligently following
Brown's words. Further along, the Treasury's chief mandarins
Sir Terry Burns and Alan Budd sat impassively. High above in
the packed press gallery were Charlie Whelan and Jill Rutter
and beside them Alastair Campbell, catching the eyes of reporters
and winking as unexpected nuggets began to appear during the
speech. Further round in the gallery, on the benches reserved
for MPs unable to sit in the crowded Chamber (or those
simply not bothered about it), Kenneth Clarke sat looking
disgruntled, reflecting no doubt on how rapidly a politician's
luck can change.

Afterwards Brown reflected on the experience of his first
Budget. 'It was more nerve-racking than most speeches. If

you speak in the House of Commons you spend so much time thinking about how you deal with interruptions, but that does not happen in the Budget so you are concentrating more on what you are saying than on what the reaction is. I wanted every word to count as much as possible.' It was a Budget for big themes, according to Brown: the people's priorities, equipping Britain for the future and a new role in the global economy, stability, investment, fairness and, of course, jobs. He felt he spent more time than he would normally have done in a speech getting his initial arguments across and was more careful than usual. He had wanted this to be a different sort of Budget, about rather more than simply dividing up the national cake. Brown noted that people tended to look at the measures on Budget Day and ask whether they were better or worse off and what was the price of cigarettes and a bottle of spirits. He himself remembered checking Budgets back in the 1960s for beer and petrol prices. 'People have not yet understood that a Budget has to be more than that,' Brown argued later and, with echoes of the Presbyterian work ethic, continued, 'It's about how all of us can improve our national effort for greater competitiveness and what a government can do about it.'

By 4.47 p.m. Brown's Budget speech was over. He sat down on the front bench, looking at the clock and trying to work out whether he had finished in under an hour. According to one of his aides, 'We worried that it might be too long – actually at 59 minutes and 4 seconds it was the third-shortest Budget speech in history.' There were friendly pats on the arm from a grinning Blair and Ann Taylor. The Labour benches, crammed with so many new MPs witnessing their first great parliamentary occasion, cheered wildly. The Tories, looking bemused, prepared to hear their own new leader tackle the most awkward challenge for any opposition, the Budget response. Lobby and economics journalists streamed out into the ante-room behind the lower press-gallery, anxious to pick up their bundles of press releases. They strained to catch the first background briefings from Whelan, Jill Rutter and Alistair Campbell.

Brown was out of the Chamber in good time to catch the early evening television news bulletins. They would carry the instant verdict and the snap headlines on his Budget. What he saw disappointed him and, by his own admission, left him depressed. They focused on excise duties and personal taxation, locked, it seemed, in the financial language and expectations of the Conservative years. The Health and Education spending packages were not highlighted as he felt they should have been. On the prompting of Charlie Whelan the Chancellor telephoned some television editors to tell them bluntly that he felt they had missed the point. Then it was off to Number 11 for the ritual of the post-Budget party. All Treasury staff who have worked on the Budget, from junior clerks upwards, are invited for drinks with the Chancellor. Brown went through the motions but felt uncomfortable, knowing that the task of selling his financial package to press and City commentators had only just begun. Sarah Macaulay joined the party that night for one of her first official appearances with the Chancellor – Whelan had quietly tipped-off a photographer to get a snap of her arriving. Later the couple slipped off to find a television. It was Yvette Cooper's maiden speech in the Commons, the New Labour MP speaking in the opening stages of the Budget debate. As she held forth on the virtues of the government's Welfare to Work programme, her fiancée Ed Balls watched with the Chancellor. Barely four years previously he and Yvette had been young journalists commenting on other people's Budgets. Now, one barely thirty, the other in her late twenties, they had their first sniff of power.

While the Chancellor and his retinue savoured the moment there were celebrations over at the Commons. It was Ann Taylor's fiftieth birthday party and the crowd of senior Labour politicians were in high spirits. The extra cash for education and health had been a closely-guarded secret and most guests at the party had only heard the news when the Chancellor told the Commons. One of those present remembers David Blunket looking particularly pleased. At interviews and press conferences for months before the election he had staunchly defended the government line that classroom standards could be improved even though spending on schools would not be increased by Labour. Now he was to inherit a £1 billion pound windfall.

On Thursday morning, the headlines glowing, Brown was

tempted to rest on his laurels. He had delivered his Budget to widespread acclaim – even Kenneth Clarke grudgingly admitted it was a clever package. (The Labour left had been muted, arguing only that the measures were not sufficiently environmentally friendly.) Indeed the Chancellor, after a clutch of early-morning broadcast interviews, forgot until the last minute that he was due to front a post-Budget press conference at the Treasury. He and Alastair Darling betrayed no sign of that, however, as they walked into the large function room crowded with journalists.

They had two lines of questioning to deal with. First, the press followed up complaints from pension funds about the scrapping of dividend tax relief. Darling parried by noting that the stock market had risen sharply that very morning, so investors could hardly be too concerned. He remarked drily that the City could not have any real complaints as shares had risen steadily since the election. Whelan, Balls and Rutter laughed at the back of the room. Then there was the question of whether the Budget should have put a tighter squeeze on consumer spending. Several commentators were arguing that Brown had missed an opportunity to put the brakes on the economy and that interest rates might have to rise more than was healthy to compensate. This clearly got under Gordon Brown's skin. Never a fan of City economists, he referred pointedly to those commentators who had claimed before the Budget that the Chancellor did not need to increase taxation. 'Gavyn Davies,' said Charlie Whelan in an audible whisper.

Brown later reflected that there was not much point in having a press conference the day after the speech. 'If the Budget speech does not speak for itself, it's not a very good Budget speech.' He realized that there were three phases to a Budget: the first-day reaction, the next few weeks and the long-term judgement. And those few weeks following the Budget – the second phase, as identified by Brown – were certainly characterized by criticism. Some argued Brown should intervene to halt the rise of the pound, others repeated the charge that Brown had not stemmed the tide of consumer expenditure. Brown's response was that people should look at the scale of his government deficit reduction plan. He used his arms to demonstrate the downward curve of the falling deficit before concluding, 'No one can say we are not being tough to get the borrowing down so we can have a stable public borrowing position.' His plea to the markets and the learned commentators was 'Judge me over the medium-term and stop arguing for temporary fine-tuning'. His frustration with the critics was only too plain. 'Don't take any notice of establishment opinion in the City because it changes with the wind' seemed to be the message he wanted to convey.

In public Brown may have found himself at odds with some sections of the financial establishment. In private he was aware of hostile manoeuvrings by the Whitehall establishment. The scars of the *Financial Times* stories and the allegations of leaks had not healed. Friction between Sir Terence Burns and Brown's adviser acolytes had become sharper in the final weeks before the Budget. Now the Treasury's boss was wondering whether New Labour's newcomers had ridden roughshod over traditions of pre-Budget secrecy. Above all he did not want his career civil servants to be tarred with the brush of the leak accusations. Robert Peston's well-informed reports had stung Burns, and he wanted to find a culprit. At a cocktail party shortly after the Budget he bumped into a senior *Financial Times* colleague of Peston's. The conversation quickly came round to the run of scoops on tax divided credits. What, Burns enquired, did Peston mean by 'a member of the government' as the source for his Budget Day story? Peston's colleague had no knowledge of the source and told Burns so. He did volunteer, though, that 'a member of the government' was used by lobby journalists as code for a minister or special adviser. Burns thought hard about his observation and reflected that a Treasury minister could hardly have briefed the *Financial Times* the day before a Budget. Special advisers, though – in other words Balls and Whelan – seemed to Burns to be more likely suspects.

Is it not clear what further enquiries Sir Terence conducted after his casual chat at the cocktail party. He did not contact Peston to enquire after his version of events. Instead he passed on his suspicions to the Cabinet Secretary, Sir Robin Butler. The result was a memorandum from Butler for the attention of the Prime Minister. It suggested that Ed Balls and Charlie Whelan were the sources of the leaks to the *Financial Times*. Blair himself, irritated by the scale of the apparent briefing taking place before the Budget, passed on a copy of the memo to Brown. An irritated Balls then called Robert Peston, who assured him that he had heard nothing from Butler or Burns, let alone revealed his source to them. The editor of the *Financial Times* wrote to the Cabinet Office pointing out that he had no idea of Peston's sources. How, he asked, could Sir Robin have reached his own conclusions? Alastair Campbell, too, appeared to accept that Peston's stories were widely-sourced rather than the result of classic brown envelope leaks. Brown's response was first to reassure Blair that what evidence there was against Balls and Whelan was inaccurate. With Burns he took a different tack, asking with irony whether such a serious offence should not result in the sacking of Balls. Sir Terence backtracked. He advised that such a course of action would perhaps be excessive.

And so the matter was laid to rest. Privately Brown's inner circle of advisers was furious that Burns had appeared to instigate a leak investigation. The already sour relations between Treasury top brass and the Chancellor's political advisers were further embittered. Treasury staff, according to one senior civil servant, were upset because they were forced to operate under very tight security. 'They have to get things typed up in a funny way on funny notepaper and put them in more envelopes than usual . . . then they see it in the newspaper and they think it is being done deliberately and they get pissed off.' The same source used more colourful language than normal Civil Service speak: 'It's like accusing people of having sex with others; you may have suspicions but you never know. Leaking is the same, it's between two people and unless both of them admit it's true you can never be sure.'

The Chancellor's relationship with his top civil servant was by now at rock bottom. And relations were no warmer with the other key member of the British financial establishment. The Treasury's chief mandarin and Eddie George were old friends and had worked alongside many Tory Chancellors. Yet now they had a Labour Chancellor in power and he seemed determined to break up their cosy cartel.

Chapter Six:
The Eddie and Gordon Show

Stocky, bespectacled and a chain-smoker, Eddie George is not a man to stand on ceremony. He is a man of modest tastes and likes nothing better than to watch a game of rugby, potter about on a sailing boat or play a few rubbers of bridge with an amply-charged glass and ashtray at his elbow. One of the only perks he allows himself is an annual skiing trip. George cuts an unassuming figure akin to an avuncular bank manager. His nickname, 'Steady Eddie', reflects a safe pair of hands and cautious instincts. But he happens to be the most powerful man in the City of London and he occupies a seat at the high table of the world's leading financiers. For Eddie George, Governor of the Bank of England since 1993, the election of the new government would herald the most tempestuous fortnight of his career and carry him from triumph to the point of resignation. A Governor and a Chancellor must together keep hold of the economic reins. The clubbable George and the cliqueish Brown were soon to find their elbows clashing.

With the New Labour Government making its golden bequest to the Bank of England in the first week in power, relations between the new Chancellor and the Governor of the Bank of England had got off to a flying start. Eddie George was keenly aware of the burden of responsibility placed upon him and his newly established monetary policy committee. He relished the opportunity to show his colours as the first independent Governor of the Bank since the war. It had come after the humiliations of the Ken Clarke years, when George had appeared to be fighting a guerrilla war with the Tory Chancellor and losing many of the skirmishes. Here was a chance to cement the Bank's reputation and hegemony in British economic policy.

Into his second week in power, however, Gordon Brown was facing up to unfinished business with Eddie George and the Bank of England. He intended to push on with plans to strip the Bank of its role as financial watchdog and police chief in the City of London. Through nods, winks and threats to pull the plug, the Bank had kept finance houses in order down the generations. Anyone wanting to run a licensed bank needed the approval of Threadneedle Street. But a string of high-profile collapses had embarrassed the Bank of England – Johnson Matthey, BCCI and Barings being the obvious examples. George himself had been in charge of banking supervision when the Middle East-controlled BCCI crashed in 1991. In opposition Brown had criticized Eddie George's banking watchdog team, accusing them of being complacent and ineffectual. Labour was committed to beefing up the Securities and Investments Board (SIB), the body which policed stockbrokers and fund managers. The election commitment was to transform it from a self-regulatory body, run by the City establishment, into an independent body with statutory powers. But Brown had decided to go further. He planned to strip the Bank of England of its role in regulating banks and award it to the newly relaunched 'super-SIB'.

Brown had warned Eddie George that he wanted to transfer the Bank's regulatory powers at their first meeting on Bank Holiday Monday. George was told then that if he was to be handed control of monetary policy he would have to accept a shake-up of the Bank's structures and functions, including regulation. The Governor was given two letters, one of which was to be made public the following day at the press conference outlining the Bank's new independent power to set interest rates. The other letter was brief. It informed George that accompanying the monetary policy reforms regulatory powers were to be transferred from the Bank to the new super-SIB. No date was given for the transfer and it concluded, 'We will of course consult you on how it happens'. George was told to keep this second letter to himself.

Brown and Balls, when they were drafting the original letter to the Governor in the final days of the election campaign, covered both initiatives in the single text. But in the hectic string of meetings during the first weekend in power they were advised by Treasury officials to keep the two policies distinct. They argued that it would be wrong to publicize the plans to strip the Bank of the City watchdog role when they might not be introduced for some time, and that delay might cause damaging speculation and uncertainty. Also, it was argued, why dilute the announcement of the Bank's new control of monetary policy? The Chancellor and his advisers were convinced. The paragraph on regulation was extracted and turned into the second confidential letter. It was a fateful decision and one which would rebound on them with near-disastrous consequences. Sources close to Brown later acknowledged they were 'mistaken'.

Treasury officials were worried that when George saw the letters and realized there were two sides to the deal he would turn the whole thing down. But he emerged after his private meeting with the Chancellor 'beaming, and saying it was wonderful news' according to one source. At that point Brown believed there could be no misunderstanding about the Government's long-term intentions. While in opposition Balls had signposted Labour's desire to revamp regulation of the Britain's banks during informal meetings with Bank of England staff. According to a source close at hand, 'Eddie knew exactly what the score on both counts was from the beginning, he knew that supervision was going to be part of the package.'

George's interpretation of that meeting was very different. He understood from the very short text of the second letter that the transfer of regulation would only happen after further consultation and, by implication, some way down the line. In any case he did not have much time to search for hidden meanings in the fine print. He had just been given twenty-four hours' notice of a seismic shift in British economic policy and his main concern was to get back to Threadneedle Street to brief his staff. It may have been an official holiday but by half past eleven that morning the Bank was humming with activity. Staff of the famous institution, accustomed to the cautious, measured pace of the Old Lady, were hauled in from their homes and holidays. They were quickly caught up in the excitement of the moment. George conveyed to them his delight that the following day they would be handed the keys to the engine-room of monetary policy and access to the central lever of power – the control of interest rates.

As for banking regulation, the Governor warned his staff that there were changes afoot. He advised them that the Chancellor intended to create a beefed-up Securities and Investments Board and that the Bank of England would in due course hand over some historic functions. But throughout these briefings George stressed that there would be consultation before changes were implemented. Effectively, Eddie George was telling his staff that there was nothing to worry about. There were some in the Bank, though, who smelled a rat. Hundreds of jobs depended on supervision of Britain's bank and finance houses. Even after consultation, some asked, would there not have to be redundancies? To Bryan Quinn, who oversaw the Bank of England's watchdog role, any dilution of these powers was anathema, consultation or no consultation. To add salt to the wound, the Bank was also to lose the technical management of government debt with the Treasury taking over the auctioning of government stocks. Ian Plenderleith, one of the Bank's other top managers, was said to be 'spitting blood'.

Brown, meanwhile, was faced with a dilemma. The State Opening of Parliament was set for 14 May. At this traditionally colourful ceremony the monarch unveils the Government's plans for the parliamentary session, the Queen's Speech containing a list of the bills which will be introduced. Labour had planned a marathon session, through till the autumn of 1999, jam-packed with measures to honour commitments made in the manifesto. The Queen's Speech had been formally drawn up immediately after the election and was rubber-stamped at Labour's first Cabinet meeting on 8 May. The Lord Chancellor, Lord Irvine, who presided over the drafting of Labour's first parliamentary programme, had allowed space only for one Bank of England bill which would contain legislation for the handover of monetary policy. There was no room for a second bill to cater for the creation of the super-SIB or the handover of the Bank's regulatory powers. A Treasury insider described it as 'a screw-up, a breakdown in communications'. The Chancellor, meanwhile, was becoming aware of the first rumours of unease inside the Bank about the removal of supervisory powers. On the other hand SIB top brass were clamouring for legislation to establish their new statutory role. Brown decided he must act quickly to prevent a damaging power vacuum developing.

What was needed was a wide-ranging Bank of England reform bill. But with the Queen's Speech already written the new Chancellor was boxed in. A bill creating a new, reinforced City watchdog authority would require hundreds of complex clauses. Lord Irvine warned Gordon Brown that such a time-consuming bill simply could not be shoehorned into Labour's first eighteen-month programme. Brown decided he would have to proceed in two stages. The move to strip the Bank of England of regulatory powers would be tacked on to the existing bill. The vision for the super-SIB would be announced at the same time but with the parliamentary legislation pushed back to the following year's session. This time there could be no triumphalist press conference at the Treasury. Brown would have to appear at the Commons dispatch box at the fag-end of the debate on the Queen's Speech to reveal his revamped deal for the policing of the City.

The Treasury was another beehive of activity on the weekend of 17 and 18 May. The adrenalin-driven excitement of the new regime was still in the air but there was also an extra air of urgency. Brown needed a high-powered leader for the watchdog body which would inherit from the Bank of England. The Deputy Governor of the Bank, Howard Davies, was to be the man for the job. Davies had been marked out as a high-flyer from the moment he was appointed to run the Audit Commission at the age of thirty-six. Married to a television news executive, Davies knew his way around the media and he got his message across effortlessly during his time as Director-General of the CBI. Gregarious and football-loving, he seemed to be marking time when he moved into the sober salons of Threadneedle Street as Eddie George's deputy. Taking command of a new financial police authority looked like a challenge Davies would accept with relish. But Brown had to get him signed up that weekend to give credibility to the package he would announce on the Tuesday and Davies was thousands of miles away on a visit to Argentina. Exasperated officials in Brown's private office clung to phones throughout that weekend trying to clear lines to South America. For a while Howard Davies could not be found. When he was tracked down Brown was getting worried. To the Chancellor's immense relief Davies said yes – even though the brief was sketchy and he would not see anything on paper until his return from Argentina.

Brown then squared up to his most difficult task. He had to break the news to Eddie George. On the morning of Monday 19 May, the Governor was summoned to Number 11 Downing Street. There, in the Chancellor's formal book-lined office, Brown and George faced each other seated in elegant high-backed leather chairs. It was exactly two weeks after their first glowing get-together on the May Day holiday. Now the warmth had evaporated, the tension was all-pervading. Brown slowly explained to George that he could wait no longer over the transfer of the Bank's regulatory role and that he would announce his intention to legislate the following day in the Commons. According to one account the Governor 'went ballistic'. His anger was plain for all to see as he marched out of Number 11. Gordon Brown's more diplomatic version of events was that he had never had a 'huge' row with Eddie George: 'The Bank always said they wanted to keep banking regulation, it's their right to say it . . . we just had a different view.'

Eddie George returned to Threadneedle Street shaken as well as seething. He felt he had misled his own staff, 500 of whose jobs were now on the line. He had promised them there would be consultation over any changes to regulation yet within a fortnight the Chancellor was presenting him with a cut-and-dried decision. The Treasury, George believed, had behaved in a cackhanded way. He felt like a company chief executive who had seen the ground cut away from him by the controlling shareholder. Back at the Treasury Brown was worried. After George's outburst the Chancellor feared that the Governor might go public with his concerns on the day of the Commons announcement. Brown and Whelan mulled over how they would present their case to the press. 'I'll have a word with Higgy,' Whelan reassured his master as he made a note to call Stuart Higgins, the editor of the *Sun*.

The following morning, Tuesday 20 May, the Governor prepared to brief the Bank of England's board of directors, the great and the good of the financial establishment known as the Court. They gathered as usual around the large oval table in the sumptuous neoclassical Court room, adorned with ornate eighteenth-century plasterwork, which is one of the architectural glories of the City of London. Now raised voices echoed around it. Members of the Court were outraged by what they heard from George – that they were no longer to be guardians of the City of London's probity. They were as angry as George had been that they had not been consulted about Brown's plan to shift the regulatory powers of the Bank. Eddie George tried to calm them down.

That afternoon Brown rose from the government front bench in the Commons. After fifteen years on the opposition side this was his first time at the dispatch box as Chancellor. It should have been an occasion for Labour back-bench rejoicing and for Brown to rest on his laurels after the dramatic reshaping of interest rate policy. But this was not time for clever flourishes or for baiting the Tories. Brown ploughed straight into his announcement on regulation of the financial sector. Supervision, he told the House, would be transferred from the Bank to the Securities and Investments Board. Later, he continued, a new super-SIB would be created to absorb the so-called self-regulatory organizations, each covering different sectors of the financial markets. Howard Davies was to chair the new authority with a budget of £150 million. MPs, having had no warning, were shocked. The media, apart from a tip from Whelan that something big would happen that afternoon, knew and guessed nothing. Pressed by the Tories to explain in more detail how the super-SIB would work, Brown ducked and wove. It came across as a hasty, last minute decision, which in a sense it was. Kenneth Clarke tore into the new Chancellor. None of this had been mentioned in the Labour manifesto or the Queen's Speech, he argued, and the Government was in too much of a hurry, 'like eighteen-year-olds in the saloon bar trying every bottle on the shelves'.

George, meanwhile, was making no attempt to conceal his frustration and irritation. With Brown on his feet in the Commons, the Governor gathered his senior staff in the Guildhall. Hundreds of them assembled in one of the City's most famous meeting halls to hear Eddie George announce that the Bank was to be shorn of one of its most hallowed responsibilities. Their jobs should be secure, he claimed, as they would theoretically move under the wing of the SIB. But George admitted there would be uncertainty and he made it absolutely clear to them that he was unhappy with the Treasury's handling of the change. Trying hard to convince them he was on their side, George revealed he had expected consultation but that none had taken place. He may have been the Governor but he was a Bank of England man and boy, having spent thirty-five years in Threadneedle Street, and he identified with these foot-soldiers. Inevitably George took flak from the floor. He was accused of selling the Bank's staff down the river. His populist pitch worked at a later stage, though, as the banking union directed its anger away from George and towards the Government.

The following day, while the media gave a favourable response to Brown's announcement, George appeared to be toying with the nuclear option. Traditionally Bank Governors are so cautious with their public utterances that they are barely reported beyond the financial pages. By coincidence the Bank of England's annual report was published that day and George was giving a rare press conference. The invited clutch of economics and banking correspondents gathered in the oak-panelled chamber used by Governors for their occasional encounters with the media. After a string of technical enquiries George was unexpectedly asked whether he had considered resigning over the regulation issue. For thirty seconds or so George waffled and rambled, all the while going over in his bridge player's mind how to play himself out of trouble. There was no preconceived strategy if the question came up and George was reacting to events on his feet.

He decided to take the risky course and came clean in front of the assembled press corps. 'All sorts of things go through your mind,' he said finally, including the thought of resigning although it had gone away 'very quickly'. The words were carefully chosen but were enough to lay bare the extent of the alienation felt by the Governor. The financial news wires were soon humming with a story which would bring silence and open mouths to every dealing room across the world's financial capitals. Rows between Governors of the Bank of England and Chancellors could send tremors through markets, yet here was talk of resignation. If George had quit Brown would have been faced with a crisis of confidence.

Far from trying to calm nerves, it appeared that the Government was ready to joust in the open with George. An unnamed source was quoted as saying that George had 'played into our hands', suggesting that the Chancellor now had just the excuse he needed to dispense with the Governor when his contract expired. The remark came amidst mounting speculation that Gavyn Davies, leading City economist and ally of Brown, was waiting in the wings and ready to inherit George's mantle. It looked to the City establishment like a politically motivated plot to ease a Labour sympathizer into Threadneedle Street. The sight of a Labour-controlled Treasury apparently trying to undermine a Governor of the Bank of England only served to sharpen these suspicions. Brown found himself under fire from leading players on the financial stage, including Lord Alexander of NatWest Bank. The Chancellor's honeymoon, which had started so spectacularly in the first week in office, had ended. Relations between Brown and George would take a long time to heal.

Once the dust had settled George told colleagues at the Bank that this cloud might have a silver lining. Another Barings crash, he opined, might contaminate the Monetary Policy Committee's reputation as a keeper of sound money. Better, he argued, to allow the task of watching over the banking system to pass to the new body with all the risk of a failure to take on board. In principle, the Governor told staff, he did not disagree with the Chancellor's reasoning for the move. He was not as dogmatic as others, like Bryan Quinn who wanted to fight the Treasury to the death over the issue. In due course he admitted to colleagues that if the full package, outlined in the two famous letters on 6 May, had been offered at once in its entirety he would have accepted it. What had angered him was that he had been humiliated and embarrassed in front of his staff for apparently giving worthless assurances. This stemmed from his interpretation of the secret letter on 6 May. At first glance that letter seemed to guarantee consultation before any final decision, although on second reading Bank of England officials conceded there was a sniff of ambiguity. The Treasury view was that 'the issue was always about the form of the transfer of powers – we said we would consult about how this would happen and not whether'. By the autumn, when the new City police force was formally named the Financial Services Authority (the super-SIB nickname forgotten), George let it be known he could live with the changes.

Gordon Brown's reform train continued to accelerate down the track. Despite initial resistance from George, Brown announced that two Deputy Governors would be appointed at the Bank. Both would sit on the new committee responsible for setting interest rates. One, Mervyn King, would take charge of monetary policy, the other would act as a link between the Bank of England and the regulators at the SIB, 'speaking for the financial regulation interest in any monetary policy discussion', according to the Treasury. That post was to be filled by David Clementi who had a strong track record in merchant banking. The Chancellor also announced the names of 'the wise men and women' who would sit with George and the Deputy Governors on the monetary policy committee. The outside experts included a Dutchman, Professor Willem Buiter of Cambridge University, and Dr DeAnne Julius, an American woman who was chief economist with British Airways. Gordon Browns advisers anticipated a hostile reaction to the idea that they would have a say in the direction of British interest rates. As one put it, 'Nobody said we've got these foreigners, it was quite astonishing.' Before alighting on Julius the Treasury had considered other women, including Ruth Lea of the Institute of Directors. In the end, though, according to one source, 'All were first choices, all accepted'. To minimize the danger of leaks they were approached only days before the announcement on 2 June.

And so George at the head of his committee began the task of charting monetary policy. They were charged by Brown with meeting an inflation target of 2.5 per cent; too much above or below and George would have to answer for the committee to the Governor. Steadily through that summer of 1997 and beyond they raised rates by a total of 1.25 per cent over six months. With clear signs of the economy overheating, their decisions were not difficult. But as investment flowed into a booming Britain the new Government faced up to an unexpected sterling crisis. Previous Labour administrations had been dogged by a plunging pound. For New Labour the problem was in the other direction, with sterling touching new heights. Holidaymakers were delighted but exporters squealed. It was a Jekyll and Hyde economy. On the High Street and in the out-of-town shopping malls customers were spraying around cash in a style reminiscent of the 1980s. Wallets were overflowing with windfall receipts after a run of flotations by building societies and insurance companies. Retailers sat back and raked it in. Their profit margins were bloated further if they were selling imported goods which, because of the strong pound, had become cheaper for them to buy. But in the belt-and-braces world of manufacturing the talk was of recession. European orders were drying up as the pound moved to levels untouched since the early 1990s. Herein was a dilemma for George and his monetary policy committee.

In the first week in August Westminster and Whitehall had slowed to a standstill after Labour's first frenetic 100 days. Tony Blair was sunning himself in Tuscany, where every pound would buy a couple more glasses of Chianti than the previous year. Gordon Brown was packing his bags to cross the Atlantic for his vacation with Sarah Macaulay. The politicians were no longer running the interest rate show.

Eddie George and his monetary policy committee could not afford to think of holidays as they agonized over whether to raise interest rates. An upward move was needed to dampen the ardour of Britain's consumers, yet higher lending rates would suck in another tide of foreign investment and the pound would drift up even more. After much debate they opted to push rates up by a quarter point to 7 per cent, the highest in more than four years. But there was a strong hint that this was to be the last move for a while, with the committee's statement noting that 'Upward pressure on the exchange rate should be reduced by the perception that interest rates have reached a level consistent with the inflation target.' George and his team were effectively saying, 'We'll sit back and stick with 7 per cent.'

Interest rates were put on hold but the problem facing the economy could not be. There were hints of a split in the committee as Professor Buiter confessed that given the difficulties of predicting the course of the economy, 'We are in uncharted territory.' Rates were pushed up another one-quarter per cent in November with business leaders screaming their dismay. By early 1998 George could no longer achieve unanimity on his committee. Half were hawks calling for a higher cost of borrowing to choke domestic spending, the other half doves sensitive to the plight of manufacturers. George was forced to use his casting vote to prevent another increase. Opponents of Gordon Brown attempted to heap blame on him. Why, they asked, had he not used his Budgets to tighten the corset on the economy and to ease the pressure on George and his colleagues to push up interest rates? As they had done in July, Treasury sources retorted that they had indeed drained billions from the economy with their taxation measures. Sources close to the Chancellor questioned George's strategy. Putting rates on hold after August, they argued, had given consumers a cue to continue borrowing and spending; the committee should have been tougher sooner.

The interest rate debate was not the only source of tension between the Governor and the Chancellor. The question of George's reappointment had still not been resolved. The delay was unsettling for George and he was puzzled by conflicting signals appearing in the media with no certainty as to which bore the hallmarks of Treasury briefings. His new five-year term was confirmed in February. Sources close to Brown tried to refute the suggestion that the decision had been made weeks earlier and that George had been left to sweat it out. They pointed out that there was an identical gap between the announcement of Robin Leigh Pemberton's appointment in the early 1980s and the formal start of his contract. Yet neither Treasury nor Bank of England denied that the personal relationship between Brown and George was cool.

Ken Clarke and Eddie George may have fallen out over interest rate policy but they could always enjoy a drink together afterwards. Both had the outgoing cheeriness of regulars in a saloon bar. George told a *Sunday Telegraph* interviewer with an expansive gesture that Clarke 'is very jolly and like that' while Brown was only the same 'to some degree'. At an informal meeting of European finance ministers in York George doffed a train driver's cap and boarded Stevenson's *Rocket* to provide the press with a dream photo opportunity. It was just the 'what do I care' gesture which Ken Clarke could – and did – pull off.

Treasury minders in York were horrified. They advised George's people that the new Chancellor would never expose himself to such a stunt. Brown and George were from different moulds and in a year of such upheaval it was hardly surprising that working relationships should be frayed. A source close to the Chancellor claimed to understand George's predicament. 'It was all a big shock to the Bank, they were big changes and the Bank was not used to changing. It all took a long time.'

The pressures were immense on Brown as he shook the pillars of the country's financial institutions. So all the more he needed the support and efficiency of a backroom team whom he could trust unswervingly.

Chapter Seven: Brown's Army

In Brown's non-stop life of politics, politics, politics, there is little time for honing his profusion of ideas into written form or dealing with the daily necessities of high office. So Brown has a backroom staff who sit at the end of a fax or a phone prepared to do everything from writing jokes to fixing up a suit or a coat. These are more than just camp followers – they are forces in their own right who have shown their loyalty to their man and their Party. Brown has reciprocated this loyalty by taking them with him into power. Just as in opposition, they still have his ear.

Writing speeches for Brown can be a thankless task. The process usually goes deep into the night, and Brown is quite capable of tearing up a speech at 2 a.m. and demanding that it be reworked first thing in the morning. His staff work together all the time and compete constantly for Brown's attention. He revels in the position of puppeteer, pulling the strings of his researchers, scribes and word-spinners. They feel at the centre of power – but they have to put up with some eccentric behaviour.

One of the team told how he was in London when he received a fax from Brown in Scotland asking him for some ideas and comment on part of the Budget. He faxed back some thoughts and then telephoned the Chancellor. No one answered the phone, but shortly afterwards he received a fax from Brown. The same process occurred on a number of occasions, and eventually it dawned on the man in London that Brown was closeted with other speechwriters in Edinburgh and did not want them to know that he was communicating with the London advisers.

Much of the philosophical exploration of New Labour takes place in Gordon Brown's office on the first floor of his North Queensferry house in the company of a doctor and a young politician. The three men, Dr Colin Currie, Douglas Alexander MP and Brown himself, share a common religious and philosophical background as well as a commitment to the New Labour cause. They are three sons of the Manse – that is, offspring of Presbyterian churchmen – and observe a strict order of service when it comes to speech-preparation and writing.

Brown presents the ideas at some length, mostly without interruption; a discussion follows, and some notes are taken down for the key phrases to be worked on. A session lasts about an hour and a half and there may easily be several in the course of a day. 'The members of the group skim given texts in advance,' says Currie.

'For a big speech, there is an immense amount of excitement – have we read this or that, who is thinking what. "I've got thirty-six books I found in America last weekend, and we will do a bit more when I have read them." There is almost a sense of seminar work.' In the middle of the 'seminar' Brown will dive into his bookcase to fish out an economic text to show to one of the coven. The conversation is constantly broken up by phone-calls, which the group accept as an occupational hazard of working for a man in the public eye.

The topics are invariably complicated but Brown's problem is not a difficulty with the ideas, but with finding a way to present them. Currie is in awe of the Chancellor's brainpower: 'He genuinely wants to think and he wants to bring you into the process, partly as someone to bounce ideas off, but also partly as a translator. The problem about getting it from this sort of symposium experience into readable or speakable prose is that the ideas are complex, the sentences are long, and there is a tendency, because the guy is phenomenally bright, to give his researchers a hard time.

'So it all gets churned together, and when he sucks it in, swirls it about and gets it out, it comes out as a sentence trying to be a paragraph and a paragraph trying not very hard not to be a chapter. So writing for him is an exercise in containment, simplification and deletion. What comes from Brown is a very large straight whisky which actually has enough in there for several whiskies; so I feel, why not add some soda water, and we can all have a nice drink.'

Currie is Brown's longest-standing and most dedicated Scottish adviser. The medical director of a healthcare trust, a consultant and senior lecturer in geriatric medicine in Edinburgh, he has no direct experience of economics or politics. His writing experience has been primarily in fiction; he has written nine novels, under the *non de plume* of Colin Douglas, featuring life in a National Health Service hospital.

Currie has known Brown for some thirty years, since they were students together at Edinburgh University. Brown was the editor of a college magazine for which Currie wrote a column. That intellectual and personal friendship has stood the test of time. Currie was also on hand when Brown wrote his biography of James Maxton. Brown promised Currie many years ago that he would ask him to write for him when he was a Member of Parliament, but the doctor cannot have been expecting to have been still writing for him when he became Chancellor.

The excitement of being summoned to write a Budget speech at Brown's Scottish home and then at the Treasury in Whitehall tickles pink the garrulous and self-deprecating doctor. As well it might. Budgets are typically written within the hallowed portals of the Treasury in an atmosphere of enormous secrecy and usually by people with three economics degrees to their name. For parts of the Budget to be written in the Chancellor's kitchen must be virtually unprecedented, and Currie admits to being slightly puzzled as to how the Treasury views this contracting out of the main speech of the Chancellor's year. 'There was lots of good minor comedy around the Budget speech, in this possible clash of expectations and expertise. Yet it came out as a smoothly managed exercise, where the Treasury did not lose face; nobody noted that the Treasury did not write the Budget speech, which is the convention. The fact that it worked made the process forgivable. If it had not, there would have been lots of painful lessons on both sides.'

A compact gnome of a man with a crisp suit, well-polished shoes, a businesslike box case and austere gold-rimmed spectacles (rather than glasses), Currie is the complete generalist, who says he is interested in ideas but not consumed by them as Brown is. All this helps him articulate Brown's thoughts in layman's language. Currie makes three sets of contributions to the Party: first, jokes; second, grammar; third, wit.

Currie says he rewrites and edits-out Brown's 'writing tics' such as overlong sentences, split infinitives and repetitious language. A grammatical pedant, he scorns the use of sentences that slip easily into Brown's rhetoric, like: 'This conference has done more in eighteen minutes than the Tories did in eighteen years.' Currie also draws attention to what he calls Brown's 'triple-rising thing, a rising Presbyterian accentuation', and tries to write for the rhythm.

The doctor is on permanent call if Gordon Brown needs a joke for a speech, and the Chancellor has been known to phone him up from a train and ask for five good jokes for the speech he is on the way to deliver. Currie takes credit, in a characteristically modest manner, for the witty reference in Brown's 1997 Labour Party Conference speech to Clare Short's outspoken statements on soft drugs.

The other Scot in the Presbyterian coven is Douglas Alexander, the newly elected MP for Paisley South and a long-term friend and colleague of Brown's. Alexander started working for Brown when he was twenty-three, just out of university. Now thirty, Alexander is thought to be destined for a high-flying political career. Brown wants him to prove himself as an MP but has earmarked him for advancement. Alexander's capacity for finding lines to fire up an audience wins him brownie points with Gordon Brown and his speechwriting entourage.

The austere, even pedantic, rigour of the Scots is tempered for Brown by his close association with Michael Wills, a former media executive who is now an MP. Wills wants to help formulate a new ideology and values based on 'historic

Labour values', but with the emphasis now on redistributing 'opportunity' rather than wealth.

Brown works with Wills as he might have worked with a student during his old days as an academic in Scotland: he gives him some notes – usually a couple of pages of rough thoughts – and tells him to go away and flesh them out and bring him back an ordered essay, incorporating Wills's own ideas, which he can then argue through. Brown likes to put the speechwriter through his paces, to see how well the thoughts are worked out.

Wills helped Gordon Brown write his speeches for the *Spectator*, the Charter 88 Group and for the John Smith lectures. Wills says Brown is rigorous about working through his ideas and he worries away at them until they are clear in his mind and he feels comfortable with them. That can mean long phone-calls at eleven o'clock at night or during holidays. Wills is a trusted and respected part of this process, but Brown is the final arbiter of the content and the form.

Wills, who is forty-five and lives in Belsize Park, north London, won Brown's attention with his capacity to conceptualize and express themes that have now become familiar through the new Clause Four. He developed some important connections early on in his career: as a producer at the *Weekend World* programme he worked with a young Peter Mandelson, a researcher at the time. The two became good friends, and this survived when Brown and Mandelson had their rift following the leadership election.

Wills stayed in television (after Mandelson left to become involved in the Labour Party) and founded his own television production company called Juniper Communications – since sold. Wills, whose father had been a Labour activist in Finchley, had wanted to contribute to the modernization of the Labour Party from the mid-1980s, and in 1988 Mandelson introduced him to Gordon Brown. The two have worked on an informal basis since then. Wills won the candidature for the North Swindon constituency in a high-profile and bitterly-fought campaign against an AEEU official.

Once Wills was provided the political perspectives on policy, Brown's academically-gifted political adviser Ed Miliband pro-vides the presentational panache. At twenty-eight, Miliband is already perceived as having made his mark. Miliband takes what Currie, Alexander or Brown himself give him, and rearranges and structures the material. That is no easy task, he admits: 'We find it is extremely difficult to do it without Gordon. He will say, for instance, "I don't like that phrase too much." If it's a passionate speech, it's very difficult to write it for him – he needs to find his own unique voice – but now that he is Chancellor he has less time to work on them.' Miliband's is a political appointment paid for by the Government, and he has worked on Brown's speeches for Party Conferences and Party meetings. His powers were put to the test when Brown decreed that his Budget speeches should be short (no more than an hour) and crisp.

Miliband has been influenced by American democratic politics in a similar way to Ed Balls and Brown himself. He went from Haverstock Comprehensive in north London, one of the area's toughest schools, to the United States, where he worked on *The Nation* magazine and in television. On his return to this country he studied politics, philosophy and economics at Corpus Christi College, Oxford, where his tutor was the Marxist economist Andrew Glyn. Glyn says: 'Edward is very clever, outstanding in fact. He was distinctly left of centre and had an orientation towards policy. I always found him very good company.'

Miliband was a researcher for the television programme *A Week in Politics* and later worked for Harriet Harman. Then in October 1994 he joined the Brown entourage, and in January 1995 was encouraged by Brown to take a master's degree in economics at the London School of Economics in preparation for playing a leading part in the New Labour Treasury.

For as long as he can remember, Miliband has thought and talked politics. His late father Ralph was a European émigré and Marxist academic, while his older brother David heads the Number 10 policy unit and is an expert in education. His partner, Liz Lloyd, is also in the Blair policy unit.

While the troupe throw out ideas and hammer out sentences and paragraphs for Brown, the Chancellor remains the ultimate arbiter. It is his act which the supporting cast follow. Their reward is to feel part of, and to provide the grist for, a philosophical and cultural revolution.

Treasury Earth Mother

Sue Nye is the mother of three young children, and recently when Gordon Brown's publicity advisers were looking for a happy family for a photocall Nye was on hand. She won widespread admiration for her patience in keeping her three-year-old son Ben still for the pose while he stood next to Gordon Brown and Sarah Macaulay as photographers and TV cameramen clicked away and barked instructions. But that has been the least of the difficult tasks Brown and his entourage have set her as they build up the organization for a smooth-running Chancellor's office.

Sue Nye has been in charge of top politicians' offices for almost twenty years and she has seen more political crises and handled more distraught politicians than she cares to remember – James Callaghan, Michael Foot and Neil Kinnock have all benefitted from her firm hand. The chance to sit at the top table of a party actually in power is a different matter and here Nye takes her lead from that tough operator of the Wilson years, Marcia Williams, alias Lady Falkender, who put the fear of God into much of the cabinet. Nye does much the same at the Treasury – she worked briefly at Number 10 when Falkender was still in evidence.

With her muted London accent and classless-girl image – high leather lace-up boots, discreet ruby ring and quirky gold-rimmed spectacles – Sue Nye bridges the gap between enlightened affluent New Labour and the old proletarian image. That is essential for her job, which is keeping the Labour Party sweet and putting the Cabinet on to Gordon's wave-length – no easy task with a professional Chancellor. Nye brings hordes of Labour MPs from obscure places through the Treasury once in a while to give them a free drink and shake the Chancellor's hand. That gives everybody the feeling that it's their own Treasury. 'Sue Nye has great political instincts, she's been around a huge amount of time, she knows what people in the Party are thinking. She knows the Cabinet, and she knows which Cabinet members we get on with and the ones we don't,' said an insider.

Nye's qualities can never have been as much in demand –

or appreciated – as they are now. There are two reasons for this: first, Nye is working for a real minister, not just a pale shadow. Second, Brown would not deny, and many would confirm, the view that he is disorganized and unworldly at the same time as being brilliant and temperamental. The challenge to the political secretary could hardly be greater.

The battle with Brown's notorious chaos does not daunt Sue Nye. She is tough; some say cold. And she stands up for herself with a vengeance. The worst insult for Nye is the suggestion that she uses her femininity to organize the men she oversees – she puts that down as 'boy stuff' and 'bollocks'. She has also told Gordon where to get off on many occasions. Once she persuaded him to attend a City meeting, even though she knew he would find it deathly dull. 'I knew that he would throw a wobbly about it. He had to do it because he was Chancellor, but I deliberately did not ask him to go outright, because I knew he did not want to. Afterwards I told him that he never has to do it again; but also that if he had not done it, it would have caused us problems for the next five years.' Brown was not ecstatic about posing at Nye son's party either, but Sue sneaked the appointment in under Gordon's nose and he was stuck.

The only other person with this sort of authority in the Chancellor's political and personal life is Brown's girlfriend, Sarah Macaulay. Her cool style and practical intelligence bear comparison with Nye's, but Nye wins out on age and influence.

Nye not only feeds the Chancellor's need for order and discipline, she also builds his guest-list, bringing together constituency people and those unconnected with his particular financial brief whom he ought to meet for his general knowledge. The Chancellor's tendency to become obsessed with a single topic irks Nye. As one civil servant put it: 'Being Chancellor is a particularly overloaded job; there are always lots of pressures on you to spend your whole time on official business. So Sue provides a good "countervailing force", which keeps Gordon's feet on the ground. Ken Clarke insisted on two afternoons a week with his constituency secretaries, ever since he got into government, to make sure he kept in contact with his constituency. There are risks of being dragged into this appalling official quagmire.'

Brown's need for a tough office manager and diplomat were brought to Nye's attention in 1992 by Peter Mandelson. He said Gordon needed someone 'to sort out his office.' This was meat and drink to the Labour party's king-pin organizer and she took on the job with alacrity. She found that Brown, who was Shadow Chancellor to the Treasury at the time, was surrounded by advisers who lacked the confidence to take in hand his disorganized energy. Nye says, 'He likes doing too many things, and the people working for him were not the sort to say: "Oh, for God's sake, don't do that, that's ridiculous!" My brief was to put order into his life.'

Nye set about arranging the Shadow Chancellor's office and appointing some new blood to allow Brown to use his efforts to better effect. But the job specifications were tough as Brown was an extremely demanding, and occasionally irascible, boss and colleague. 'He really needed someone who was respected already, and who could operate on his behalf. Someone he could trust.' Nye commissioned a head-hunter to conduct a search for two jobs, one an economist, the other in public relations: many people came for interview but no one was taken on. In the end, Nye and Gordon went to their own friends and contacts and Gordon came up with Ed Balls as his economics adviser, while Sue's friend Peter Mandelson came up with Charlie Whelan to be Brown's press officer.

Brown's relationship with Nye was an early success story. The Chancellor's furiously-paced but unfocused office was quickly put into shape by this 'frighteningly efficient' (according to her husband) administrator. Within a short time, the present Chancellor had given her wide authority. 'I know when I have to ask him something, and when I can say yes or no on his behalf.' Nye was able to take the sting out of the Chancellor's notorious gruffness. She also had the mettle to take his flak, knowing that he trusted her to do the right thing.

Nye has never been far from events at the centre of the government, and at the takeover of power on 2 May she was critical. The civil servants wanted the other leading Cabinet ministers' phone numbers and, according to Nick Macpherson, the Chancellors principal private secretary, Nye had a large database of contact numbers built up in opposition and was able to provide them very quickly.

In her twenty-year-long career, Nye has seen at close quarters almost all Labour's leaders ground down by opposition. But while they went by the wayside, she survived the journey into power and now works for the first time for a leading member of a government.

Sue Nye was born into Labour politics, but at a relatively humble level. The daughter of a London trades union official, she entered politics as a temporary secretary at Number 10 during Jim Callaghan's tenure as Prime Minister. Her efficiency was quickly recognized and the Civil Service gave her a job in Callaghan's Private Office. When Labour was defeated in 1979, she was part of the line-up that clapped Margaret Thatcher into Number 10. But she was politically unsympathetic and wanted out. Callaghan invited her to run his office in opposition and she accepted, keeping the job when Michael Foot became leader.

While Nye was working for Jim Callaghan she met her husband-to-be and showed herself to be a shrewd judge of men. At the time, Gavyn Davies was a young economist working in Callaghan's office at Number 10. Over the course of twenty years he went on to be chief economist at the American investment bankers Goldman Sachs. He is also a partner of the firm and is thus extremely rich; on the company's imminent sale he is set to become a millionaire many times over.

Nye's and Davies's political affilations with old Labour socialism initially puzzled Gavyn's plutocratic partners at Goldman Sachs. Now, Sue says, they understand the Party more easily. 'If you explain Labour is like Democrats,' she says, 'you don't get the baggage.'

At one time the partnership between business and New Labour looked capable of wafting Davies into high office, perhaps even as high as the Governorship of the Bank of England itself. Such a move would have been far from unusual in Goldman's boardroom – former senior partner Robert Rubin became Clinton's finance secretary, for example, but nothing tangible materialized for Davies who may simply be too close to Nye and New Labour. Davies himself had his fingers badly burned by *The Times*, which claimed his firm had used information leaked from the Treasury by Nye. Nye sued the paper and the suggestion was retracted.

Davies says he is deliberately maintaining his distance from Party officials. Keeping conversation away from sensitive matters tests Nye's discretion, as she admits she is often privy to secret plans such as the decision to make the Bank of England independent. But she claims that she and her husband stick to the topic of their growing family rather than the economy.

When Foot was replaced by Kinnock, Nye followed the new leader and worked with him for his entire period as leader of the opposition. She got particularly close to Glenys Kinnock and remains a soul-mate, sharing an interest in Third World development issues. Nye sat next to Glenys on the platform when Neil Kinnock gave his Conference speech at Bournemouth, laying into the Trotskyite Militant Tendency's antics in Liverpool. Supporting the Kinnock household was the act of a dutiful friend in time of stress. 'We were all very nervous what the reaction would be to his speech. We did not know what people would do. They could have stormed the platform! Bear in mind we had had lots of meetings in Liverpool and there was a lot of intimidation and threats of physical violence. We knew what was coming, we were looking at the hall and asking ourselves, "What are the buggers going to do? Neil knows that I am on the platform and will look after Glenys, he doesn't have to worry about that."

Nye also put up with Kinnock's notoriously painful speech-writing process. This often went on late into the night, with nothing happening until the former leader banged his head against the wall and said, 'I've got no words.' At that point the poetry flowed, and they could all go to bed.

Brown's speech-writing style has some similarities to Kinnock's – except he does it on a keyboard while Kinnock used a typewriter or pen and paper. Brown, Sue Nye says, agonizes over every word late into the night and involves all around him in the process. 'You can't just give Gordon a draft and he will say, "Oh, that is fine." Every single word will have had to have come from him. What he likes best is to be killing a keyboard, but have people around, challenging them: "What do you think of this bit?" Then he will split the screen into three and know which version was the best.' Where the self-flagellatory style scores, of course, is that by the time the speech is ready for delivery, the speaker knows it so well that he does not need to refer to the text and can deliver it with truly theatrical force. Nye says Brown's conference speeches have gained their force as a result.

When Neil Kinnock left the leadership, Nye knew better than to go with John Smith. It was a wise decision which she took partly out of loyalty to Kinnock, for whom she had worked for eight years, and partly because she doubted Smith's ability to continue the pace of Party and policy reform she thought was necessary for Labour to be elected. The Party was much more deeply split at the time than most were prepared to admit publicly. Given the widespread grief at Smith's tragically early death, Nye says that joining Smith would have been seen by Kinnock as a 'great betrayal'. Nye's career appeared to be out in the cold – until Peter Mandelson came to the rescue.

Mandelson was Sue Nye's lodger at the time – and had been for two years – and the two were close political as well as personal friends. Those days are long since gone and now she snipes at the political 'fixer' who was once also very close to Brown. 'He came to us for six weeks, and stayed two years; the big joke was that we had to knock down Peter's bedroom (when we refurbished the house) to get rid of him. Then he bought a flat in the next square so that I could pop over to tell him how to use the washing machine.'

The internecine dispute between Brown and Blair which followed John Smith's death soured Nye's relations with key members in the Blair camp. It was not a comfortable time. 'Relationships went slightly awry,' she says. 'Gordon and I had a tie and threads and relationships [with members of the Blair camp]. We had all the baggage of past relationships, and that had to be worked through.' In fact, Nye appears to have been a crucial conduit between Brown and Mandelson when Brown's relations with Mandelson cooled after the election of Tony Blair.

Nye's friendship with Mandelson duly broke down, although Nye says that on a personal level something of it remained. 'You can't rub out years of friendship. Politics isn't that important. Even now, Peter and I still have the most blazing rows about politics, current events, and we could say some terrible things to each other. However, I think – I know – were I to be taken ill in hospital, no matter how gruesome our last argument, the first thing he would do would be to visit me in hospital (or vice versa).'

The rift with the Blair camp rankles. Sue Nye was, and is, particularly friendly with Anji Hunter (Blair's old college friend and now a political ally) whom she calls 'one of her closest friends'. The two had worked very closely together, having similar roles in their respective masters' offices. Keeping that friendship open has placed great strain on the two women, but it has been critical in ensuring Nye's channels and influence at Number 10.

Nye may not have made it to be the Prime Minister's *chef de bureau*, but her efforts and achievement in building up the Chancellor's office are proving a match for all that Number 10 can throw at it. Nye's role in the selection of Charlie Whelan has ensured that Brown's profile in the Government and the country has been as high as that of the Prime Minister, and arguably at times even higher. Both are large personalities and both are completely committed to Gordon Brown. Nye will remain the 'earth mother' and great provider.

While in opposition, Brown's back-up team had been developing a programme and an economic approach as well as the tactics and methods to build up their man. Now the time had come to put the New Labour economics into effect.

Chapter Eight: Go-Go Economics

The old socialist battles between state and market, government and companies are over. Long live the new economics, where efficient markets serve the State by creating wealth while government ensures the people have the opportunity to benefit from it. Few people know it yet, but Britain has a radical and interventionist government whose aim is two-fold: first, to make economic institutions more transparent and efficient; second, to put wealth into the hands of those who government thinks really need it. Otherwise, government's role in the economy is to lay a framework for enterprise and leave the entrepreneurial, within limits, to get on with it. The problem is that not many people understand what is going on, let alone are ready to play their part.

They will have to, if Gordon Brown is going to succeed in bringing economics and the market into people's lives and a new 'commercial realism' into the national culture. In his own words: 'Individuals have the right to expect that government will increase employment, education and training opportunities – economic opportunities generally – and give people the right to participate in the political decisions which effect their lives, and to have more access to the culture of society.'

Old Labour-style taxation and spending have no place in this economics adventure, and if Gordon Brown and Tony Blair have their way, the new individualism and entrepreneurism will replace the old socialism for good. But Brown also has a strong ethical commitment to the welfare of the poor and disadvantaged. His ability to find expression for this alongside the newly enlightened business culture will be the touchstone of the success of his period at the Treasury.

Britain's key financial institutions were the first to feel the blast of the new 'fairness' and 'transparency' objectives. Changes at the Bank of England, in financial regulation, in monopolies policy, in rules about selling pensions, have shaken up the establishment. Gavyn Davies, who worked for the last Labour government in the late seventies and has been close to the Brown project, is amazed at the changes but shocked by the ignorance: 'Gordon has implemented large chunks of his framework, and people haven't realized it yet! The depth and profound nature of what he has done to the macro-economic nature of this country is hardly realized. Macro-economic management, as understood by the Treasury for the last twenty years, has almost ceased to exist.'

Davies says Brown is an activist who wants a firm hand on the economic tiller. 'Labour does not believe that we should just take our hands off the economy, set a money target, and let the economy deal with it. Gordon's policy is activist and interventionist – but only within certain compartments: welfare, labour market, regulation, competition policy, education. It is not a laissez-faire approach.'

The gap between government and business will be bridged as Labour beds down its politics: bureaucrats will be expected to be businessmen, old monetarists, managers and long-time socialists, stockholders. Equally, businessmen will be brought in to fire up welfare schemes and entrepreneurs used to shake up government departments. Those with jobs will be encouraged to improve their skills for this dynamic world we live in, while those without jobs will be told you cannot leave the market economy for ever. Like the poor, the global market will always be with us and to ignore it puts an individual and a country at peril, believe the new men at Whitehall. In this brave new market economy, people power reigns and every individual is being encouraged to fulfil his or her potential, with government support on the one hand, and the market discipline and reward on the other.

Enter here one of the men who fashioned New Labour. Robert Reich is a brilliant and diminutive American academic from the East Coast, who was Labor Secretary in Clinton's first administration. Reich taught Ed Balls and has been a visitor at Number 11 Downing Street in the course of the year. His Third Way or Three-legged 'Stool' may sound mystical, even millenarian, but it has infused some in the Labour government with a theory which has gripped the imagination. As Brown shows, the Third Way actually provides a means of bringing together market and state, Mammon and government. 'The middle way must recognize that you're in a market economy which must work in the public interest, that there is a lawful government, and the rule of government does not suppress the market. Government's role in this model is to equip people for a global marketplace, where public services are the rule, and they are absolutely crucial – they must be the best, and not simply the basic minimum. Government also pursues policies that maximize equality of opportunity and that is the only way to create more social justice and a more dynamic economy.'

The Third Way has strong American connotations but Britain has adopted it because it is thought it makes sense within our economic culture. Like America, Britain is looking for liberal alternatives to monetarism and free-market philosophies without throwing the baby out with the bathwater, and going back to antiquated nationalization or red in tooth and claw free markets. According to Michael Wills, MP for Swindon North and one of Brown's close colleagues, 'The Third-Way approach is the result of a similar response to common phenomena like globalization, new markets and the need for the highest possible level of skills. It is misleading to say Labour economics are borrowed from America. Gordon developed it as a key tool in Labour's modernizing agenda early in the 1980s because it was a practical response to the real world.'

The crux of the Third Way is its focus on the individual, encouraging him to take what he can from the markets, and to receive what he needs from government. It has connotations of the supremely rational 'golden mean' and Brown suggests the right balance has profound implications for people and their countries. 'Nations can rise and fall depending on the government's ability to work with people and have them adapt. The nations that succeed are those that will invest in people and will be prepared continuously to adapt.

'America has solved some of the problems of economic opportunity by creating jobs, but it hasn't solved the problem of social protection, or social cohesion, because it's got massive poverty. Europe has got a better record than America on social protection, but it hasn't got a good record in job creation. The challenge of the modern economy is to combine policies for social cohesion with policies for economic opportunity.'

Those theoretical terms translate in practice to two sets of actions that the government has taken in the last year. The first have been the big picture changes to institutions and economic practice, the sort of things that government do with the aim of social cohesion and transparent governance. The second are the smaller-level pushes and prods to stimulate enterprise and boost welfare.

On the first score, the government has turned the Treasury and the Bank of England upside down by wresting the power to set interest rates out of the hands of politicians. That brings the country in line with international practice, and takes political interests out of an economic decision that ought to be dispassionate. According to one source, the Labour Party finds this particularly convenient when it is in power. 'The Labour Party starts with nil credibility, and credibility is everything when it comes to setting interest rates.' It should also help deal with another Labour bugbear of old – pay negotiations.

The inflation target is intended to indicate to employers and unions what government believes the economy can afford. At the moment it is no more than a useful guideline rather than an enforceable limit as the timing of pay negotiations, let alone their outcomes, differs from one employer to another and even from one factory to another. So Ed Balls, the Chancellor's economics adviser, is thought to be studying a tripartite arrangement which brings unions, employers and government together to decide an affordable pay increase. This could then be enforced in a single settlement. Says Martin Wolf, the economics leader writer at the *Financial Times*: 'Balls had a quasi-corporatist view of the pay-bargaining process. By expressing the inflation target, the government hopes that wage and corporate bargainers will be aware of the likely path for inflation, and that it will guide their expectations.'

The matter gained added urgency in the middle of 1998 as pay increases in the private sector leaped and inflation leaped ahead of target. This prompted the Chancellor to warn that the price of high wage increases would be paid in numbers of unemployed.

The sensitivity of the inflation target set by the Bank of England committee cannot be exaggerated, and the Government believes it is essential there are mechanisms in place to check that the committee is playing fair. As Ed Balls puts it: 'The more the policy is set in an open and transparent institutional framework, with targets and clear goals, the easier it will be to say on particular occasions that we can make exceptions. If you don't set up a framework, then every time you make an exception, people will complain that there are no rules.'

Making exceptions to the targets is fraught with hazard, as it raises question marks over the sustainability of every subsequent target, but some situations are so grave that a well-managed change will be acceptable. Balls: 'If there was a huge and unexpected shock to the world economy, such as a ten-fold rise in oil prices, then over the following years it would be impossible for any economy to meet a 2.5 per cent inflation target. The system now in place allows inflation to go outside the target range in the short-term while you take steps to get back to the original target.'

Foreign exchange rates have been the biggest bone of contention in the Labour government's first year, but Balls takes a dispassionate view of their importance, seeing them as a neutral 'shock absorber for instability', reflecting inflation, growth or fiscal concerns. Such an approach to economic management will give scant comfort to exporters who have spent the first year beefing at government indifference to the high pound against the deutschmark. 'When we came into government, the Treasury said that inflation would be 4 per cent, and they wanted interest rates to go up immediately. That is what drove up sterling. If sterling had not risen, inflation would have gone up.'

Inflation is not the only evil in Brown's sights. The newly activist Treasury takes its role as policeman of companies and markets very seriously, and the decision to bundle the financial regulators into a single organization may be a prelude to a new crackdown on the monopolistic and the crooked in the financial sector. Says Brown; 'Part of our job is breaking up the vested interests of monopoly, not least in the utilities, to ensure proper competition in airlines, telecommunications, agriculture. Pro-competition and pro-equality policies go hand in hand.' Balls says he expects corporate governance – the term used to describe procedures to make sure companies act honestly and properly – to become tighter. 'We want to make markets work better, but information is basically imperfect. A lot is to do with short-term expectations . . . Even if there is no obvious market failure, government can still have an impact by working along the grain of the market and bringing a more long-term perspective.' This contrasts with the classic American role for government as the friend of business who only intervenes in the market when business cannot sort out its own affairs.

Government is making these big changes to company and Treasury practice to get to the bottom of Britain's greatest economic unfairness: inflation and unemployment. Brown: 'Inflation is the enemy of the poor and the weak. It is those on low incomes and fixed incomes who suffer most if it rises. It is the insecure and unemployed who suffered most from the consequences of macro-economic policy mistakes.' Brown has a strong ethical interest, over and above simple economic efficiencies, says Neil MacKinnon, a left-wing economist close to Brown's Treasury team: 'Gordon Brown wants to move beyond cyclical considerations in the economy with structural reforms which raise the level of potential output and have the objective of getting unemployment down and doing something about poverty.'

While the attacks on the inefficient institutions have been undertaken through dramatic changes, the attacks on poverty and joblessness are being carried out piecemeal. But this is because the two approaches are working hand in hand to gain the maximum effect. Economists see a ratchet effect, so that inflation and the big picture of money supply are not threatened by the government spending money on welfare and employment pushes whose effect may be long term.

Lord Eatwell, now President of Queens College Cambridge, is Neil Kinnock's former economic adviser. He says Brown has been more foresighted than the former unlucky leader of the Labour Party by finding a route to job creation without upsetting public finances. 'Brown has linked a policy dealing with supply of resources, and people with the right skills, or physical capacity, like machines, to macro-economic strategy. He expands the economy, as far as you can, against an inflation restraint. Then you shift the inflation restraint by making the economy more productive.'

The supply-side policies – that is, policies affecting production in the economy – to boost employment and industry are now motoring at the Treasury, where teams of managers have been directed to visit companies to see what jobs they have on offer for the young unemployed, and to visit universities to look for opportunities and new technologies. Gavyn Davies sees the government adopting 'a very, very strong supply-side, reform-oriented programme to create new employment, and to boost the economy's efficiency'. There are two parts to the supply-side enthusiasm. One is investment for long-term economic growth. The other is support of welfare programmes, for short-term social cohesion.

Investment is now the name of the game, for state as well as private sectors. The correlative of investment is long-termism and this has now become the boringly repetitive mantra for all things good and efficient. Brown: 'Neglect of investment is the consequence of macro-economic errors . . . We have had short-termism and inconsistency in monetary policy.' Brown does not tire of repeating that UK rates of investment lag behind competitor economies. A non-oil growth rate of just 1.7 per cent over twenty years is 'too low, and the British economy is too small with too few successful firms and a too narrow range of technologies'. This was confirmed by the recent McKinsey study on the efficiency and productivity of British companies and industrial sectors, which found that most of Britain's industrial sectors, except supermarketing and drugs, seriously lagged behind those of the developed world.

Investment policy goes in three directions: first, government is being encouraged to stimulate investment and follow financially adventurous criteria in its own departments. Second, companies are being given incentives and stimuli to invest more of their profits. Third, both government and the private sector are being pushed to make links and joint ventures between themselves. According to Brown, 'The mixed economy is a partnership between public and private sectors rather than a conflict in which there was a truce between public and private sectors. The two sectors have a shared interest. The breakthrough for the Left is to recognize that markets are an essential and efficient element of society; they do not automatically work in the public interest, but there is a public interest in making markets work more efficiently.'

Facilitating investment is one of the conundrums which Gordon Brown is working on, says Eatwell. 'There is no one single great policy on speeding up investment. Rather, a raft of small policies, all tending in the same direction. So it is not just an approach to labour market; there is policy on the capital side as well.'

Third Way philosophers see a straight continuum between the two sectors, and the faster the escalator between state and private, and vice-versa, the better. While the Treasury is seeking to build closer bridges to the private sector, to help the private sector with capital raising and skills development, government is benefiting from private-sector financial disciplines. As the state seeks to unload some of the risk of large-scale investment projects, the private sector is receiving increasing stimuli to expand its own investing base. The way to achieve this is to re-invest profits, rather than hand them out to shareholders in the form of dividends. This was said to be the reason for the advance corporation tax, and the withdrawal of tax credits for pension funds announced in the second budget, says Eatwell. 'There is a bias in this country towards dividend distribution. By this tax move he has made retention less expensive and tackled a bias against investment.' The view was not shared by the pensions lobby who saw the measure as a straightforward raid, netting the Exchequer £50 billion over ten years. One leader writer for the *Guardian* wrote: 'The Chancellor seems to have ignored the fact that pension-fund money is people's money. There can be few worse examples of short-termism than raiding people's long-term savings in order to finance today's government expenditure.'

Balls's own Oxford University economics tutor, Tim Jenkinson, also questions the measures. 'I don't think some of the tax changes have been very well thought through. The removal of tax credits on pensions was justified on an inconsistent basis, that it would increase investment. In fact I think it will reduce investment. It was a tax rise hidden under a cloak so that the general population would not spot it, at least for a while. I told Ed that it was silly to rush it through so quickly.'

Private and public sectors are being pulled together by the Private Finance Initiative, where the state becomes a stakeholder with the private sector in initiatives like the development of the London Underground, the redevelopment of the Treasury building itself or hospitals. Says Brown: 'The Treasury must ensure the public and private sectors co-operate to inject dynamism into the PFI to encourage the private sector to raise capital and manage projects. And equipping everyone with the wherewithal to compete in the modern market place means ensuring an equal opportunity to compete.'

International standards of best practice in management, both in the public and private sectors, underpin the Chancellor's enthusiasm for the micro-economic activism. Brown: 'The only way that a modern economy can work as a knowledge-based economy in an information age is by getting the best out of people's potential. And the only way that can happen is by having policies for equality of opportunity. The premium is on having skills to create technology driven precision products which depend on the ingenuity and dedication and commitment of the workforce.'

Those individuals who cannot reap the benefit of the market economy, by enjoying its opportunities for work or investment, see its darker side. That is unemployment, and the evil it wreaks on families and communities cuts the Chancellor to the quick. He frequently mentions that some one in five households has a breadwinner out of work. The macro-economy pays the price, says Eatwell: 'The unemployed can represent a constraint on an expanding economy, because they lack the work experience or skill. Bank clerks who lose their jobs because of automation in the bank industry are often quite intelligent people, so they can be moved up quite effectively. Similarly, there are an enormous number of arts graduates, often with modern languages, who find it extremely difficult to get a job. They can also be taught high-skilled jobs. So this notion that the unemployed are a great lumpen proletariat is just not true.'

Unemployment causes instability at a community level, but also distorts the labour market, because the larger the pool of unemployed, the lower the wages of those at the bottom of the working ladder. Martin Wolf, a friend and former colleague of Ed Balls, says: 'Liberal Americans have started to be very concerned with the fact that the economy had been doing quite well, but there has been a worsening of the earnings distribution and there are a lot of working poor and that was associated with many social problems. The collapse of family structure among the poor was linked to this.' The American experience has been extensively researched by the new Treasury, and in particular by Balls, and its lessons and remedies applied to the UK. Balls argues that the growing number of people moving in and out of the market and taking short-term work on low wages has required a rethink of the tax and benefit system.

Adoption of a minimum wage– an approach first used in the United States – gives some protection from exploitation to those at the bottom of the wages ladder but it is still an open question whether this will increase or decrease job stability. So Labour's principal route to dealing with the unemployed and the poor with jobs is the provision of training and skills. Wolf says New Labour's key messages are: 'We must improve education. We must shrink the pool of unskilled labour if earnings are going to improve.'

Models for schemes to encourage the unemployed to return to or stay in the labour market originated in the United States. The scheme to get the young jobless back to work was called the New Deal – a name taken from the great 1930s experiment implemented by Lyndon Johnson under the aegis of President

Roosevelt. The price of the job is that the unemployed youth is not able to reject it without losing benefit. The scale of the funds allocated to the schemes far eclipses anything spent by previous government on numerous unsuccessful work-creation schemes; £3.5 billion is available for the welfare to work programme, but it was raised not from current expenditure but through a hypothecated windfall tax (that is, a tax where the proceeds are directed at specific spending needs, not general Treasury use). The schemes have been greeted with some approval, although sceptics question employers' commitment to the new jobs once the subsidies run out. There is also a genuine fear that an external event, such as a recession in 1999 or 2000, will submerge the new jobs created through the schemes with a large surge of new jobless.

Brown's approach to the problems of work, and the Chancellor's determination to push through the schemes, have won some trades union approval, says John Monks, General Secretary of the Trades Union Congress. 'There's quite a lot of confidence in him because he's put unemployment at the top of his agenda, even if there are some authoritarian echoes to it. We think his heart on that issue is in the right place.'

Such enthusiasm may not be sustained when the schemes start to bite in the homes of the incurably lazy, says Martin Wolf. Britain does not share the American willingness to put the workshy and unfortunate on to the street as the price for their inability to earn a wage. But the logic of the policy is that benefits will eventually dry up for those who cannot keep jobs provided by the state subsidy.

The real political test for the Third Way, and its American proselytizers, is to transfer this piece of transatlantic culture to a largely ill-informed but also cosseted country. Even pushing the British along the road to benefit reform is going to be a huge challenge, according to Martin Wolf. 'We start from the position of a highly articulated welfare state – more than the US – and a much stronger commitment than the US to equality and to avoiding destitution. We have a much less developed view of personal behaviour than the US. That raises very tricky problems in how far the new government can get with welfare reforms. The British are generally not prepared to take the view that if you don't work you starve, it's that simple. The new Treasury don't want to persuade people to work, they want to force them.' That is the big cultural jump, that suggests to some that new Labour is more Thatcherite than the queen of the monetarists ever was.

The work schemes also fulfil another part of the American agenda: the need to take people out of benefits and so shrink the state's role in the personal finance of its citizens. Under the new Working Families Tax Credit employers provide the instrument for the delivery of social payments to the low-paid. The scheme has been straightforwardly translated from the United States, where it is called Earned Income Tax Credit, and is based, says Wolf, 'on the belief that people should work, but they need to get decent incomes from that and the way to do that is to link the benefit system to work. The solution is to provide in-work benefits, and this fits beautifully with Gordon's ethical view, mania, for getting everybody to work.' But Wolf is not convinced it is workable. 'The shift to the tax basis for family credit rather than the social security benefit basis is just window-dressing. I don't think it will make any difference.' Will Hutton, the author of *The State We're In* is also sceptical. 'We are asking our bottom 10 per cent or 20 per cent to accept American policies in the context of European immobilism. That is a lethal mix which the politicians do not understand.' Balls is more optimistic. 'We know the Earned Income Tax credit scheme was helping to create a dynamic labour market in the United States. We also saw ways that it would not work for us, and we came up with a British solution.'

The desire to curtail state budgets – a response to the decline in levels of personal taxation – is also prompting the government to study massive changes in state provision of pensions, and this is arguably the biggest challenge now facing it. Balls likens it to the American need to find a resolution to the country's healthcare problems. But it is a long-term issue, which will not be rushed. 'This is a poverty problem, not an affordability problem. It is a distribution issue, and one that will need to be solved over the next ten years.'

The push to reduce the size of the state is the last and most controversial part of the American influence on government policy. It is also the Party's greatest political and economic shift, says Gavyn Davies. 'Because Labour's tax and spend policy was notorious, and increasingly unpopular, the new men in charge have set their minds against managing demand through changing taxes here and there, public spending here and there, or doing it in a clandestine way within the Treasury.' Tax and spend were the by-words for Labour's traditional approach. Now they are like rotting BSE carcasses that the Party wants to bury. Says Brown: 'Old Labour was caricatured as a Party that had as its goal equality as equality of outcome, to be realized by ever-higher levels of taxation to support ever higher levels of public spending. This is completely wrong.'

In fact Britain's taxation levels have fallen back to levels where old-style spending is out of the question, says Andrew Dilnot of the Institute of Fiscal Studies. UK levels of personal taxation – currently 37 per cent of national income – are approaching American levels of 33 per cent – far lower than in France and Germany where personal taxes are around 46 per cent of income. Dilnot worries that the government wants to have its tax cake and eat it – low personal taxation, with high quality of state services. 'The government seems to want to keep taxation low, while spending rises. But they can't have everything, like free comprehensive healthcare and education. We need to face up to what this means. NHS spending is now growing by 1.5 per cent a year, compared with GDP growth of 3 per cent – it is simply not sustainable. So we could have higher taxes.'

Hutton would agree with that. 'Blair likes to say the Welfare State does not work because the poor are still with us. Well, one reason for that is that the state is so goddam mean. We are asking those on Income Support to put up with Victorian living standards.' But demands for redistribution and higher taxes continue to surface from Labour's old school. The most vocal advocate for a return to Labour's former policy of raising taxes from the rich so they can be redistributed to the poor is the former shadow Chancellor Roy Hattersley. Brown rebuts them out of hand, neatly twisting the redistribution knife. 'Jobs, education and the reform of the welfare state are the key to equality rather than tax rates. Redistribution within the existing budgets for public spending will have a higher priority than increases in public spending.' Elsewhere Brown showed some of that notorious hairshirt when he commented that: 'Nobody ever said that in the first two years we were going to make it easy for people.'

Brown's tight grip on the state purse has produced predictable, and very personal, animus from his ministerial colleagues. As one top TUC official revealed: 'The spending department ministers are all fed up with the Presbyterian lecture from the son of the manse when he tells them they mustn't put at risk our wonderful economic achievements. He gives them a sermon. He's got them so they are very loath to ask for anything. It is a sermon not from the Mount, but from the Treasury . . . They find him totally unyielding, impervious, uninterested . . .' Brown for his part will not be moved: 'Our toughness on the public finances is toughness for a purpose, so we can move resources to high-priority areas. It is a toughness so we can get the long-term and substantial improvements in health and education in particular that we want to see.'

Brown makes no apology for wanting to work to a tight budget. 'Our aim will be to save money before we spend money. I want our government to be remembered as wise spenders, not big spenders.' All taxation will need to be costed and justified, and Brown has brought down from the mountain two 'Golden Rules' with which he can beat his colleagues over the head if they show any sign of profligacy. Golden rule number one on borrowing says that over the economic cycle, government will only borrow to finance public investment and not to fund public consumption. 'Current spending on consumption will have to be met by available revenues.' Rule number two says: 'As a proportion of national income, public debt will be held at a prudent and stable level over the economic cycle.'

Labour's would-be big spenders balk at the new Chancellor's severity, arguing that if the government cannot have ambitious schemes when the economy is growing and it is at the start of its term with a landslide majority, when can it have them? But Brown had made two key guarantees on taxing and spending before he had entered office to win political credibility, and he was determined to stick by them: first, there would be no rises in income tax rates in the Parliament; second, government departments had to work to the spending levels set by the former Conservative government. Once in office, Brown announced an additional guarantee of fiscal rectitude. This would be a vehicle established to supervise the policy. The 'code of fiscal stability', modelled on New Zealand's Fiscal Responsibility Act, will compel the government to give regular details of its budgetary targets for at least ten years ahead. A new statement of economic and fiscal strategy will be published at the time of each Budget.

Gavyn Davies compares the code's objectives to the decision to give interest rate setting to the Bank of England, namely to increase transparency, and to avoid manipulation of currency for electoral purposes. 'The new code will make it more difficult to stimulate demand before an election by cutting taxes because you will have to explain what you are doing in terms of targets. This is the short-term/long-term thing that he is always going on about.'

Balls concurs, saying that toughness should not be confused with meanness; it is not a matter of principle so much as good economic planning, he says: 'Left of centre governments need to favour tough fiscal policy because from time to time, if economic crises occur you may have to relax that. But first you have to build up the credibility and the means to do so.'

Brown has not been quite as austere as some would claim. Politically embarrassing issues, such as the growth in NHS waiting lists, have required him to put an additional £2 billion into the National Health Service. He has also served the government's overriding social mission to stimulate education by putting a further £2.5 billion into education in the course of his two budgets.

In fact, Brown is a passionate believer in equality, and he sees all policy as an ethical activity, where the cost of government capital is measured in human as well as financial terms. He is fired by the need to produce equality (his intellectual heroes are left-wing thinkers like Tawney and Hobsbawm, among others) but he sees it not simply as a straight line with a fixed beginning and end, but a process on which government can encourage all citizens to embark. Government is egalitarian when it treats all citizens in the community equally, but it cannot provide a cocoon against all the woes and unfairnesses of life. The new government wants to ensure that the individual has the 'opportunity' to attain a goal, but it would be rash, and perhaps wrong, to promise that it will be attained. Those who like to identify philosophical differences between Brown and Tony Blair, however, say that the two differ in the extent they believe the state ought to help the individual achieve his goal, with Brown preferring greater support, Blair less.

Inevitably the Third Way approach has its critics. Many contend that it is no more than a fudge, designed to find a means of balancing differing political prejudices of the left and right of the Party, who intuitively favour more or less government involvement in the economy. To them, the Third Way seems more like a middle way to take politics out of economics, a sort of safety valve for the old discussions about hot socialist potatoes like redistribution and interventionism. But Brown asserts most forcefully that the Third Way is not just an economic and industrial approach, but a moral and philosophical theory with appeal to socialists and libertarians alike. 'The breakthrough for people who used to be sceptical on the left, is to recognize that equality of opportunity, which used simply to be an ideal for people who believed in social justice, is now actually an essential component of a philosophy about how you can create an efficient and strong economy.'

Fundamental changes to a country's economic and political philosophy of this individualistic kind are bound to be greeted by the media with incredulity. What has shocked observers is the lack of wider understanding of the new concepts. Balls says this is due partly to the need to advertize and explain, and this will happen when the schemes are implemented over the next few years, and there is still time. 'If, by the next election, people still say, "We do not understand how it fits together," then we will have failed. The chances of people completely understanding the new schemes until they affect them are small.'

The optimism of the new men at the Treasury will be justified if companies and government departments play ball and if world markets favour Britain with a soft landing in the face of a slowdown in growth. But that is far from guaranteed, and

John Monks warns of dangers ahead. 'The economy has been good up to now. Unemployment has been falling, inflation has been low and public spending is moving into surplus. But it looks as if it will get choppy as growth slows down and inflation starts increasing.

'Our forecast is that unemployment will rise and that is a difficult thing for any government, but it is especially difficult for a Labour government, committed as Gordon is to high and stable levels of employment.'

Brown's optimistic approach borders on the philosophical and will be appreciated by the more visionary folk in the Treasury and the population at large. But the only justification for clever talk will be if it leads to the application of policies that ensure the British people find their purses full, and their houses appreciating in value. Brown in turn will judge his contribution by the economy's capacity to create and secure the jobs that underpin the spending power, and the greater sense of general well-being.

Implementing his economic prospectus in the first three months in power had been enormously exhilarating and desperately tiring. By the end of July, the workaholic Chancellor was looking forward to a holiday where he could recharge both his intellectual and physical batteries.

Chapter Nine: Cape Cod Holiday

It was a supremely relaxed Gordon Brown who set up home for a holiday in Cape Cod in the summer of 1997. With three months of non-stop activity behind him, the newly empowered Chancellor could lay aside the duties and cares of government and enjoy the fresh sea air. It was also an opportunity to do the reading from which government red boxes distracted him, and to recharge his intellectual batteries worn down by the grind of daily management of the economy.

Gordon Brown's holidays had become part of legend even before he entered Number 11 Downing Street. It was always said that he went to the United States with suitcases full of books and decamped to Harvard Library, where he caught up on the reading which he had missed during the political year. Needing to be briefed on the most recent economic theories, he had the advantage of close contact with the great experts in the subject who lived and worked on the Harvard campus – people like Robert Reich and Larry Summers. These holidays gave Gordon Brown free access to American culture, the source of much New Labour thinking.

The life of the academic mole which Brown enjoyed before he entered politics, when he taught at Edinburgh University and wrote books, worked better in opposition than in government. The responsibilities of a government minister never

cease while he holds power, and Brown had to arrange his
holiday where he could be easily contacted and benefit from
good communications.

As a figure of great public prominence, second only to the
Prime Minister himself, Brown also has to think about visibility.
The place chosen had to be discreet, to ensure minimal chance
of recognition by a member of the public. Brown is probably
less at ease with his public role than many of his colleagues,
and becomes very uncomfortable when people point him out
in the street.

When push came to shove, there was little doubt where
he would take his holiday in 1997 – the same place he
had gone to for many years. This was Cape Cod in the
north-eastern United States. The area's remoteness famously
attracts American politicians (John F. Kennedy established
the pattern for Democratic politicians with his well-known
vacations at Hynannis Port), while its location on the East
Coast also puts it within an hour or so's flying time of New
York and Washington, as well as Boston – ideal, should a
political crisis occur.

Cape Cod had its usual clutch of famous visitors in summer 1997, most notably President Clinton himself who was
vacationing at Martha's Vineyard, only a few miles up the road
from Gordon Brown. There was no question of Brown visiting
the President, however, despite their political friendship, as
Clinton was making his visit painfully conspicuous, conducting
well-publicized meetings with local government officials and
residents. Brown's desire for obscurity could not have been in
greater contrast.

There was plenty of scope for the British Chancellor to burrow
himself away out of the public eye in Cape Cod. Much of the area
is covered in dense woods and sand dunes, and towns like East
Harwich where Brown was staying – pronounced in America
exactly as it is spelt, with a 'w' – are sleepy backwoods with
a few trendy shops and large numbers of retired American
residents who would be unlikely to recognize a visiting British
politician, let alone have the bad manners to point him out
and make him cringe.

The loose ends of the Scottish devolution campaign still needed to be tied up just before his scheduled departure for the States and Cape Cod, so Brown allocated mundane tasks like booking flights and accommodation to the two people who take care of his daily requirements – his girlfriend Sarah Macaulay and his brother Andrew. His intellectual soulmate and close political friend, Geoff Mulgan, was given the task of building a holiday reading list and tracking down the tomes. Mulgan had worked in opposition in the late eighties as political adviser to Brown. When he left to set up the Left-leaning Demos think-tank, he was replaced by Ed Balls. But Brown continued to stay in touch with a man whose breadth of ideas in social and political science and economics he much respected.

After undertaking the nitty-gritty holiday arrangements, Sarah Macaulay joined Gordon in Cape Cod. She was already known publicly as his official girlfriend and had made a number of carefully timed media appearances. She was still slightly uncertain of her role and could seem forbidding, keeping her words to a minimum in case she put a foot wrong. A discussion about pop music over breakfast gave Sarah the chance to get one up on the omniscient Brown, who is thirteen years her senior. She patiently explained about the sad fate of pop singer Kurt Cobain (who committed suicide) and his band Nirvana. When Brown failed to show any interest in the subject, she repeated the information. He was clearly not well briefed and expressed surprise at his partner's knowledge. 'You're very well informed,' he remarked to Sarah, with a suggestion of irony rather than outright admiration at her knowledge of this, to him less than critical subject.

Sarah accompanied Gordon Brown on his entire month-long holiday in Cape Cod, but she only took responsibility for organizing the first two weeks when the couple retreated to a wooden bungalow in a well appointed residential holiday estate with identical bugalows, tennis courts and other amenities. Such man-made privacy – in classic American style – served Brown's need for anonymity and peace. The couple did not entertain friends or visitors during this part of their stay. Brown spent most of the time reading and writing.

Arrangements for the second two weeks, which were more public, were undertaken by Brown's brother Andrew. Andrew is five years younger than Gordon and has grown up with a strong sense of obligation, verging on awe, that a younger sibling may sometimes feel for an older one, especially one as imposing as Gordon Brown. Andrew is a Channel Four programme editor – his wife also works in television. He is a paid-up member of the Labour Party, but is not actively involved in politics. A sense of family duty is powerful in the Brown household, never more so than at times of need, and Andrew was a source of moral and practical support following John Smith's death.

The second half of the holiday would also be a little more complicated, and noisier, than the first, as Gordon would have the company of Andrew, his wife Clare Rewcastle and his young family – Alex aged two, and Patrick who was just a few months old at the time. He would also be joined by his elder brother John and his rather older family. The three brothers appeared to be extremely close. 'They are a fantastically strong family,' says one friend, 'very easy with each other, and very mutually supportive'. The holiday would be a chance for Gordon to catch up on developments with his brothers and their children, and for Sarah to get to know Gordon's family – possibly her future in-laws – better.

The Brown family's holiday residence in Cape Cod, called Goodfellows, was a substantial wooden house, like many in the area covered on the outside by clapboard planks, set back from the road and surrounded by forest. The unpretentious exterior and the modest drive which was open to the road gave no hint of the identity of the occupants for this particular fortnight in August.

While the atmosphere at Goodfellows was informal and at times rowdy, Gordon would not be drawn into the chaos generated by young children. Handling the practicalities of everyday life is not his strong card, as those around him are the first to agree. At a barbecue the Browns hosted, for example, he made small-talk and filled wine glasses while his brothers struggled with the hot coals and grilling meat.

Later, he would make polite conversation while his brothers hovered. Politics was surely on everyone's mind, but no one ventured any such talk in front of him, in case it ever were to put him in an embarrassing position. Brown determined what he considered to be politically acceptable conversation in front of strangers, in this case the antics of his deniable source Charlie Whelan. The Chancellor recalled how Whelan leaked to the press the fact that the Royal yacht *Britannia* was due to be scrapped. Brown was transparently gleeful at Whelan's talent for making mischief.

Away from the focus of activity, the real politics of emotion and angst were seething. They bubbled to the surface when John Brown, who lives in Scotland and works for Glasgow City Council as its public relations executive, started beefing about the Labour Party's position on devolution. 'I've tried to persuade Gordon about this, but he won't listen,' he muttered under his breath. He didn't speak too loud, out of loyalty, or perhaps fear.

After the barbecue, the television was switched on. Gordon was slumped in an armchair, taciturn, Sarah was sitting on the other side of the room. Reasonably enough, American television held little appeal for the Brown brothers or Sarah, as one of the nephews surfed the channels. But interest was momentarily excited when an American preacher came on the screen calling for donations and selling membership of his Church, or suchlike. This prompted Gordon to break his silence with a sardonic remark. To the sons of the Manse, this marketer must have seemed like Satan.

The party prepared to go to bed at 10 o'clock, with Sarah saying that they were all very tired. They had been roused at 5 o'clock that morning (10 a.m. British time) with a call from Scotland. Apparently the devolution campaign had hit a rocky patch following revelations over the suicide of the Scottish MP Gordon McMaster. Other mornings were similarly interrupted with calls from Italy and France, where Tony Blair was holidaying.

In the brief gaps between phone-calls, serious reading and meetings, Brown found time for the thing in life that really mattered to him, other than politics: football. He had found a local bar with a satellite receiver shortly after arriving in East Harwich, and watched a few European football games in the course of his visit. The reception was impressive and he was constantly looking for opportunities to see more.

When in London, Brown gets his exercise doing light weights and using an indoor running track at his Westminster flat, but on holiday he preferred to play tennis. He and Sarah were equipped with the appropriate white gear and Sarah looked sleek, Gordon sprightly – despite the fact that his socks did not match. Once they had moved into Goodfellows, and out of the bungalow estate, they lost access to the private tennis courts but occasionally sneaked in unnoticed when no one with a valid pass wanted to play. On these occasions, Sarah drove Gordon there in a sporty white rented car. The snappy little motor had no CD player, a source of momentary irritation to the Chancellor, who loves classical music, in particular Bach, Mozart and Beethoven. Sarah had just bought him a CD of Bach's Concerto for Two Violins, and he was keen to listen to it. He searched the car for a player, in the hope of cruising through the New England countryside to a lush lyrical background, but found none. Andrew searched the car too, even looking in the boot, but without success. As a desperate last resort, Gordon began listening through headphones, but after a moment Sarah rebuked him, saying, 'That's rather rude.' He muttered, 'S'pose you're right,' and switched off the music.

Gordon chivalrously played tennis with his girlfriend, who had said earlier that she could not claim to be his equal on the court. She was duly conquered. He then went on to beat his brother Andrew, but did not have the same success with another opponent. Brown won his points by a number of guileful volleys at sharp angles to the net, rather than by force of serve or power of shot. Before he had a chance to recover his losing situation, other players appeared and, on the assumption that they would have a greater claim to use of the court than the Brown party, the Chancellor's group beat a hasty retreat.

Gordon returned to Goodfellows to relax after the game. On reaching the house, he retired to the veranda and hastily removed a laptop computer marked as Treasury property and some papers. The computer was not very good, he grumbled, even if it did have its own printer. Talk ranged widely; he disparaged the book about the 1997 General Election campaign by the BBC reporter Nicholas Jones, somewhat haughtily and unfairly calling him a 'day-by-day news chaser'

Labour's big hitters: the 1997 election campaign.

Tony Blair and Gordon Brown inside Number 10.

The first Budget,
July 1997: Brown with
Rosyth apprentices.

First day at the Treasury, May 1997: Sir Terence Burns greets the new Chancellor.

Gordon Brown's changing moods.

The second Budget, March 1998: Brown with Treasury ministers. (From left to right) Alastair Darling, Dawn Primaralo, Helen Liddell and Geoffrey Robinson.

Gordon and Sarah enjoy a night out. Arriving for a reception at Number 11.

The famous pre-Budget photo opportunity: Gordon and Sarah pose with
Ben Davies.

Brown with the Governor of the Bank of England, Eddie George.

Brown's right-hand women:
Sue Nye (left) and
Sarah Macaulay.

Brown meets with the committee of the Diana, Princess of Wales Memorial Fund.

Brown on the move with Ed Balls (left).

New Labour's dream
couple: Ed Balls and
Yvette Cooper MP.

Minister Without Portfolio:
Peter Mandelson.

The Paymaster:
Geoffrey Robinson.

Scottish Television's presentation for their recent documentary.

The Spin Doctor:
Charlie Whelan.

rather than a serious commentator. Suggestions were thrown around about the management of the world economy; weren't companies using the buoyancy of the global stock markets to borrow recklessly, putting investing institutions at risk, the Chancellor was asked. His tone altered from the small change of parliamentary gossip. He wanted evidence. 'Which investing institutions?' he demanded. 'Who was going to crash as a result?' The argument stopped there (although in the wake of the Asian crash the question may have had some merit). But for the Chancellor, serious ideas demand serious thought, and must never be posed lightly.

Gordon Brown brought out a Diet Coke for himself, and in this exceptionally relaxing environment was able to break all his normal rules of reticence about his private life. His tennis, he admitted, was not so good, but then he only has one eye, and that limits his vision to two dimensions. He explained he lost his eye in a rugby match when somebody scraped their boot across his face. The retina of his left eye was detached and he had three operations with local Scottish surgery to try to put it together again. He recalled how he was required to lie completely horizontal and virtually stationary for a matter of months, as the doctors believed that if the eye and the retina remained completely still they would bond back. For that period he was registered blind, and he appeared to shudder just thinking of it. In fact, within a matter of weeks, the cells bonding the retina on his left eye died, and he lost its use.

Three years or so after the loss of the left eye, his right eye appeared to be failing too, and an investigation revealed that its retina was also detached. The prospect of losing this eye as well was devastating, but then Brown was introduced to an Edinburgh-based Asian eye surgeon, Dr Hector Chowla, the head of the eye department at Edinburgh Royal Infirmary. Chowla had learnt the latest laser technology in America and was due to return to the States shortly. Catching him before he left had been a stroke of luck. Brown had an operation, and Chowla was able to hold the eye together with what Brown called a form of sellotape. The memory understandably still sends shivers down his spine, and he mentioned the fear he experienced several times. Mr Chowla remains a friend; he has visited Brown in North Queensferry, and Brown wants to entertain him at Downing Street in the next year. That would right a wrong that Brown thought the surgeon had suffered; he had not received the respect and rewards he was owed by the Edinburgh establishment.

The eye injury still has a constant impact on Brown's daily life; although he has a driving licence, he does not drive, and he prefers not to lift heavy weights. Despite his love of sport, until recent years he had not been physically active. Tennis is a risk he is prepared to take. But despite the seriousness of his eye problems, there is almost no immediate visible evidence of it, no squint or sign of uncertainty. In conversation, it is impossible to discern which eye functions and which does not.

This has not always been the case, however. Some years ago, a cataract grew over the unseeing left eye, and although this was not visible in natural light, when television lights were shone on the retina it became opaque. This was disturbing to viewers and Brown had a contact lens made to counter the effect. Brown talked for a long time about having the cataract surgically removed, but happily five years ago it disappeared of its own accord, and the contact lens is no longer required.

Friends say that Brown's compulsive political urgency is the result of his knowledge that even his good eye will deteriorate with age. 'He is a politician in a hurry because he fears that one day his vision will greatly worsen,' says one.

Brown's conversation ranges widely from the state of his parents' health – both were once very active but now are ageing and increasingly infirm – to his own view about family and parenting. While in opposition, he had brought together for dinner the Chief Rabbi Jonathan Sacks and the *Guardian* and *Observer* journalist Melanie Phillips to discuss the future of the family. The result of the conversation was an enhanced respect for the sanctity Rabbi, whom Brown felt was intellectually impressive, but whose intellectual approach led him to overstate the case for the sanctity of the family. This relaxed Gordon Brown seemed a quite different person to the assertive public figure.

There was none of the preachiness or haranguing that can characterize his public mode of address. The private man speaks quickly, quietly and volubly, in a low voice, about personal and private concerns: the importance of family life, the ills of unemployment in the household, the value of opportunity – all these are part of his instinctive discourse, coming naturally to him. He has no love for the Westminster cauldron and says how sad he is that his holiday is passing so quickly and that his return to London is pending. Friends say he has never seemed so relaxed as he was on this holiday.

In the evening Gordon and Sarah planned to go to the movies. Gordon changed from his tennis gear into a sporty shirt and slacks – nothing showy, but well-fitting. Sarah, looking svelte and glamorous, placed a tenderly guiding arm around his shoulder. In fact they missed the movie and instead took out a video from the local video-rental store of the film *The People Vs Larry Flint* (the American publisher of *Rustler* and other soft-porn publications who fought a campaign for press freedom).

The stay on Cape Cod was not without its political moments. These tended to happen at the Wequasset Hotel – the plushest inn in the area – which was situated round the corner from Goodfellows, on the main Route 6 through Cape Cod. One notable British guest during August, staying for three nights, was the Paymaster General, Geoffrey Robinson, a good friend of the Chancellor. Gordon Brown liked to hold his meetings in the breakfast room where he could point out to visitors a spectacular view over the Atlantic Ocean through a giant window. The wide view over the sea shared some features with the extraordinary vista of the Firth of Forth from Gordon's own house at North Queensferry – the great marine landscape and the steely sky. The array of breakfast food at the Wequasset was enormous – more yoghurts, mueslis and pancakes than one would ever want. But Brown was content with a cup of coffee and a roll.

Another guest Brown entertained on his holiday was Gavyn Davies, who passed through Cape Cod on his way to a partners' meeting of his firm in New York. He 'crashed down' on the floor at Goodfellows for a night, putting up with rather less comfort than his wealth and status would normally entitle him to. Brown also spent a day, and played tennis, with the TV newscaster Jon

Snow and his family who every year swap their London home for a comfortable house on Cape Cod. The two men are not politically entirely aligned, for, in the words of one observer, Snow is definitely more 'Old Labour'.

When Brown left Cape Cod his suitcases were even heavier than when he arrived. He had bought books like crazy on many visits to bookshops in Hyannis. Between government red boxes and Cabinet meetings, the Chancellor was determined to keep up with the latest ideas. US theory had been crucial to the birth of New Labour and the newly elected Labour Government looked to Americans for guidance in their practice of power.

Gordon Brown broke his return journey from Cape Cod in Washington, where he met up with a US Government Welfare to Work committee. The spell of Cape Cod had been broken; business was returning to normal.

Brown came away from Cape Cod not only much more relaxed and ready for the new push ahead, but quite also a bit closer to his partner and girlfriend, Sarah Macaulay. The uncluttered time spent together also gave Sarah a better idea of the man she was courting when he was not pulled hither and thither by the Westminster treadmill.

Chapter Ten: 'A Great Big Teddy Bear'

The Chancellor is on the phone when the expected visitors arrive at his North Queensferry home. The heavy wooden door of the secluded old house with its wonderful view over the water is opened by an attractive woman, casually dressed in blue jeans and a simple shirt. Sarah Macaulay shows the guests into Gordon Brown's sitting room, invites them to sit down and then, in the absence of her partner, chats about her life and work.

Sarah has just come back from a Brown family Christmas at the home of Gordon's elder brother in Glasgow. It was convenient for Sarah to have a warm family hearth to gather round at Christmas, she notes, as London is lonely and her own family is scattered round the world, some in the United States and her mother and stepfather in Bangladesh.

But the visit to Glasgow had another agenda, of course. It was Gordon's first opportunity to introduce his latest girlfriend to his parents, who had travelled down from Aberdeenshire. It was important that the formidable Reverend John Ebenezer Brown and Elizabeth Brown liked Sarah, and they did. Privately the elderly couple will have hoped, prayed even, that this would be the one with whom Gordon would settle down. He had, after all, introduced them to a number of very suitable girls and each one in turn had slipped through his fingers.

Gordon was the middle of the three Brown sons, but both his brothers had married and had children – he had yet to commit himself. As decent and respected folk in their community, the Browns had never quite got used to this perplexing behaviour, but Gordon's mother had long given up trying to push or pressure him. She had always thought her son was a law unto himself.

So too was the young woman now playing the leading romantic role in Gordon's life. The 34-year-old Sarah had acquired a mind of her own early on in life. She had been brought up in a literary household; her father was a publisher and her mother a teacher. Her stepfather was an academic and an expert in the economics of development. At the state school she attended in the cosmopolitan area of Tufnell Park in north London, she had been part of a group of kids whom less accomplished mates called the 'trendies'. They stood out with their advanced liberal opinions, outrageous dress, riotous behaviour and sheer determination to be cleverer than the herd and different.

The school did not meet Sarah's intellectual needs, so for the sixth form she progressed to the highly academic Camden Girls' School – Emma Thompson's old school. Sarah went on to Bristol University, the fashionable alternative to Oxbridge, where she studied psychology and passed her exams with ease. Armed with her upper-second degree, Sarah looked for a job in the media. In 1987, she was taken on by one of the country's top design and marketing consultancies, Wolff Olins, to write annual company reports and brochures. Her clients included the Department of Trade and Industry, the Midland Bank and the Design Museum in London.

In 1988, at the height of the Thatcherite period when everyone was encouraged to think of themselves as entrepreneurs, Sarah joined the bandwagon and, together with three friends, formed her own design agency to provide companies with carefully designed logos and branding. Spirit Design flourished at the peak of the booming economy, and went down with some acrimony, if reports are to be believed, with the recession in 1994.

But Sarah's interests in commercial public relations had been waning in any event. In the early nineties she had begun to appear on the left-wing circuit, and when she met an old schoolfriend, Julia Hobsbawm, the daughter of the distinguished Marxist historian Eric Hobsbawm, and a very live wire in her own right, she set about building a more congenial career. The two women launched a PR agency whose task was to promote politically-responsible clients. At the PR agency Hobsbawm Macaulay Communications she can work with the clients she likes, where she likes and with the colleagues she likes. Her clients have included Emily's List (the campaign to increase the number of female MPs), the *New Statesman* and various charities.

The New Labour team acknowledged Sarah's PR skills and she became friendly with another formidable New Labour lady. Sue Nye had recently been given the job of running Gordon Brown's political affairs, and in 1994 she invited Sarah and Gordon Brown over to dinner at her home near Farringdon Road in central London.

The occasion was fortuitous as both Sarah and Gordon were on the rebound from relationships. Gordon Brown's partner had been the Scottish television interviewer Sheena Macdonald. He had first dated Sheena way back in 1977, but the two split after a couple of years. Then they tried again. Again it was not working.

Sarah Macaulay's partner was a very different kettle of fish. He was a soldier in the Parachute Regiment who had fought in the Falklands War when he boasted that he killed an Argentinian in the line of duty. The couple had a relationship which developed as Sarah was helping him with the publication of a book on his Falklands War experiences. Sarah found the situation increasingly trying. An old friend recalls: 'She had a difficult time. He was an unsavoury fellow, and merely served to demonstrate what a decent and nice person she was. He messed her around.'

The witty politician with ideas and opinions pouring out two-a-penny came as an enormous relief after such a trauma. Brown in turn was captivated by Sarah's raffish looks and intelligence. 'She corresponds to Brown's type,' says one old friend. Her sculpted facial features, thin frame and straight hair are similar to those of his old flame from the late sixties and seventies, Princess Margarita, the daughter of former King Michael of Romania.

Sarah also had the strong protective streak that any woman involved with Brown needs. Carol Craig, a long-time friend of Brown, who knew him in his Edinburgh University days, and is very conscious of his foibles and eccentricities, says, 'Yes, he is a great man. But he obviously has lots of weaknesses. He is the sort of man that you feel you would have to take to have a haircut or get the right shoes.' Brown's unworldliness, says Craig, is precisely what's attractive to women. 'He doesn't give much back, but he is so clever, thinks he is so important, that was enough. It is a very attractive combination of this very clever person with an emotionally vulnerable side.' One woman who found him immensely attractive and fascinating (although the interest was not reciprocated) felt: 'He's like a great big teddy bear. You want to button up his shirt for him, he seems so vulnerable.'

But there is a downside to a relationship with Brown, as any woman who gets close quickly finds – dedication to politics leaves little room for much contact, let alone for the emotional side of a relationship. 'There is a problem for women who have got involved with him because of his lack of commitment to a relationship,' says one old friend. 'Sure as hell he wasn't putting the women in his life first. Any woman who got involved with him had to realize that she would be incidental to some extent. She would have a role in his life, but it wouldn't be the most important thing. I don't know if it was a great deal for the women who did get involved with him.' The thought was put more succinctly and less kindly by one other observer, who said, 'Any woman marrying Brown would be number five, after politics, the Labour Party, Ed and Charlie.'

That was what really upset Brown's first long-term partner, ironically (for Brown as a socialist), a scion of one of the great royal families of Europe. It was at Edinburgh University that he met and dated Princess Margarita of Romania who was said to have been infatuated with him. But she wanted him to see her as number one. He refused. 'I never stopped loving him, but one day it didn't seem right any more. It was politics, politics, politics, and I needed nurturing,' said Margarita.

But the friend says the woman who expected more by way of commitment than she received had only herself to blame – Brown never pretended to offer much, certainly not marriage. She believes Gordon was always straightforward and wouldn't lead a woman along for the sake of it: 'If he had been the ambitious opportunist that a lot of people make him out to be, he would have done it years ago and to hell with the consequences. He is quite an honourable guy. If he was going to do that it would have to mean something.' Friends speculate that in refusing to get committed, Brown may also be rebelling against his religious background and all the early parental pressure.

In fact Brown came close to making a commitment to his longest-standing girlfriend, Marion Caldwell, whom he saw over a twelve-year period in the eighties and early nineties. Caldwell was a television researcher when she met Brown, but she turned to law and prospered; in due course she became a senior lawyer in Scotland. Friends wonder whether Brown was happier going out with a lowly researcher and found the more confident career woman less attractive. In any event, there was endless discussion between the couple about buying a flat together, but Brown never thought the moment was right, and Caldwell eventually went off and bought her own flat. Said one good friend of Caldwell: 'I don't think it was machiavellian, it was simply Gordon procrastinating, and not being able to make the commitment.'

Caldwell's departure left Brown with both a personal and professional gap. Brown the man needed the company of women for physical and emotional comfort. Brown the politician needed a woman for official reasons. In the early nineties, there seemed to be a real possibility that Labour might take power, and Brown started thinking about the consequences of being without a partner. Did he really want to be another cold fish like Ted Heath, attracting all the innuendo? According to a former aide, 'In 1991 and 1992 we were discussing what you needed to get to the top in politics. I told him he had to lose one or two stones, as he had got big and jowly. I also told him, "You've been umpteen years with Marion, why don't you bloody well marry her?" He did start going to the gym to lose weight, but as for the other thing . . . well, you know what the Scots are like with their private life, very buttoned-up.'

Brown has been no exception. Increasingly inquisitive journalists started to notice how he would 'twitch like a half-dead fly' whenever he was tackled about his marital state. A typical reply to the 'Marriage' question: 'The fact I'm not married is just the fact that things didn't work out, or haven't so far. Things will change.' – 'Do you want to get married?' 'I think it would be quite good.'

This comparative indifference to something even modern and liberated politicians have to pay attention to fuelled rumours that he had something to hide. Might he even be gay? Before the 1992 general election there was malicious talk about a police file on his sexual activities. Tabloid reporters appeared outside the door of his North Queensferry home. The same baseless rumours were recycled again in the week before polling at the 1997 election. Even in the City of London, the slander was being repeated.

Opponents exploited this lingering doubt by spreading rumour and innuendo in the leadership campaign in 1994. Many MPs, uncertain whether to support Brown or Blair, were telephoned by Blairite colleagues and asked: 'Do you really think we need another Scot, and one who's unmarried, for leader?' The venom was whipped up much later by Sue Lawley who repeatedly challenged Brown to come out of the closet on *Desert Island Discs*. Brown's fumbling replies and denials did not help his cause. He was thought to be less upset for himself by such insinuations than he was for his devout parents, who he felt would be mortified at the very suggestion.

Brown has repeatedly been counselled by colleagues to take his bachelordom in hand, for the sake of his career if nothing else. One MP, whose personal, as well as economic, advice Brown usually appreciates, reminded him that he had had three apparently suitable girlfriends: 'If there is a 51 per cent chance of the marriage succeeding now, for God's sake take it.' Needless to say, the advice was shrugged off. Anthony Howard, a canny observer of the British political scene, knows the risk of a mysterious private life to the inquisitive public: 'There is something wrong with an unmarried politician, dedicated to his trade, who does not recognize that he must get married. Brown is an obsessional politician and if you eat, sleep and drink politics as he does, it seems amazing that the penny did not drop till he got to his mid-thirties.' Howard notes that there have been only two bachelor Prime Ministers in the twentieth century and both have been Conservatives. 'The fact that Blair was married with children was an asset to him.'

The loss of the leadership and the near-certainty that Labour would gain power were two catalysts for Brown to take his private life in hand in the mid-nineties. In April 1995, the first rumours surfaced that Brown was seeing Sarah, although neither would say anything to suggest it could be serious. Some urgency crept into the coverage at the beginning of 1997, when, with an election looming, it started to be put about that Sarah had proposed to Gordon at the end of December, that they were secretly engaged and would marry after the forthcoming election. That looked like the wishful romance of the spin-doctor, as nothing happened. Brown remained eminently eligible as well as highly electable.

Brown's July budget was the occasion for another spin of the media wheel. A photograph of the couple in a Soho restaurant called Vasco and Piero's Pavilion appeared in the *News of the World*. The two were pictured at a discreet corner table and readers may have gained the impression that this was a snatched shot of an intimate liaison. In fact it was posed and as close to an 'official picture' as there was ever likely to be. Afterwards it was reported that the photographer was not happy with the first roll of film he took, and asked Brown and Sarah to remain in pose for another one. Charlie Whelan was at the adjacent table and they willingly complied.

As the year progressed Gordon and Sarah have given the spin-doctors increasing opportunities to promote them as a couple. They were reported during the Party Conference to have boogied the night away at a discotheque next to Brighton's Metropole Hotel. Gordon was prepared to be photographed with Sarah at Ed Balls's wedding in Eastbourne, where they were seen strolling on the promenade with Geoffrey Robinson and his Italian wife. But on other occasions he's been more shy;

he went out of his way to avoid photographers at a high-profile Labour fund-raising bash.

Behind the scenes, Sarah has been doing her best to promote her consort to opinion-formers whom he would find good company now, and future supporters in any political contest. The results have not been entirely satisfactory. Sarah assembled one group, including *Guardian* editor Alan Rusbridger and Football Association executive David Davies, for a cosy Number 11 dinner party. But the Chancellor was completely uninterested and ill at ease. Sarah will have realized something that Carol Craig knew twenty years earlier from Edinburgh days. 'Gordon hated dinner parties, he wouldn't go to someone's house if they were having a dinner party. He would go to a party, and he liked big parties, and you could always count on Gordon to be at your big party. But you didn't invite him round if you were only having six or eight people.'

Sarah has been at Gordon's side at a series of receptions at the official residence. After the 1997 Christmas party for journalists, she and Brown escorted guests round the flat at Number 10. Some see this political socializing as empire-building, but he is unlikely to be over-worried. He seems to quite like being seen as a risqué Chancellor, who has some fun by taking a tilt at the stuffy establishment. For example, he spends little time in the formal flat above Number 10, preferring to be at his old Westminster flat or with Sarah. She has kept her south London home, with her cat and collection of country music records.

Formal dress has never been a strong point with Gordon Brown, and friends say it was completely predictable that he would resist sprucing himself up in the proper finery for the Lord Mayor's City dinner. Brown has always detested wearing dinner jackets or other formal clothing and Brown is said never once to have worn a dinner jacket and bow-tie until 1994. He broke the rule at the instigation of his brother John, who had invited him to toast the 'immortal memory' of the great Scots poet at the Strathclyde Region Burns Supper. Wearing a dinner jacket and bow-tie is absolutely a three-line whip to the person who gives this awesome toast and a mortified Gordon did what he was told. But there was a last-minute panic when he forgot to pick up the outfit from the dress-hire shop in London. The fact is, says an old friend, 'He hates anything that smacks of élitism.'

The other challenge for the new public relations lady in Brown's life is to smarten up his personal image. She has begun the mammoth task by organizing for the complete repainting and redecorating of his splendid house in North Queensferry. Sarah began the job by having a new kitchen installed, but now the whole house has been spruced up and made fit for a Chancellor. Sarah is now watching Brown's wardrobe and ensuring there are no repeats of the recent embarrassing occasion when his trousers split as he climbed on to a platform during an election rally in north London during the May local elections, revealing a pair of blue underpants.

She also has a bit of sorting out to do of Brown's interpersonal skills. He upset one little group of Scottish friends many years ago by buying up ten copies of his favourite book at the time – *The Best and the Brightest* by David Halberstam, an account of the Kennedys and the Vietnam War. As each of their birthdays came along he gave them an unsigned copy until the pile had run out. While the friends recognized this as a piece of typically cackhanded Gordonism, Brown himself could see nothing wrong. The new broom may be expected to insist he make an inscription at the very least.

Sarah's task in revamping the unworldly Chancellor is a tough one. But behind her, and pushing hard, is the Chancellor's office manager and powerful factotum Sue Nye. Nye arranged for Brown and Sarah to be photographed with her son Ben at his third birthday party, just prior to the March Budget. Under protest, he agreed to shed his regulation navy-blue suit and tie for an open neck shirt and jumper – the first time in his political career he had been photographed looking so casual. The aim of the spin-doctors was to promote Gordon the family man to a slightly incredulous public. Political commentators greeted the scheme with derision, but Charlie Whelan riposted that it worked: every paper had used the photo on their front page.

As the first year of office drew to a close, Brown found interviewers less interested in the great political projects than in his matrimonial plans. His stock answer was, 'I'll let you know when I have something to tell you.' Once he would have blushed and stammered, now he is able to smile and embrace the possibility of tying the knot. This gives spin-doctors hope that Brown's remaining political hurdle can yet be cleared. But others see the delay as fairly standard Brown procrastination.

As Gordon's mother Elizabeth might yet be heard to murmur, 'It's up to you, son.'

Romance and relationships had never ceased to figure in Brown's life, but these were not always of the personal kind. Some five months after taking power, relations between European countries and currencies would come to the forefront. For Brown, these would prove as sticky as those of the heart.

Chapter Eleven: The EMU Row

The wine was flowing as it always did when political players dined with journalists at a Party Conference. It was the final night of the Conference in Brighton, the scene was a Chinese restaurant where Ed Balls and Charlie Whelan were enjoying a relaxed night out with Phil Webster, Political Editor of *The Times*, and his deputy, Jill Sherman. One throwaway remark made here, over the chopsticks and willow-patterned plates, set in train one of the great political dramas of Labour's first year in office. Disaster turned to triumph during an extraordinary month as the new Government wrestled with the challenge of the European single currency.

Webster was affable, popular among colleagues and MPs and an excellent sportsman. Equally at home on the golf course, the football field or the cricket pitch, he was described by one friend as 'a Peter Pan character refusing to let go of his youthful obsession with sport'. But few political journalists doubted that he was one of the canniest operators around the lobbies of Westminster. Webster and Ed Balls were old pals with longstanding Norfolk connections – Norwich City was their mutual passion. Webster would occasionally persuade Balls to run out for the political journalists' football team. By mutual agreement their Conference dinner was deemed to be off-limits, with nothing said that could be usable by the journalists, let alone attributable. They settled down for a pleasant meal laced with the latest gossip from around the Conference and its fringes. Webster and Sherman were winding down as much as their guests and they had no prepared agenda or questions as they would for a normal meal with political contacts. The conversation inevitably meandered towards Europe, the main talking point among Labour Party *apparatchiks* and camp followers.

The previous Friday, 26 September, the *Financial Times* had triggered near panic in the stock market by suggesting that the Government was considering a more positive approach to the single currency and possible membership soon after the official launch in 1999. 'It is now clear that we must indicate our willingness to be in there,' according to an unnamed minister quoted. The pound plummeted as dealers contemplated an early devaluation to bring sterling into line with other European currencies. Shares correspondingly rose in anticipation of a low pan-European interest rate. The story had been penned by Robert Peston, whose informed punt on the abolition of tax credits before the Budget had caused consternation in Whitehall. Peston's track record and the prominence given to the story by the *Financial Times* suggested an authoritive basis to the report. There was much speculation that Balls himself, or Charlie Whelan, had briefed Peston in line with Gordon Brown's supposed pro-European leanings. Whelan denied it then – 'a package of bollocks' was the typical Whelanism regaled to inquiring reporters. Balls too was robust with his rejection of what Peston's sources had suggested. He had even called Webster who was travelling up to Norwich for the weekend to 'assure' him that the story was not true.

Despite the denials there were whisperings around the Party Conference in the week following the *Financial Times* story. The new Government's official position at this stage was not dissimilar to John Major's 'wait and see'. Other European nations appeared to be doubtful about the viability of the project. Since the election Britain under New Labour had opted to take a back seat, ruling nothing in nor out. But Gordon Brown, so the theory went, was trying to bounce his colleagues into early membership of the single currency and the

Financial Times report was part of his strategy. Inevitably the Thursday night dinner-table conversation between the *Times* duo and Brown's aides touched upon this line of speculation. Denials were repeated, Whelan scoffing again at the *Financial Times* story. But Webster was struck by a casual expression from Balls: 'If anything,' he said, 'Gordon is leaning the other way.' It was a throwaway remark but to Webster it suggested something rather different from the popular image of Brown as the single-currency enthusiast. He made a mental note of the comment before the group left the Chinese restaurant and returned as usual to the crowded main bar at the conference hotel, the Metropole.

From the point of view of Brown and Balls the *Financial Times* story could not have been further from the truth. In the middle of September, a couple of weeks before the flurry of excitement over Peston's report, Balls and a handful of Treasury officials had begun fleshing out a possible line for the Government to adopt over the single currency. Jonathan Powell, Blair's Chief of Staff at Number 10 Downing Street, was kept informed of these highly sensitive discussions. Reflecting Brown's thinking, they came to the view that joining the single currency at the projected start date in January 1999 would not be feasible for the UK economy. Much of the rest of the European Union was moving slowly out of recession, interest rates were low and the currencies weak. In contrast, the UK was approaching the peak of the economic cycle, inflation was rising and interest rates were moving steadily upwards. Locking sterling into a fixed exchange rate grid with common interest rates across Europe would be highly risky for the British economy. The buzzword was convergence. Hitching up to the single currency would not be sensible until UK economic performance had 'converged' with the rest of Europe. That might happen in the year 2000 but it would need a year or more to be certain that all the lines on the economic charts were pointing in the same direction.

And then there was the political argument. Did Labour really want a highly divisive single currency referendum to colour its first term in office? The Government would have to take sides against the Eurosceptic Murdoch press in the referendum campaign. The fallout from that would certainly pollute the atmosphere of the next General Election battle. Tony Blair was acutely aware of the political risks: 'Tony doesn't want all this to get in the way of a second term . . . he is more concerned about fighting the election on domestic issues,' said one Labour insider. Some were arguing that there should be an early referendum on the principle of joining EMU but 'in Gordon's view this was completely mad', according to a Treasury source. If it was not going to be possible to assess the economic viability of the project there was no point in having a referendum. 'You've got to have the smallest possible gap between the referendum and going in,' Brown's aides argued.

All these arguments pointed to the same conclusion, that joining the great single currency venture could not take place during Labour's first term in office. But once the election was out of the way all options could be re-opened. Labour, Party strategists reasoned, could go to the polls arguing that Europe was out of the equation and an issue to be left to a forthcoming referendum: 'We'll make the right economic decisions and the people will decide.' If that election took place in May or June 2001 and Labour won, a referendum could be organized within months. A lightning Yes campaign, backed by the Government, could then deliver a mandate for the UK to join in 2002, the formal launch-date for the Euro notes and coins. Such was Gordon Brown's tactical thinking. It drove the detailed economic calculations which were being made inside the Treasury.

Mindful of the need to kill-off corrosive speculation, the Chancellor and his advisers agreed that they must reveal their hand sooner rather than later. They decided that the Government's stance on the single currency would be unveiled with a flourish in early November. Brown would address the CBI conference in the morning and assure delegates that Labour was committed to signing up to monetary union when the conditions were right. This was certain to play well with the pro-European leadership of the CBI, especially after the endlessly confused positions adopted by the Conservatives. That same afternoon in November it was planned that Brown would travel triumphantly back to Westminster to set out the full Government position to the Commons. MPs would be told that, barring exceptional circumstances, joining the single currency was not envisaged in the lifetime of the five-year Parliament. That evening Tony Blair would set the seal on a historic day for the New Labour Government with a speech at a glittering white-tie dinner in the City of London.

The *Financial Times* story about possible early entry to EMU dropped into this carefully plotted scenario like an uninvited relative at a wedding. Balls was as curious as anyone about the source. It could not, he reasoned, have been from inside the tight-knit circle of just five people who were plotting a very different strategy. Perhaps it came from a minister on the inside track but not privy to the Treasury discussions. Brown himself claimed later that 'there was no evidence of a leak from the Treasury – it certainly did not come from the Treasury, no minister that I know'. As Brown went on to the airwaves to deny the story, a Cluedo-style game began around the Members' Lobby and the Parliamentary Press Gallery. Who briefed Robert Peston with the single-currency story was the question. The suspects in the frame were ministers deemed to be pro-European and with an interest in pushing early entry as a policy. Peter Mandelson's name cropped up in conversation along with his ally Roger Liddle, the Downing Street policy adviser. Doug Henderson at the Foreign Office and Lord Simon the Trade Minister also came into the reckoning. Even Peston's own father featured in the lobby gossip; he was, after all, a Labour peer who had once sat on the Party's front bench in the House of Lords. It was also noted that Peston had lunched with the Paymaster-General, Geoffrey Robinson, a few days before his big story.

The pursuers of Peston's source were chasing up a blind alley. The *Financial Times* man insisted that he had talked to a number of contacts and sources and that his story reflected accurately the varied opinions across the Government in late September. There clearly were ministers, Peston argued, who at that stage were in favour of joining the single currency sooner rather than later. He regretted the fact that his sub-editors had cut out two paragraphs at the end of his story which stressed the arguments against early entry, including the concern about the stance of Rupert Murdoch's newspapers. Overall, though, and even with the benefit of several months hindsight, he claimed to be standing by his story. As for the suggestion that he had been briefed by his father, he dismissed it as preposterous. Lord Peston did not hold office in the Government. And given the obvious sensitivities of our positions, he argued, we make a point of not talking shop.

Beyond the public denials Brown and his cohorts decided there was not much more that needed to be done about the Peston story. After all, it did not reflect official Treasury thinking, they reasoned, so there was no cause for concern about leaks. But the denials had not been robust enough as far as the press was concerned. Like a slow-burning fuse, stories about Brown's pro-single-currency leanings continued to spread. They were always contrasted with Tony Blair's reported caution towards the monetary union project. On Monday 13 October, the *Daily Mail*'s Paul Eastham reported that Blair and Brown were poised to announce that Britain would sign up for the single currency soon after its launch in 1999. This represented 'a victory for Gordon Brown . . . who had put enormous pressure on the Prime Minister'. Downing Street suspected this was a Treasury-inspired briefing. That morning Brown, Balls and Whelan were in-flight to Luxembourg for a meeting of European finance ministers. At their hotel there were messages to call Number 10 urgently. Campbell demanded to know what was happening and what the official line was. He had been irritated by the storm whipped up over the *Financial Times* story; now the *Daily Mail* report had made him angry. Brown's people, calling from a hotel room in Luxembourg, assured him they were not responsible.

The following morning the *Independent*'s headline was 'Blair, Brown clash on the biggest issue of all'. The doyen of lobby journalists, Anthony Bevins, reported in a full front-page splash story that the Treasury was trying to bounce a sceptical Blair into killing off the pound. He speculated about an open split developing between Numbers 10 and 11 Downing Street over the most difficult decision facing the Blair Government. The language used may have been overblown but the story was doing no more than reflecting the tension between Blair's and Brown's offices. One source close to the Chancellor thought he had detected what was going on: 'It was clear there were people at Number 10 who said, "Oh my God, Brown's got an agenda", people who either don't understand the Gordon–Tony relationship or have an interest in it being not as close as it is.' A torrent of similar stories picking up on the same theme now seemed likely. Peter Mandelson urged Blair to 'close it down'. The Chancellor, too, decided it was time to act.

On Wednesday 15 October they met in Blair's eyrie at Number 10, the tiny ground-floor study once used by junior ministerial aides but now commandeered by the boss. Blair as usual was sitting on a sofa surrounded by his paperwork. Brown ran through his thinking on the EMU debate and briefed Blair on the secret preparatory work underway in the Treasury. He argued that the Government must state its intention to stay out of EMU during the lifetime of the current Parliament whilst acknowledging that if the project was a success Britain would join at a later stage. Blair's initial response was to question the need to go so far in ruling out membership in the short term. Why, he asked, should the government not continue to keep all options open? Brown pointed out that the Conservative Government had been undermined by the endless speculation about joining the exchange rate mechanism in 1989 and 1990. 'We will join when the time is right' had been Thatcher's formula. The debate had crippled the Government and taken the Cabinet's eyes off the ball. Better, Brown argued, for the new Labour Government to set aside the EMU issue and concentrate on domestic priorities.

The Chancellor's team later observed that 'the whole media discussion centred on Brown trying to bully Blair into going in early. The split was supposed to be Gordon going over to EMU and Tony not going that far. In fact they felt it was the opposite of what was going on.' Behind the closed study door inside Number 10 Downing Street Brown was in reality taking a very cautious stance. Blair had told colleagues soon after the election that if the single currency was right for Britain his Government would sign up. Here his Chancellor was suggesting that not only should the UK stay out at the formal start date in January 1999 but remain on the sidelines for some time longer. As one source put it, 'Gordon was persuading Tony, Tony was asking do we need to go as far as saying we are not going in . . . Gordon said yes.' Their discussion turned to presentation. Brown and Blair agreed that rumours about early entry must be killed off and that an unequivocal signal must be sent out to the media.

Since the Labour Conference Phil Webster had been badgering Balls and Whelan about their conversation in the Brighton Chinese restaurant. Each time he was keen to write about what Brown really thought about monetary union. Each time he was asked to hold off. But on that Wednesday afternoon the Chancellor's advisers discussed once again Webster's interest in Government thinking about the single currency. They put it to Brown that in an interview with the *Times* political editor he could set the record straight and lay to rest the damaging innuendo of a split between Chancellor and Prime Minister. The strategy was agreed. Webster was informed on the Thursday morning that he would be granted an interview with the Chancellor for publication in the Saturday edition. In the frenzied climate of gossip and argument about a rift over European policy an exclusive interview with the Chancellor was a potential goldmine and Webster knew it. He asked his editor literally to 'clear the front page' for the Saturday paper. It was a rare request but when Peter Stothard, editor of *The Times*, heard what Webster was offering he was delighted to oblige. It only remained to hear exactly what Brown had to say.

By the Thursday afternoon the Chancellor had refined the message he wanted to convey to *The Times*. He would make it clear that joining the first wave of the single currency in January 1999 was not feasible. He would then argue that the British economy needed a period of stability before entry to the European monetary project could be considered. For 'period of stability' he hoped Westminster insiders would read 'in the lifetime of this Parliament'. He was dropping the broadest possible hint that the Labour Government would stay out until the next election. This form of words, Brown believed, would take the heat off the Government and buy time while a full statement was worked on and finally presented to the Commons in November.

That evening Brown asked his private office at the Treasury to make contact with Number 10 Downing Street. Blair was in the middle of a sensitive meeting with another member of the Cabinet but the Chancellor insisted that he was put through. He spoke on the phone with the Prime Minister for five minutes and explained his decision to do the interview with *The Times*. They discussed a short form of words which would reflect their thinking. It was to be turned into a draft paragraph on monetary union which would be dictated to Phil Webster. Blair indicated he was satisfied and before returning to his meeting asked Brown to 'have a word with Alastair'. The draft words were faxed from the Treasury to the Prime Minister's press secretary and agreed after some minor changes. That evening Alastair Campbell and Charlie Whelan chewed over the strategy. Labour's twin masters of media manipulation looked forward to another presentational triumph. A chance to kick EMU into the long grass appealed particularly to Campbell's instincts, attuned as they were to the Eurosceptic tendencies of the popular press.

Early on the Friday morning Webster received a call at home from a senior Government source. 'Are you ready to gain your place in history?' the *Times* man was asked. He was told the interview was on but that first he would be supplied with a quotation from the Chancellor relating to EMU. Cancelling a game of golf he had planned with the *Sun*'s political editor, Trevor Kavanagh, for that afternoon, Webster hurried into the office, excited by the prospect of a dramatic scoop. He was phoned separately by Alastair Campbell and Ed Balls. They briefed him on the latest thinking about the single currency and the practical problems implied by British membership. Webster was not surprised to learn that joining at the start in 1999 was being effectively ruled out. There had been briefings to this effect before. He was left in no doubt though that the new Government had no desire to enter until their first term of office was complete and that the Chancellor would soon make a formal announcement to this effect. Webster knew he was on to something. He took a shorthand note of the prepared quotation from Brown. These words referred to the need for a breathing-space for the British economy before any decision was taken on joining monetary union. That afternoon Webster spoke on the phone to Brown, by this time up in his constituency. There was no spinning or extra briefing. The

Chancellor was providing a predictable interview about the state of the economy.

Early on the Friday evening, Webster had finished writing up both a front-page splash and his full interview with Gordon Brown for the inside pages. Whelan called to check how the story was shaping up, Webster talked through the outlines and the angle he had taken. The *Times* man was emphasizing that the Chancellor was on the verge of ruling out membership of the single currency before the next election. Whelan did not demur. Later he and Alastair Campbell passed on the same line to the editor of the *Sun*, Stuart Higgins. Crucially, neither Campbell nor Whelan checked the headline being prepared by the *Times* sub-editors. It read: 'Brown rules out single currency in the lifetime of this Parliament', the words 'close to' or 'on the verge of' left out. Upon these few words, or the absence of them, hung the calamitous events of the following ten days and the unravelling of the new Government's credibility. One Treasury aide reflected later on the extraordinary semantics of this episode: 'The story was supposed to be, Gordon Brown hints if we don't go in in 1999 we will be out for a period of stability while we prepare, and the clearest signal that Labour is not planning early entry. The problem was the word "if" got left out and it got hardened up.'

The Red Lion is a traditional London pub, unspoiled by the ravages of tourist exploitation and fast food. Here civil servants rub shoulders with political researchers, journalists and other Westminster hangers-on and enjoy a real pint. Close to the Cenotaph and opposite the Foreign Office and the Treasury, the Red Lion has a fine outlook on the comings and goings of political life. Television producers sometimes ask permission to position cameras in the upper rooms for the view across Whitehall. Indeed, the landlord's bedroom was once rented by ITN as an *ad hoc* television edit suite. On the evening of Friday 17 October, the Red Lion was to make political news as never before, its name forever to be associated with the Labour Government in turmoil.

Like many other ministerial aides, Charlie Whelan found the Red Lion a convenient watering-hole and a useful sounding-board for the latest political gossip. He would often step in with colleagues from the Treasury press office on the way home. That Friday evening was no different. He considered he had put in a good day's work, *The Times* had been taken care of and it was time for a drink. Inside the bar was packed. It was a warm evening and many drinkers had spilled out on to the pavements. As ever, Whelan's pager was humming every few minutes. There were messages to call the BBC's *Newsnight* programme and ITN urgently. They had been tipped off by Phil Webster. He was happy to share his scoop with them as both would be on air after ten o'clock, by which time rival newspapers had sent their first editions to the presses. Whelan stepped outside the pub to return the calls. Both news organizations asked whether *The Times*'s interpretation of the Chancellor's remarks was correct, specifically whether Gordon Brown was set to rule out entry to the single currency until the next Parliament. Whelan said simply, 'Phil Webster is a respectable journalist.'

The sight of Charlie Whelan speaking animatedly into a mobile phone outside the Red Lion was not unusual. Westminster insiders milling around on the pavement, drinks in hand, would not have given it a second thought. This time, however, the gist of his conversation was overheard by a young Liberal Democrat press officer. He pieced together the few words coming from the Chancellor's press secretary. Whelan's cover had been blown. In a world where briefings are non-attributable and sources anonymous, to be seen and heard at work by a political rival is like being spotted by an enemy sniper. Having inadvertently put his head above the parapet, Whelan had become a sitting duck. The strategy pulled together by the Chancellor's team was beginning to fall apart.

The Lib Dem aide got on to his Party's Treasury spokesman, Malcolm Bruce, and reported what he had heard. Armed with this information, Bruce made his way to the *Newsnight* studios for a live interview on the single currency. After their tip-off from Webster, *Newsnight* had been trying to sniff out more on the story. They contacted the duty press officer at the Treasury who told them the Government's policy had not changed, in other words, that options were being kept open. At the Treasury those outside the inner-circle of Brown's advisers had no reason to think otherwise. But *Newsnight*'s suspicions were aroused. Here, it seemed, was a Government information officer denying any change of tack while the Chancellor's press secretary was signalling a new policy. Fuelled by Bruce's account of Whelan's activities outside the Red Lion, *Newsnight* went to town. Just what was Government policy on the single currency, they demanded to know, and who was making it?

The Prime Minister himself was wondering who was saying what. As usual he had retreated for the weekend with his family to Chequers, the official country residence in Buckinghamshire. That night he was phoned by Peter Mandelson. The Minister without Portfolio, well known for his pro-European leanings, was spitting blood. He was horrified when he heard what *The Times* was reporting and he told Tony Blair how he felt. He had not been privy to Brown's thinking and the activities of Campbell, Balls and Whelan over the previous forty-eight hours. Ruling out British membership of the single currency for effectively five years went right against the grain for Mandelson. Tony Blair replied that he and the Chancellor believed policy should be clarified. Pointing out that the Minister without Portfolio had called for the speculation to be closed down Blair said, 'I thought you wanted it.' Mandelson argued that *The Times* headline went too far. Did the Prime Minister, he asked, really want to come out with a firm statement of policy there and then?

It was Blair's turn to hit the phone lines. He instructed staff at Chequers to find the Chancellor of the Exchequer. Downing Street's renowned Switch system was called into play. Wherever they were in the world and at whatever time of day or night, ministers would be traced and connected by Switch. But not on this occasion. The Chancellor was on a round of constituency engagements near Dunfermline. Mobile phone reception was at best patchy in this corner of Fife. That night even Switch could not make contact with the phone in Brown's car. Blair and Brown did talk later, when Brown had returned to his house.

By Saturday morning the Conservatives were on the offensive. They pursued the line taken by *Newsnight*, demanding to know if policy had been changed and if so, why the House of Commons had not been informed first. Parliament should be recalled, they thundered. The Chancellor's and the Prime Minister's aides were

not greatly perturbed. Tory demands of this nature served only to
unite Labour factions against the common enemy. The following
day, though, the ripples turned to waves crashing against the
Government's defences. The Sunday papers were full of the
drama and confusion allegedly overshadowing policy towards
European monetary union. Charlie Whelan's cameo role in the
Red Lion appeared in the paper. It was classic Sunday newspaper
fare. Labour's spin-doctors hoped still to lie low and watch the
storm blow over. But those hopes were dashed when the genial
figure of Frank Dobson, the Health Secretary, appeared on the
BBC's *Breakfast with Frost* programme. Dobson, like others in
the Government, did not know of Blair's discussions with Brown
the previous week or the background to the *Times* story. When
asked for his view he repeated the line which ministers had
spouted up until then: 'We may not join in 1999 but we will
keep our options open after that.' Dobson spoke with the best
of intentions but unknowingly he had contradicted the briefings
coming from Number 10 and Number 11 on the Friday night.
Far from being killed off, the 'Government in confusion' story
was running again.

Charlie Whelan knew they were in trouble, so much so that
he cancelled plans to go to White Hart Lane for the Sunday
afternoon match between Spurs and Sheffield Wednesday. He
had a personal invitation from the Tottenham chairman, Alan
Sugar, by now an ally and unofficial adviser to the Chancellor.
Whelan's passion for Spurs was well known. Telling Sugar he
could not get to the game was painful. But his energy was quickly
diverted into a fire-fighting exercise. There was a conference
phone-call with Alastair Campbell and Peter Mandelson. They
agreed to sit tight and wait to hear BBC Radio's treatment of the
story on *The World This Weekend*. As one of them remembered
later, 'The programme was bad, they were all over us.' Soon
afterwards there was another conference call. Whelan and Balls
joined the Chancellor at his flat near Westminster Abbey.
Alastair Campbell came on the line, then Peter Mandelson
and finally the Prime Minister. It was a tense few minutes,
Mandelson making plain his irritation that the others had
blundered into trouble without consulting him. Here were the
most powerful players at the court of King Tony in a tight spot

and uncertain how to get out of it. They decided that Brown must try to hold the line in an interview for television news. That line was 'Gordon will not be bounced', in other words there would be no emergency statement to the Commons.

Whelan's task was to get his master on to the airwaves and he wasted no time in trying to make it happen. He called the BBC newsdesk, and told them Brown would do one interview to be pooled among the broadcasters. He asked them to have a reporter and camera crew at Westminster by the early evening. The venue for the interview was, unusually, to be the Chancellor's Westminster flat – Whelan reasoned that summoning a television crew to Number 11 Downing Street on a Sunday would suggest an atmosphere of crisis. Brown fended off the questions about policy on the single currency and repeated again and again that he would not be bounced by the Tories into a recall of Parliament. Nerves were steadied as Brown's interview set the tone for the broadcasters' coverage in their late news bulletins. But the Chancellor and his aides knew their sternest test would come the following day. By an uncanny coincidence it was the tenth anniversary of 'Black Monday', the 1987 stock market crash. Already stockbrokers and currency dealers were predicting a bloodbath in the markets because of the clouds of uncertainty over the Government's intentions towards the single currency. That night there were real fears in the Treasury that there would be a big slump. For the Government, not yet six months in office, the nightmare was another Black Monday caused by its own gaffe.

There could not have been a more inappropriate engagement in Brown's diary for the morning of Monday 20 October. He had been invited to launch the Stock Exchange's new paperless trading system. The Chancellor was supposed to press the button and a new era of automated share-dealing would burst into life. But as Brown mounted the platform a few minutes before trading formally opened, the financial pundits were predicting a market meltdown. Whelan and Balls grimaced as they watched their man ushered to a position in front of a giant screen. Here was a presentational disaster in the making and one over which they had no control. At precisely half past eight Brown declared the system open and the screen flickered behind him. The movement of each of the top 100 shares was marked blue for upwards, red for downwards. Inevitably a wave of red flashed across the screen as the Chancellor pressed on with his speech. He spelled out a holding position on European monetary union, stressing that the Government would act in Britain's economic interests. Clips from the statement were put out on news bulletins within the hour. The image of a Chancellor on the defensive during a crisis with red lights flashing around him was every television producer's dream.

After these early tremors the stock market calmed down. Share prices crept back upwards although they remained below where they were before the weekend. The financial fallout was contained, but the political shockwaves were still pulsating. The Commons' summer recess was not due to end until the following Monday, but the Tories bayed at the Government's door demanding an emergency recall of Parliament. Inside Whitehall there were harsh words, recriminations and the jabbing of fingers of blame. Neither the Foreign Secretary nor the Deputy Prime Minister had been consulted about the new line on the single currency. Sources close to Robin Cook and John Prescott made it plain that they were not happy. Other Labour insiders alleged that no proper groundwork had been done on the new policy. Some even argued that the Prime Minister had never guessed when he gave his blessing to the Chancellor's *Times* interview that it would result in a new statement of policy.

Charlie Whelan himself was now in the firing line, the spin-doctor stung. Lurid reports of his power and influence at the heart of New Labour were spiced with embellished accounts of his performance at the Red Lion. Although Whelan had not been involved with the original briefings to *The Times*, a convenient consensus had it that he had single-handedly changed Government policy while leaning on the bar. His swaggering manner encouraged his critics to suggest that the Chancellor's press secretary was calling the shots and that he was solely responsible for *The Times* interview fiasco. Radio news-reporters thrust microphones in his face. Eminent commentators called for his head. He was even the subject of the main leader in the *Daily Telegraph*, headlined

'Charlie Whelan, Chancellor'. *Channel Four News* dispatched a producer to purchase a child's spinning-top. Shots of the toy were superimposed on footage of Whelan on a telephone.

While Whelan was exposed to a hail of media bullets other heads were kept well down. There were few questions asked about those who had actually briefed *The Times*, in other words Ed Balls and Alastair Campbell. Those who pointed out that Whelan and Campbell would only act in accordance with their masters' wishes were drowned out in the clamour. The messenger not the master was taking the shots. Later on the Monday Campbell went on the offensive. At one of his briefings for parliamentary journalists the Prime Minister's press secretary let fly. 'You people depend on spin-doctors to brief you,' he cried, 'but now you're biting off the hand that feeds you'. Later Campbell floated the idea of on-the-record briefings with the source of information to be made explicit. Stories from then on would be attributed to him as the Prime Minister's official spokesman rather than the vague catch-all 'Downing Street sources'. Whelan wondered whether this was a dig at him and an attempt by Campbell to distance himself from the *Times* interview.

On the Tuesday Blair called a council of war at Number 10. Brown and Whelan sat across the table from the Prime Minister, Mandelson, Campbell and Jonathan Powell alongside him. This was the very core of New Labour, the men who had trounced the Conservatives in the battle for the affections of the media in the long election campaign. They were masters of presentation and proud of it, envied by their opponents. Yet now they had been humbled. The hastily devised plan to quell talk of a rift between the Prime Minister and the Chancellor had backfired spectacularly. In doing so the seeds of a new tension between the two men had been sown. The interview with *The Times*, far from killing speculation about the Government's intentions towards the single currency, had revived it. As one of those present was to admit later, 'We should never have done it, we got things wrong,' a remarkable concession from one of New Labour's apparently invincible chieftains. Blair brought the meeting to heel. 'This must never happen again,' he said curtly, 'we're in this together.' Their task now was to get out of it.

The first and most pressing decision was over when the Chancellor would explain the new single currency policy to MPs. Word had come from the Speaker's Office that Betty Boothroyd was not amused by the drama of the previous weekend. She made it clear she expected a full statement to the House of Commons. The Chancellor's aides privately feared that an emergency recall of Parliament that week, before the official end of the recess, would smack of panic and give the Tories the moral high ground. Yet waiting until November, as originally envisaged, was now out of the question. Blair's diary for the following week was a nightmare and fitting in a statement seemed impossible. There was, however, to be an auction of Government gilt-edged stock on the Wednesday of that week. Treasury officials pointed out that ministers could be accused of creating a false market if they withheld the announcement of the new policy till after the auction. Government business managers predicted that the Conservatives would use the ruse of a private notice question to force the Chancellor to the dispatch box as soon as MPs returned on the Monday. Better, they argued, if the Government had already announced there would be a statement that day. Monday, then, was decided upon, though it would be kept secret until the weekend. That left precious little time for the policy itself to be fleshed out.

Over the next few days Downing Street and the Treasury hummed with activity. Meeting followed meeting as officials agonized over phrases and paragraphs. They knew it would be one of the most important parliamentary statements of Labour's first term of office. It had to be watertight, immune to the jibes of the opposition and robust enough to stand up to scrutiny in the years leading up to a final decision on joining the single currency. And while the civil servants toiled, the politicians wrangled. Gordon Brown wanted a clear-cut decision from the Government, either to go in at the start in 1999 or not to do it before the election. Having decided that 1999 was not practicable, Brown wanted to send an unequivocal signal that Britain would hold off till the early years of the millennium. Others in the Government, most prominently Peter Mandelson, were worried that this would play badly with business leaders. They argued that a loophole must be left open, allowing the

Government to join if it wished during the lifetime of the Parliament. Mandelson also wanted to reassure pro-European Labour MPs like Giles Radice, who saw in the *Times* interview as a large and undesirable lurch towards Euroscepticism.

Behind the scenes there were extensive discussions involving Brown and Mandelson with Blair as referee. The shifting debate within the Government was reflected by contradictory briefings flying around the Parliamentary Lobby and Press Gallery. One political editor remembers, 'I was told by the same minister on successive days completely different policies on Europe.' Meanwhile Phil Webster, whose scoop had detonated the crisis, endured an agonizing week. 'It was the best story I've ever had,' he said later, but he could not be sure until Brown made his formal statement to the Commons. Webster dreaded the possibility of the Government changing its mind. He was phoned a couple of times by a senior source who warned him that he would live to regret his splash the previous Saturday. The *New Statesman* described it as 'one of the most extraordinary news stories in political history'. The journal went on to predict that the Government would not rule out membership in the lifetime of the Parliament but would review the state of economic convergence with the rest of Europe 'on a regular, perhaps annual basis'. Brown's team thought they detected the fingerprints of friends of Mandelson on the *New Statesman* story. Friends of Mandelson denied it.

On the Thursday morning Tony Blair and his entourage departed for the Commonwealth Summit in Edinburgh. Blair left his most powerful generals behind him still jostling for position over the preparation of the Commons statement. Back in Downing Street twelve of the leading players gathered to review the work being done, Brown and Balls, Mandelson and Campbell among them. Sources close to Brown claimed later that 'Mandelson saw the light' as he realized that notwithstanding the refusal to sign up to EMU in the lifetime of the Parliament the Chancellor was positive about the project in the longer-term. Friends of Mandelson in contrast claimed that they had to reel Brown back from total rejection of British membership before the year 2002.

The final days of preparation were arduous. Numerous drafts

were prepared and circulated within the tightly knit circle of Government ministers and advisers. Fax machines worked non-stop as the texts were sent to Edinburgh for the Prime Minister to consider. Blair was not happy with the first two drafts and ordered changes. He was concerned with maintaining a balance, as one source put it 'treading a tightrope between early entry and shutting it down'. Four hundred miles from Downing Street, he instructed his old allies Peter Mandelson and Lord Irvine, the Lord Chancellor, to get involved in consulted work being done at the Treasury. Brown, deciding it was time to build bridges, made his own overtures to the Minister without Portfolio. He advised Mandelson about what the Prime Minister would find acceptable. The Chancellor, on Blair's prompting, also consulted Lord Irvine. The lines between the Treasury and the Lord Chancellor's office were kept busy. Indeed a fax was dispatched late one night to a private residence where Irvine was dining, the Lord Chancellor scribbling notes on the text and firing back a response.

Brown's familiar speech-writing team was ordered to report for duty. Dr Colin Currie cleared his desk at his Edinburgh hospital and caught the first shuttle down to London. As usual he was put up by Geoffrey Robinson at his flat above the Grosvenor House Hotel, but there was no time to enjoy the Paymaster-General's five-star hospitality. Currie rolled up his sleeves and joined Balls, Miliband and Whelan in the Chancellor's private office. In all their years crafting prose from Brown's machine-gun bursts of ideas this speech was the most difficult. Brown as always paced the room, churning over the momentous challenge before him, striving to channel his thoughts. He could not rest until he was comfortable with every sentence. As Currie remembered it, 'Gordon is at his best when he is in trouble – his back was really against the wall at that time.' The speech writers were chivvied and chided as they struggled to capture the ideas flying around them. After the débâcle of the *Times* interview they could not afford to fail; this statement had to press all the right buttons.

One question vexed them. Should the Chancellor apologize for the uncertainty and market turbulence caused by his interview with Phil Webster? Downing Street wanted him to do just that and a suggested opening paragraph was sent over to the Treasury. Brown was expected to say sorry for allowing policy on the single currency to leak before the Commons was informed; but he refused. An apology was an admission of failure and he was determined to turn the extraordinary developments of the past week to the Government's advantage. As a source close to him put it, 'He thought we had to get out on to the high ground, we need to get out of this problem in a big way.'

Brown and his aides had noted a tactical shift by the Conservatives that very week. Facing threats from his Eurosceptic colleagues, William Hague persuaded his Shadow Cabinet effectively to oppose the single currency for ten years. At the Treasury there was astonishment and delight. Brown and Balls believed the Tories were consigning themselves to the margins of the European debate. Indicating a preparedness to join the single currency within a few years, they reasoned, would allow them to cement an alliance with big business, historically the friend of Conservatism but never able to countenance such a hard-line rejection of monetary union. Even better for Labour, there were signs of new Tory fissures over Europe just at a time when the opposition could have been uniting to attack the Government's apparent turmoil. That weekend the arch Tory pro-European Peter Temple indicated enough was enough and he was ready to cross the floor of the house.

By half past three on Monday 27 October the Commons was nearly full. It may have been the first day of business since the summer holidays but MPs had made much effort to get there. The Speaker, Betty Boothroyd, paid tribute to Viscount Tonypandy after his recent death and announced there would be a re-run of the election in the Winchester constituency. Then she announced to a hushed House that there was to be a statement from the Chancellor of the Exchequer. Gordon Brown rose in front of the dispatch box and in near silence delivered the lines fleshed out so laboriously with his aides. The decision on the single currency was, he said, 'the most important question the country is likely to face in our generation'. He went on to reject the constitutional argument which ruled out ever signing up to monetary union, and in doing so committed the British

Government for the first time to the principle of the single currency: 'If, in the end, the single currency is successful and the economic case is clear and unambiguous, the Government believe that Britain should be part of it.'

Much of Brown's speech was devoted to the five economic tests which he said would determine when Britain should enter the single currency. Convergence of British and European nations' economies was the first and most important, flexibility of the labour market and the impact on investment were two more. On the basis of these tests, Brown continued, British entry at the start date in 1999 could not be justified. The Liberal Democrat spokesman Malcolm Bruce later described the tests as 'so elastic they could stretch to the moon and back'. Privately that was the way many Treasury and City economists felt. The tests were to a large degree a smokescreen to mask the basic decision by Brown to rule out entry for the whole of the first Parliament. But he preserved himself the loophole of a 'fundamental or unforeseen change in economic circumstances' to allow earlier membership. Setting up a committee to oversee preparation for EMU, Brown urged businesses to start thinking through the practicalities of using the Euro. He was effectively telling them it might not be happening for a while but it would happen in due course.

The Tories' response was tentative. The Shadow Chancellor Peter Lilley dwelt at length on the confusion over the *Financial Times* and *Times* stories. He could not resist dropping references to the Red Lion into his speech and calling for Charlie Whelan's resignation. This focus on the process of Government rather than the policy itself did not quite hit the mark. Brown in his response to Lilley simply ignored the questions about Whelan. He taunted the Tories for their outright rejection of the single currency because of 'division, dogma or anti-Europeanism on the part of the Conservative Party'. Most observers agreed that by the end of exchanges on monetary union the Chancellor had convincingly seen-off his Shadow.

The following morning Tony Blair chewed the fat with Gordon Brown at Number 10. The statement had been well-received in the press, the pro-Europeans finding as much to be cheerful about as the Eurosceptics. The Red Lion now seemed like a red herring as pundits and commentators got their teeth into the meat of the dramatic new policy announcement. The obsessive interest in spin-doctors and presentation had waned. The Prime Minister was pleased with the outcome. The Cabinet Secretary Sir Robin Butler later told one minister, 'With one bound you are free.' Brown himself later argued that 'what we did in October will actually be seen as the turning point in Britain'. It had been a turning point too for the new Government. Wounds between Blair's and Brown's rival courts had festered. The renewed rancour would not easily be forgotten. But the Government had staggered through its first real wobble and survived. Lessons, particularly about spinning stories that went beyond the words of an interview, had been painfully learned. Most important of all, the Government could encourage preparations for joining the single currency without attracting political approbrium. A referendum soon after the next general election and scrapping the pound by 2002 was the aim. Labour's chiefs could in the meantime concentrate on winning what no other Labour administration had done, a second full term in power.

Chapter Twelve:
The Communist and the Capitalist

In the 1970s Charlie Whelan and Geoffrey Robinson were on opposite sides of the great industrial divide, one a Communist student activist, the other the boss of a great British corporation. With the passage of time and the blurring of class-lines under New Labour they would find themselves together at the heart of the Whitehall establishment. They were united by unswerving devotion to their Chancellor and the blokeish intimacy of Brown's inner circle. Charlie Whelan and Geoffrey Robinson were in their own ways indispensable to Gordon Brown. Each generated acres of hostile media coverage and regular calls for their heads. Whatever the embarrassment or short-term pain, Brown repaid them with his loyalty.

Whelan and Robinson, as much as Ed Balls, hover at Brown's beck and call. There is a friendship and trust between them borne of the intense struggle of opposition. Working and playing together, there is little time for another life. As one acquaintance put it, they are bound together by 'the gym, football and policy'. After-hours they will as often as not repair to the Grosvenor House hotel, one of London's finest. On one of the uppermost floors the Paymaster-General Geoffrey Robinson keeps a spacious apartment. It is an alternative nerve-centre for the Brown team. In opposition it was their master control room. Speeches were crafted, strategies honed. Politics consumed them twenty-four hours a day as they pursued power.

In the dawn of election victory they retreated to the Grosvenor House from the Party's official celebrations at the Festival Hall. There was time for champagne and self-congratulation but the talk was more of their imminent arrival at the Treasury. In power the apartment has become their refuge. Here after an exhausting thirteen hours at the Treasury they relax together with 'a pasta and some wine from room service'. They will watch live football on television and keep an eye on the late news programmes. Exercise is an obsession. The Grosvenor House gym is the scene of many a late-night Treasury workout, Whelan sometimes joining Robinson who aims for 3 miles per session of 'brisk walking.'

As a former director of Coventry City Football Club, Geoffrey Robinson is well-known and welcomed in the directors' boxes of the Premiership. Tickets are not a problem and Commons researchers and journalists have benefited from Robinson's generosity. His contacts allow the Brownites to indulge their passion for 'the people's game'. Together they watched many of the European Championship games at Wembley in 1996. Whelan once dreamed of a career as a footballer and had trials with QPR. As a fan, though, his first love is Tottenham Hotspur, and Brown's acquaintance with Alan Sugar, Chairman of the club, has taken them more than once to White Hart Lane, home of Spurs. While Brown, Balls and sometimes Robinson might sit in the directors' box, Whelan prefers to sit with his mates elsewhere in the stand. Over the years Whelan has berated and threatened newspaper editors but he has only once ever written a letter for publication. That was to complain that a profile in the *Independent* marked him down as an Arsenal fan: 'In all my time as Press Secretary to Gordon Brown, I have never experienced such a disgraceful allegation.'

The autumn of 1997 was not a happy time for Whelan. The Bank of England move and the first Budget had left Brown and his aides on the crest of a wave. In terms of politics and presentation they had scored highly. But the EMU saga had severely dented Whelan's confidence. Inside the Treasury and at Number 10 there was agreement that the right policy had been reached in the end, but the events before and after the infamous interview with *The Times* were regarded as a fiasco, and Whelan appeared to be single-handedly taking the blame. Insiders knew it had been a collective decision, indeed Alastair Campbell had said, 'If Charlie goes, I go too.' But the media, encouraged by nods and winks from enemies of the Chancellor, continued to blame Whelan. He knew there had been pressure from friends of Blair to have him sacked. He was chastened and resolved to keep his head down. For a time he steered well clear of the familiar journalistic haunts around Westminster. For the gregarious and usually self-assured Whelan it was purgatory.

Whelan's critics were also tut-tutting over his role in a Scottish Television documentary. The two-part production shown in a prime slot on ITV during the Party Conference season had followed Gordon Brown through the last year of opposition and the first months at the Treasury. The project was conceived by Alastair Moffat, a senior Scottish Television executive, who was a friend and tennis partner of Gordon Brown's. Moffat had negotiated with Brown to allow a fly-on-the-wall camera team into Labour headquarters and later the Treasury. Whelan's task was to make it work. There were many headaches during the election campaign, with some senior Labour strategists objecting to the presence of the camera crew in sensitive meetings. Taking the documentary-makers into Downing Street and the Treasury was even more complicated. Immediately before and after election day Whelan had been involved in tortuous negotiations with civil servants. A television camera on the new Chancellor's elbow seemed to the senior mandarins to be an appalling prospect. A tense compromise was reached, with Treasury staff given the right to veto their own appearances in the finished programmes. Well before it appeared on air, though, a climate of suspicion about the documentary had evolved.

To ITV chiefs and many ordinary viewers outside Westminster the two-part production was a great success. Ross Wilson, the director, had got behind the scenes of a political world unknown to millions and conveyed an unusual inside view of power. Whelan appeared on camera almost as much as Brown, and Balls was also prominent in many scenes. This may have been inevitable because so few of Brown's meetings were for public consumption, but to the political audience it looked as if Whelan was hogging the stage. His critics seized upon his comment on screen that 'you have to be economical with the truth – you should never lie but it's very difficult'. Here, they claimed, was confirmation of dangerous manipulation by the powers behind the Chancellor's throne. The Red Lion drama was the opportunity to throw it all back at Whelan and make him the scapegoat. The documentary was soon being portrayed as another presentational own goal by Brown's team.

The controversial aside about being economical with the truth in fact related to a specific event before the election which, as it happened, was one of Whelan's greatest coups. With Brown's blessing he felt he had led journalists up the garden path to extract maximum reporting of a key Labour policy.

It happened in January 1997 when Brown was due to make a series of speeches setting out Labour's plans for public spending and taxation. After months of ducking the issue the Shadow Chancellor had let it be known that he would reveal the Party's intentions regarding the basic and higher rates of income tax. Behind the scenes Brown and Blair had wrangled for months over the issue of taxation for the wealthy. Brown was keen to raise the higher rate for top earners from 40 per cent to 50 per cent in line with most leading industrial nations. Blair was worried that any proposed tax increase would play into the hands of the Conservatives. Brown was left to announce their joint decision the tax rates and in doing so wrong-foot the Tories.

Charlie Whelan's strategy was a near-perfect demonstration of spin-doctoring. Rule Number One was to split the announcement in order to get more than one day's worth of coverage. The Sunday newspapers were briefed that Brown in his speech the following day would promise to stick to the Conservative Government's planned spending totals. There was no mention of tax, but the spending story was enough to occupy much of the Sunday and Monday morning front pages. Rule Number Two was surprise. Only a handful of people, not even the Shadow Cabinet, knew about the tax plan, so the dangers of a leak were minimized. Whelan's tactic was to keep the tax story from national newspaper reporters but to spring it on the Monday morning on BBC Radio's influential *Today* programme. In that way it was sure to dominate the day's television news. The newspapers would of course report it in great detail for the following morning, guaranteeing favourable headlines for a third successive day.

The plan worked and the venue for Brown's speech that Monday afternoon – the Queen Elizabeth II Conference Centre near Westminster Abbey – was packed out with television and radio teams. The tax and spending plans dominated the day's news schedules as Brown was dubbed the Iron Chancellor. The Tories were caught unawares and were unable to come up with a convincing response. In the pre-election phoney war this was a defining moment: Labour seized the initiative and appeared to shed the tax-and-spend image which had derailed the 1992 campaign. It was a triumph for both Gordon Brown and his media lieutenant.

Whelan had been playing for high stakes and won. But he had left some journalists feeling bruised. Some had specifically asked the night before whether Brown would cover personal taxation in the speech and been told 'No'. According to the BBC correspondent Nicholas Jones in his book *Campaign 1997*, Whelan revealed that a reporter had accused him of being 'evil for lying to him when I said tax wouldn't be in the speech – but I've apologized. I couldn't tell him. I had to do it.' This was the context of the infamous clip from the documentary which came to haunt him during the EMU row when it became a convenient stick to beat him with.

The documentary certainly lifted the lid on the black arts of the spin-doctor. *Brewer's Dictionary of Politics* defines the term as an official attached to a candidate or party 'to channel facts to the media which put the best possible construction on events in an effort to build momentum.' Derived from baseball, 'the term, relating to the spin given to a ball in flight to fool the recipient, originated in America in the 1980s'. If the *Dictionary* ever sought to include a list of leading practitioners, Charlie Whelan's name would certainly appear next to that of Alastair Campbell, the Prime Minister's press secretary and acknowledged master media strategist. Their contribution to the stunning general election success of New Labour was incalculable. For years the Tories had led the field when it came to slick PR and presentation. In the 1997 campaign they were left standing by Campbell and Whelan and Labour's ruthlessly disciplined campaigning machine.

Unlike Campbell, Whelan clawed his way through the Labour movement into Government, whereas the Prime Minister's spokesman made his name as a Left-leaning political commentator and correspondent with the *Mirror* and *Today* before becoming Blair's media man in 1994. Whelan joined the engineering union, the AEEU, in 1980 as a researcher. He became personal assistant to Jimmy Airlie, the charismatic Scottish organizer, and cut his teeth on some of the best-known disputes of the 1980s, like Ford Europe and TIMEX Dundee. At Tower Hamlets Trades Council he played his own part in the industrial strife of that era. He organized and chaired a mass meeting supporting the miners' strike. Strikers were put up at their East London home by Whelan and his partner Philippa Clarke, an official with the Fire Brigades' Union. More than once he appeared on the Wapping picket line during the ferocious clashes between the print unions and Rupert Murdoch's News International. Latterly he became the Engineering Union's press officer, under the leadership of Bill Jordan and Gavin Laird. Promoting them was his chosen task and he worked tirelessly to do so. He would compare notes with other union press advisers about how many times their leaders had been mentioned in that week's papers. In Thatcherite Britain it was a triumph to kindle any flicker of media interest in unions. To succeed in this infertile territory Whelan had to develop any number of 'schemes and scams'.

He came to the attention of the Labour leadership during the heated debate over one member one vote at the 1993 Party Conference. The AEEU swung behind John Smith and Brown, his Shadow Chancellor, as they struggled to push through the reform which would kill off the old union block vote. The leadership line prevailed and Whelan's contribution as a backroom fixer was noted. A month later he received a call from Peter Mandelson and a simple question, 'Do you want to come and join us?' Whelan replied he would 'only consider working for Tony or Gordon'. Shortly afterwards he was invited by Sue Nye to meet Brown. They got on well, Whelan's claims having already been advanced by Brown's brother. As *Channel Four News*'s business producer Andrew Brown had seen and admired the Engineering Union spokesman at work. Whelan needed time to think the offer over, aware that it was 'a big step which changes your life'. But within weeks he was installed in the Shadow Chancellor's office. One of his first acts was to cut down the reams of press releases being disgorged by Brown, 'the opposite of the AEEU where I was desperate for any mention', as Whelan noted later with a chuckle.

Whelan was now under the wing of a Shadow Chancellor preaching austere financial rectitude. But as with Airlie, Laird and Jordan he offered unstinting loyalty to his chief. Coming from the Communist Party represented an intriguing political journey, though he was not alone in making it. The young Charlie Whelan had run the Party's branch at the City of London Polytechnic. Fellow travellers in student Communist politics included John Reid, later to become a very New Labour defence minister. One of Whelan's political opponents then was Graham Allen, later a member of Tony Blair's Whips Office. Ask Whelan how he squares his early convictions with a New Labour Party freed of so much historical baggage and he will growl, 'But I'm not New Labour.' Pressed harder he will argue that Jimmy Airlie was a precursor of much of the Party's fresh thinking.

While Whelan's politics remain enigmatic he revels in his colourful and sometimes contradictory past. Brought up in Surrey, he was educated at a boarding school – Ottershaw, near Woking. It was a 'state boarding school' offering a lifeline for those who, like Whelan, had failed the 11-plus. From Communist politics at college he moved in and out of different jobs. He worked at a wine warehouse which was exposed for selling fake Beaujolais and went bust, then as a lorry driver. Later he donned red braces and took a job as a foreign exchange dealer. Two decades later he would sit at the high table of economic policy-making, his Communist past raising eyebrows among the senior mandarins. There were hiccups, but Whelan was cleared with the security services vetting procedures. But he is quite at home in other corners of the British establishment, enjoying membership of the all-male and ultra-exclusive MCC.

Charming or blustering, coaxing or bullying, Whelan will do whatever it takes to promote his master. Firefighting hostile media coverage is his speciality. Killing off a story can be just as important as creating one. While his day may be spent in Treasury meetings or accompanying the Chancellor on trips away from Whitehall, he comes into his own as the evening wears on. With newspaper deadlines and prime-time television news programmes approaching he will usually be found in a bar, in the parliamentary press gallery, perhaps, or over at the broadcasters' haunt, the Atrium on Millbank. Chain-smoking and sipping a Pernod and water or a spritzer, Whelan berates and pleads. He enjoys a 'nosebag' with journalists but even in the smartest political eateries like Shepherd's Whelan will break off from the oysters to bark into his mobile phone. Friday, when most MPs have fled to their constituencies, is usually his busiest day. The agenda-setting Sunday newspapers are taking shape and Whelan wants to steer them. A huddled group of Sunday correspondents joins Whelan in the press gallery bar. A bottle is uncorked and a briefing that never took place takes place. There is a forced silence as other journalists wander in, linger and then get the message to move on.

While Downing Street wants favourable news coverage for Tony Blair, Charlie Whelan wants it for Brown. Sometimes this can be agreed amicably. Once Whelan and Alastair Campbell decided that 'Gordon was getting better coverage than Tony' and organized some fine-tuning with briefings to political commentators. Whelan has undoubtedly been a great asset for Brown in both opposition and Government. 'Charlie works like a slave and Gordon is totally dependent on him,' according to one insider. But often there is tension and Whelan has made enemies in high places who abhor his style, 'Charlie guns for people and is quite reckless,' claimed one detractor. The same source acknowledged Whelan was a skilful press officer but with no wider responsibility to the Party or the Prime Minister: 'If he was working for the Government we would do well.' Those who want him dislodged appear, though, to have accepted that with the Chancellor's patronage he is a fixture: 'He's a disgrace to the Government but he's there and he's going to remain.'

Whelan's powers of presentation were tested to the full in November, not by his responsibilities to the Chancellor but by stories generated about a hitherto little-known Treasury minister. The position of Paymaster-General is not one which traditionally attracts great interest from journalists until, that is, Geoffrey Robinson took on the job. Robinson's wealth was well-known to fellow Labour MPs and Parliamentary journalists. But revelations about a multi-million-pound trust in Guernsey set in train a nightmarish sequence of events which were deeply embarrassing for the Government – as much as for Robinson himself.

They started to surface when the *Independent on Sunday* alighted upon the Orion Trust. This held a legacy believed to be worth £12 million bequeathed by a Belgian millionairess, Joska Bourgeois. Robinson, at the discretion of the trustees, was a potential beneficiary. Questions were being asked about why the rights to buy shares in his own engineering company, Transtec, a company specializing in commercializing academic ideas, had been acquired by the Orion Trust. Adding spice to the story was the fact that Robinson as a Treasury minister was himself overseeing taxation of trusts on behalf of a Government which had promised to close tax loopholes.

In the inner sanctums of the Treasury Robinson turned to Whelan for advice. Yes, he said, the whole arrangement had been cleared just after the election by Tony Blair, Gordon Brown and the two senior mandarins, Sir Robin Butler and Sir Terence Burns. Whelan was not aware of the arrangement and advised Robinson that with hindsight it might have been better not to have been a discretionary beneficiary. However, the press secretary was confident that he could mount an effective firefighting operation. He suggested to Geoffrey Robinson that he should 'cough the lot' and get the full facts into the open as quickly as possible. Whelan knew only too well the dangers of a slow-dripping story which might run for weeks. His plan was to spike the *Independent on Sunday*'s exclusive by issuing a full statement to the Press Association which would be available to all the

Sunday papers. Robinson duly coughed and the statement was
released.

Two days later Robinson was due to launch the Government's
plans for Individual Savings Accounts (ISAs). By this time
his name had been extensively spread across the newspapers,
laced with sensationalized accounts of the offshore trust, the
millionaire's tax haven and Madame Bourgeois. It was galling
for Robinson and a headache for the Chancellor's advisers.
Robinson's press conference on ISAs could, they agreed,
degenerate into a free-for-all on his personal finances. On the
other hand, replacing him with another Treasury minister would
give the impression that the Paymaster was running away from
trouble. Brown resolved that Robinson must push on with the
launch. The Chancellor, Ed Balls and Charlie Whelan spent an
hour with Robinson running through the type of questions that
might be asked. This was uncomfortable for Robinson, who was
not accustomed to the rough-and-tumble of a Westminster press
conference. As one source put it, 'Geoffrey's not a streetwise
politician.' In the event he need not have worried. He may
have had a hard time from his own colleagues but the press
conference passed off without one hostile question on his
financial background. There was certainly sceptical probing
of the Individual Savings Account plan but at this stage that
was not the main concern of the Chancellor and his team.

If Robinson hoped that his opening statement on the Orion
Trust wold lay to rest media interest in his personal wealth he
was to be greatly disappointed. He endured another Sunday
newspaper barrage and then turned to his lawyers. The result
was a letter to certain Sunday newspaper editors demanding
retractions and raising the possibility of libel action. But the pack
was not seen off, indeed it continued to pursue the quarry. By
the following weekend Geoffrey Robinson had abandoned the
smart solicitors' offices and turned again to Whelan. Together
they plotted a charm offensive, with the Paymaster-General
providing a series of interviews for the Sunday newspapers. He
believed he had nothing to hide and that there was everything to
gain from getting across his side of the story. Robinson pointed
out that he had paid £1.5 million pounds worth of income tax
in the previous five years on his substantial UK earnings. He

acknowledged that he had had made 'suggestions' to the Orion Trust about investments in Transtec and Coventry City football club, but said that ultimately the final decisions were made by the trustees.

Robinson's interviews were given extensive treatment. He was still 'the man in the news' and very much in demand. Extraordinarily, he arrived in his chauffeur-driven car early on the Sunday morning at BBC Television Centre. Whelan had told him the previous evening that the *Frost Programme* might want to interview him. Although nothing had come of it Robinson assumed he was still required and reported to reception at the BBC. Here was the chance of a major scoop, an interview with the minister at the centre of the storm. However, the *Frost Programme* team decided they were happy with their line-up and said no to Robinson. It was only as he was driving away that the BBC's political correspondent Jon Sopel heard what had happened. Quickly he called Robinson on his car-phone and arranged to meet him for an interview later that day.

Whelan was by now becoming exasperated with the Robinson affair. The charm offensive had not kicked the story into the long grass. Questions were being asked about Robinson's admission that he made suggestions to Orion Trust and Whelan muttered to himself that 'Geoffrey had said more than he needed to.' Robinson's bizarre appearance at the BBC and subsequent deal with Jon Sopel came as a shock to the press secretary. It was completely at odds with his determination to keep the story away from television and radio. The broadcasters would only keep it running. Whelan was already frustrated by Robinson's apparent naivety with the media – it seemed extraordinary for a man who had been in politics for move than twenty years. The previous week he had encountered the *Times* reporter James Landale trying to 'doorstep him' in his constituency. There was no brush-off, Robinson instead inviting the reporter to join him in the car. Driving around Coventry he proceeded to give Landale an off-the-record briefing. That, and now the Sopel arrangement, left Whelan wondering whether it was possible for anyone to handle the Paymaster-General's press relations. He had hoped for a day off as he attended a friend's memorial service in Sussex, but all day he was badgered by constant inquiries about Robinson.

For months Robinson endured the taunts of the Tories. When it came to the Budget speech in March he kept himself out of opposition view. As the Tories scoffed at Gordon Brown's crackdown on offshore trusts they shouted, 'Where is he?' Robinson stood out of their sight behind the Speaker's chair.

As his first tempestuous first year in office drew to a close Robinson claimed not to be bruised by his ordeal. 'There's no resentment, if you're in public life you accept it,' he said of the press coverage of his affairs. The only thing which really upset him was that his sister had been cornered by reporters early one Sunday morning and that his brother's business in America had been investigated by the press. He argued that his position had been misrepresented and that as the Orion Trust was a settlement by a third party abroad he was powerless to do anything about it. The wealth he had built up in the UK shares in Transtec, was, he argued, 'all risk capital earned myself and totally unprotected from the British taxman'. Robinson claimed there was no conflict of interest between his potential interest in an offshore trust and his capacity to take a neutral view on tax policy: 'After all lots of people in the Treasury have PEPs and that doesn't stop them overseeing investment taxes'. At no time had he discussed the question of resignation with the Chancellor. But the media consensus, reflecting the views of some well-placed Labour insiders, was that Robinson would be moved in a Government reshuffle.

Gordon Brown never let slip any hint that his Paymaster-General should quit. In his view, 'The press were looking for the first minister to have to resign and looking for the first split in the Party.' Crucially Robinson had 'not sent money out of the country to deliberately avoid tax . . . he has been paying all his taxes in Britain'. To Brown the problem was, 'If you are a rich man, can you be in the Labour Government? . . . It ought to be possible.'

Robinson has established a critical role in the Brown team. His business brain made him an ideal troubleshooter for the Chancellor. Cambridge- and Yale-educated, Robinson joined British Leyland as a financial controller in 1970. He became

Chief Executive of Jaguar Cars before entering Parliament at a by-election in 1976 just in time to see Harold Wilson give way to Jim Callaghan. Two years later he worked unpaid as Chief Executive of the Triumph Meriden motorcycles co-operative. In the early years of opposition Robinson held front-bench portfolios on science and trade before appearing to fade into obscurity after the 1987 election. Indeed, one profile described him as 'rarely heard, low-profile, self-retired'. Finding opposition a chore, Robinson disliked the late nights and hanging around at the Commons. During this time he was building up Transtec. He had dealings with the tycoon Robert Maxwell and Transtec took over a Maxwell company. Robinson's holding in Transtec was thought to be worth £35 million.

But with Labour's ascent up the polls and Blair's accession to the leadership, Robinson raised his profile with the purchase of the *New Statesman*. He scented an opportunity for a role in Government and renewed an acquaintance with Gordon Brown which went back to the time when they overlapped in Labour's Shadow trade team in the mid-1980s. In the last two years of opposition Robinson became a frequent visitor to the Shadow Chancellor's office. Slowly he was absorbed into Brown's inner circle. Robinson opened doors to the leading firms of accountants in the City of London and with Balls they pieced together the corporate tax reforms and the windfall tax. Robinson believed the Labour Government could raise more than £6 billion from the windfall tax. At the time Blair and Brown were anxious not to impose an unreasonable burden on the utilities and settled for the figure of £5.2 billion. But a year later in Government they might have been glad of an extra billion given the scale of problems in Health and Education.

The detailed work in opposition under Robinson and Balls paid off handsomely. The windfall tax and corporate reform would raise £16 billion over three years. When it came to ISAs they did not work up detailed blueprints. It was only in Government that they started thinking through how the policy might work. The result was one of the Treasury's biggest mistakes in the first year. Soon after the launch of the ISAs in November Robinson's outline consultation document came under fire. Ministers, aware that the cost to the Exchequer of the Conservatives' personal equity plans (PEPs) was growing too fast, had set a limit of £50,000 for the new accounts. There were howls of protest from the financial services industry. Many ordinary savers had built up PEPs plans for retirement or mortgages which would in time be worth considerably more than £50,000. Labour appeared to be penalizing them. By the time of Brown's second Budget a U-turn had been announced and existing PEPs holders were protected. The Chancellor's explanation was that he had listened and reacted after the consultation period. It looked like a climb-down.

Robinson took his share of the blame for the ISAs débâcle. He and the Chancellor had put their names to the consultation document so there was no escaping their liability as ministers. Privately Robinson rued the fact that he had not done his own private research before the election. The Treasury's data on PEP holders turned out to be inadequate, and civil servants had pressed for the limit to be below £50,000. As Robinson put it tactfully, 'If you leave it to go through the Civil Service machine you don't get it as quickly as you'd like it.'

The Treasury for its part has warmed to Robinson. He is a different kettle to that of the colder fish who passed through during the Conservative years. Clerical staff appreciate the time he takes to listen and ask about their families. 'Call me Geoffrey,' instead of 'Paymaster-General', is the order of the day. Perhaps it is his experience as a motivator and leader in business that enables him to cut across the grain of Whitehall's 'Yes Minister' culture. One civil servant who worked with him was shocked when Robinson called him up and outlined a problem with another department: 'I said the usual Civil Service thing and offered a draft letter to the Secretary of State and he said, "Oh, that will take for ever, give me his number" and he made the call immediately, did the deal and we wrote a letter afterwards to confirm it.'

Probing some of the lesser-known eddies of policy-making, Robinson has operated on a semi-freelance basis across Whitehall. He brokered a deal to use lottery money and some Government cash to extend admission to museums and galleries. Curators were called in to see Robinson and explain why they were losing money. According to one source it was a refreshing change for the arts lobby to find the Treasury as 'facilitator rather than inquisitor and denier'. A rescue package for the coal industry and a financial structure for London Underground numbered among Robinson's other achievements. His speciality was the Private Finance Initiative. What Robinson brought to the Treasury, said a friend, was 'a quick mind, he gets to the point in ten seconds while the rest of us are trying to figure it out'. Others are impressed with his drive: 'For a man who is sixty he has the energy of someone twenty years younger.'

Treasury insiders are struck by the informality and intimacy of Brown's closest confidants. As one put it, 'Robinson, Brown, Whelan and Balls have developed a huge bond of trust and draw a great deal of strength from each other's presence when probing an issue.' Civil servants have realized that Robinson is central to the decision-making process and they have to bounce ideas off him as much as off Ed Balls. Robinson is nearly twice Balls's age and has a paternalistic affection for him. He sees in the younger man an intellect that surpasses his own. As John Monks, the TUC's General Secretary, noted wryly, 'Geoffrey's an avuncular lad.'

Labour may have discovered over the first year that there are some drawbacks in having a businessman in a sensitive Treasury position. But they have also realized there are benefits, and they have made use of them. For example, Robinson's apartment in Cannes has been used by Gordon Brown and his brothers' families for tennis-playing holidays, while Robinson's Italian villa has been lent to the Blairs for their summer vacations.

The passage from opposition to Government, from comparative obscurity to the highly visible redoubt of power, had been painful for both Whelan and Robinson. Their capacities to build on the harsh experiences of the first year in office would determine their future roles in Government.

Chapter Thirteen:
Routledge and All That

Cock-up or conspiracy, the events of early January 1998 exposed a deep-running fault-line running right to the core of the Labour Government. On one level there was little more than the usual smoke and mirrors of squabbling spin-doctors. But on another, the simmering suspicions and resentments between the leading players of New Labour were brought under the public gaze for the first time. A biography of Brown by the political journalist Paul Routledge was the catalyst. Then there was an innocent mistake by the staff of John Menzies at Glasgow Airport. The ensuing drama, sometimes descending into farce, had within days caused a rift at the highest levels of the Government. That most crucial of political alliances, the Prime Minister's with his Chancellor, appeared to be on the rocks.

Conspiracy theorists have argued that Gordon Brown had deliberately poisoned the political well with his grudges and grievances. He had used the Routledge book, so the argument ran, as a vehicle to revive the claim of betrayal by Tony Blair and to air again the suspicion that the man once seen as the junior political partner had broken promises not to run against him in a leadership contest. That was certainly a view taken by some Blair acolytes and commentators. Why now, they cried, and why was Gordon digging up long-dead corpses from Labour history? The truth is that there was no conspiracy, no carefully plotted political script. It was more a case of panic, over-reaction and a spiralling news story which Labour's masters of media manipulation could not contain. A brittleness in the New Labour project was revealed and the complexities of Brown's relationship with Blair were made plain.

Paul Routledge had a long and respectable track-record as a Labour and political correspondent, first on *The Times*, then the *Observer*, then the *Independent on Sunday*. Alongside that was a developing and deserved reputation as an author and biographer, with Arthur Scargill, Betty Boothroyd and John Hume among his subjects. Routledge's old Labour contacts were impeccable, honed in Annie's Bar and other watering-holes around Westminster. A Yorkshireman to the core, complete with moustache and glasses and inevitably with a pint in his hand, Routledge was everyone's idea of the typical hack. But he was a good operator who knew his way around the Labour movement. He had guided a young colleague on the *Independent*, Yvette Cooper, through the jungle of Labour politics towards an eleventh-hour adoption as general election candidate in the safe seat of Pontefract. On his travels Routledge had got to know Charlie Whelan, a friendship forged during Whelan's days at the Engineering Union. Routledge's acquaintance with Gordon Brown, as well as his links with Whelan, had sown the seed of his idea for a biography of the Chancellor-to-be. It would focus on Brown's little-chronicled youth and rapid rise through the ranks of the Party, culminating with an account of his first days in office. The notion was well-received by Whelan and there was agreement in very general terms that some access would be granted, assuming Labour won the election. On 3 May Routledge signed his contract and got to work.

As Brown moved on at the gallop with his reform of the Bank of England and his first Budget he gave little thought to Routledge's book. He met the author four times for interviews – once in a car on the way to Heathrow Airport – and was aware that Routledge, after finishing his research and talking to friends of the Chancellor, was aiming for publication in late-January 1998. But as he worked out at his favourite Westminster gym on the first Tuesday of the New Year, mulling over the launch of the pilot schemes for the young unemployed, Brown was given some surprising news. Alongside him on a gym treadmill was George Galloway, the Scottish Labour MP for Glasgow Kelvin, bronzed from his frequent political trips to the Third World. Galloway told the Chancellor he had seen a copy of the book on sale and had read it. Brown was shocked and later instructed Charlie Whelan to investigate.

A few copies of the Routledge book, *Gordon Brown, the Biography*, were on display in a John Menzies outlet on the departures side of the barrier at Glasgow Airport. They were the first of a batch distributed by the publishers in advance of release at the end of January. An over-zealous, or alternatively dozy, Menzies representative had put them on the shelf several weeks too early. They were spotted by Galloway as he browsed away a few minutes before a flight to London. Like any self-respecting member of the Westminster club he turned to the index to check for any references to himself. There were a couple of entries relating to the internal feuds of the Scottish Labour Party after the 1979 election defeat when Galloway, as a scion of the Left, crossed swords with Brown. Galloway did not like them. He made his displeasure plain in a call to Routledge. Later he passed on his feelings about the book to Seamus Milne, Labour editor of the *Guardian*. Milne knew the biography was in the pipeline but was intrigued to hear of its premature and unofficial appearance at Glasgow Airport. The *Guardian* man sniffed a story and set about trying to find a copy.

On Thursday 8 January Routledge enjoyed a good lunch with his old headmaster and a schoolfriend at the Oxford and Cambridge Club in Pall Mall. In this, the first week of the New Year, the political world was still dormant and MPs were enjoying the last days of their festive break. Tony Blair and his entourage were preparing for an official trip to Japan but otherwise there was little for a lobby correspondent to get stuck into. Routledge was uneasy that the book had been seen by Galloway and possibly others. But for now he could relax, not for a moment suspecting that his own handiwork was to blow like a typhoon through these political doldrums. By late afternoon Routledge and his guests had repaired to the Red Lion. His pager went off with the message 'Call Charlie immediately'. It was an unusually blunt message from his old friend and contact so Routledge knew something was up. He hurriedly made his excuses and within minutes was at the Treasury.

Whelan, it transpired, had been contacted by Downing Street who were aware that Milne was preparing to run a story in the *Guardian* about the book. This was news to Whelan and he was unable to help when Alistair Campbell demanded a copy of the book: he simply did not have one. This was later to prove a bone of contention, with Number 10 claiming that Brown's people had deliberately refused to release the text. Arriving at the Treasury that January evening, Routledge found Whelan agitated and anxious for an explanation. Offices were closing and Routledge took a while to track down his editor at his publishers, Simon and Schuster. There was an exclusive serialization deal with *The Times* at stake so there was every incentive to stop the *Guardian* hijacking extracts. But Routledge's publishers warned him there was little they could do. They discussed a late-night High Court injunction but decided it was an option they could not pursue.

Seamus Milne, meanwhile, was developing his scoop. He had tracked down one of the few copies of the biography in circulation and carefully read the chapter on the death of John Smith and the highly charged aftermath which set the tone for the leadership race. He filleted enough facts and quotations to prepare a front-page splash headlined 'How Blair broke secret pact'. There was, for example, Routledge's suggestion that Brown's 'closest advisers' believed there was a secret understanding that Blair would not stand against Brown in any leadership contest. Routledge's argument that 'privately, Brown's friends believe Blair let him down and there can be little doubt that they represent his feelings accurately' gave Milne further meat to chew on.

Routledge's most dramatic revelation focused on Peter Mandelson's role in those turbulent and emotion-charged days immediately after John Smith's death. He disclosed that Mandelson had written to Brown warning that his candidacy would damage the Party but that he would, if he had to, act as Brown's campaign manager. It was cleverly pitched to touch a raw nerve, the sense that loyalty to the Party came ahead of personal ambition. And for the biographer of Maxton, steeped in the history of the Labour movement, it cut to the core. It was an intervention which according to Routledge's sources had 'upset' Brown. Then there was the 'revelation' that Brown's eventual decision to stand aside was taken not over dinner with Blair at the ultra-chic Granita restaurant in Islington but on the previous night with his allies at the brasher Joe Allen's in Covent Garden. That set the seal on an inside story which, according to Milne, highlighted the 'continuing rawness of the Chancellor's personal and political wounds and the tensions with Mr Blair and other ministers'.

The *Guardian* man then relayed his story to a 'well-placed Government source' who professed himself baffled about Brown's apparent collaboration with Routledge. As reported by Milne the next day, he accused Brown of opening wounds and aggrandizing his role vis-à-vis the Prime Minister. A second source made more hostile noises about the Chancellor. Later, there were rumours that some of these quotations came from Peter Mandelson. The touch-paper had been lit and the tone had been set. A row had been sparked off and as such was an ideal story for a political media, starved of real news during the parlimentary recess. What's more, it had been generated before Brown's office had been contacted and weeks before any copies of the book were in circulation. There would now be no chance of a joint Treasury/Downing Street response or a concerted attempt to kill off the story.

The final ingredient in this bizarre cocktail was the heavily contested suggestion that Routledge's book had been authorized by Gordon Brown. The dust-jacket blurb said 'written with his full co-operation', which Milne claimed had been confirmed by Charlie Whelan. It added to the impression that Brown had personally instructed his friends and allies to stir up the murky waters of the 1994 leadership race. Whelan claimed that Milne never contacted him personally but had used a journalist on the *Guardian* diary to check the status of the biography without revealing the newspaper's intentions. Angry calls were made to the editor of the *Guardian*, Alan Rusbridger. There were mutterings about legal action. The following day Whelan sent a lengthy letter to the *Guardian* protesting that 'full co-operation' was not an accurate depiction of the Chancellor's involvement in the Routledge book. He denied that Gordon Brown had ever told Routledge of a sense of betrayal by Tony Blair.

But the distancing operation had come too late. *The Times* hurriedly tried to make something out of what they had thought was their exclusive. They headlined their story 'Revelations in Brown book start Labour feud' and quoted allies of Mandelson accusing the Brown camp of provocation. A prominent Blairite minister even told *The Times* that the idea that the book was not authorized was 'complete balls'. *Scotland on Sunday* took up the baton and devoted a large amount of space to what was now being billed as a row between Blairites and Brownies. The Scottish press particularly savoured Routledge's contention that Brown had been done out of the leadership by an Islington mafia who had briefed against the son of the Manse and spread dark rumours about his private life.

Against this backdrop, MPs would return to Westminster believing that a Gospel according to Gordon had been published. With Labour members eager to catch up on the gossip after the seasonal lay-off, the atmosphere around the tea-room and bars could hardly have been better for conspiracy theories to blossom. Talk centred on the Chancellor's motives rather than what was actually in the book. Some, as before during the single currency row, were eager to paint Whelan as the villain. As a friend of Routledge, they pointed out, Charlie must have been pulling the author's strings and taking a chance to settle old scores. It was unwise, they opined, and Gordon should have known better. In a normal week, Campbell, Mandelson and Whelan, the main participants at the morning meeting of Downing Street advisers and spin-doctors, might have agreed to argue in private and presented a united front to the media. They might have decided it was in everybody's interests to kill off the story or even to laugh it off. But it was not a normal week. The Blair entourage, including Alistair Campbell, was still in Japan and at a distance suspicions could only fester. Downing Street staff had faxed the reams of press cuttings to Campbell. They had done nothing to dispel his belief that Whelan and the Treasury were covertly encouraging speculation about Brown's relationship with Blair. Campbell called Whelan in the middle of the night London time and blasted him down the phone-line. The Chancellor's man, in his pyjamas, cursed back. They slammed down their phones simultaneously. Relations were so bad that they would not speak again for six weeks.

So what was all the fuss about? Taking away the media coverage and going back to Routledge's original text points to the conclusion that there was a row over not very much. Indeed some Westminster insiders were muttering, 'So what's new, didn't we know most of this already?' John Rentoul's biography of Tony Blair, written in 1995, had covered much of the same ground as Routledge in relation to events in the weeks after John Smith's death. Rentoul argues that at the time of the Shadow Cabinet elections in October 1993 'Gordon was still widely, if wrongly, regarded as the "bus" candidate [should John Smith fall under a bus or anything else happen to him]. It was understood that Blair would not stand against him.' Brown came fourth and Blair sixth in the Shadow Cabinet poll. Rentoul goes on to state that there was a pact or understanding between the two dating back to 1992: 'They agreed it would be disastrous to stand against each other in a leadership election, and in 1992 they shared the view that Brown was in the stronger position.' This understanding, Rentoul points out, had not been discussed since and he acknowledges that Brown's supporters could be justified in thinking that the agreement with Blair had not been superseded.

The existence of the Mandelson letter to Brown was revealed for the first time by Routledge. But Rentoul notes that Brown believed that Mandelson had abandoned his former ally and had been promoting Blair behind the scenes from the start. 'As a means of identifying a scapegoat,' records Rentoul, 'this charge had the advantage of being true.' In other words, the 1995 Blair biography contained the kernel of the contentious passages of the 1998 Brown book and there was not a squeak of protest from anyone when it was published. Rentoul's account is less colourful than Routledge's and not as fully developed, but it does take in the dinner at Joe Allen's restaurant at which Brown and his advisers finally decided they would not run against Blair. Perhaps three years is long enough in politics for memories to fade to nothing. Those who berated Brown and his people for what they read about the Routledge book must have forgotten or never read John Rentoul's comprehensive work three years earlier.

The Prime Minister and his inner circle flew back from Japan on Tuesday night to find the political press feasting on rumours of a rift at the heart of the Government. Routledge was finding himself the victim of a dog-eat-dog operation. Lobby journalists looked to him to explain the extent to which the Chancellor's fingerprints were on his book and what level of inside guidance he had received. Some even likened Routledge on Brown to Andrew Morton on Diana, a sounding-board for a subject baring a soul. He was later to complain that it was a nightmare week, with fellow reporters pursuing him around the Palace of Westminster – even on one occasion to the sanctuary of the Lords' bar. Others remarked that there was no such thing as bad publicity when it came to raising the profile of a book. All this with the book still not officially released, although Simon and Schuster was frantically rewriting schedules to get stock on to the shelves. Under pressure and increasingly exasperated, Routledge decided it was time to break cover and put the record straight. In doing so and by his own admission he made a serious error which made life yet more difficult for the Brown camp.

Jet-lagged and with nerves on edge, Alistair Campbell and the Downing Street team awoke on their first morning back from Japan to a new splash: 'Chief Whip named as source of Brown book'. Routledge had granted the *Scotsman* an exclusive interview. Attacking what he called 'the sneering put-downs from Tony Blair's creatures', he argued that his story was accurate and he had no doubt his sources from among Brown's close friends and family were speaking the truth. He explained that the Chancellor had refused to talk about the leadership contest but had referred him to Nick Brown, the Chief Whip and a close ally of the Chancellor. As Routledge put it, 'He spilled the beans about the leadership contest,' a phrase which was quickly buzzing around the Westminster bush telegraph. Routledge's intention had been to shift the focus away from Gordon Brown and to establish that his book was based on other well-placed sources. The effect of the *Scotsman* interview, however, was to imply that the Chief Whip had sided with the Chancellor in a web of intrigue against the Prime Minister. From Blairite loyalists there were mutterings about treachery and even isolated calls for the head of the Chief Whip. Nick Brown, whose loyalty to Blair could never be questioned, was livid. Later he stressed that his interview with Routledge had been off the record and that there had been no background briefing. 'They were his conclusions, not mine, and not my views on the question of betrayal and broken pacts.' Routledge, who afterwards admitted it had been a mistake to talk of spilling the beans, was still trying to make his peace with Nick Brown several months later.

With Nick Brown dragged into the torrent of speculation and the Tories making hay at Prime Minister's Questions on the Wednesday afternoon, patience in Downing Street was wearing extremely thin. One course might have been to rise above the fray and laugh-off speculation about the tortured events of 1994. But sources close to Number 10 decided to intervene. Spin-doctors often try to use columnists to plant ideas which are not specifically news stories. In that way they can be dressed-up as unsourced opinion. The intention was to drop some disdainful views of the Chancellor and his cronies into the system. A high-level source contacted Andrew Rawnsley of the *Observer*. They had a lengthy conversation; Rawnsley was left in no doubt that the Prime Minister was not impressed with his Chancellor's behaviour. There would be no traces, though, to suggest this was an officially inspired slap-down.

Rawnsley did not play ball in the anticipated manner. Sharp-suited and always sporting an eye-catching tie, Rawnsley was never shy of expressing an opinion. As a seasoned broadcaster he revelled in the role of a detached and heavyweight observer of the ebb and flow of British politics, above the grubbier world of hard news. But he had a well-honed news sense and knew a good story when it was dangled in front of him. Here, after all, was a high-level rubbishing of the Chancellor. Even in the dog days of the last Tory Government, differences between John Major and Kenneth Clarke had never been set out quite like that.

Rawnsley wrote it up in a centre-page piece entitled 'What

Blair really thinks of Brown' and he did not make much effort to cover his tracks. He referred to 'someone who has an extremely good claim to know the mind of the Prime Minister'. This 'someone' had let it be known that Blair still had a high regard for Brown's talent but he was wearying of the Chancellor's misjudgements. It was time, according to this very thinly disguised source, for Mr Brown to get a grip on his 'psychological flaws' because the Government could not afford further 'lapses into this sort of nonsense'. And, what's more, the real disasters of the Labour Government, the single currency row, the Geoffrey Robinson affair and the mishandling of lone parent benefit cuts, were the fault of the Treasury. All this, Rawnsley concluded, was too good to stay buried in the centre pages. It was transformed into a front-page splash headlined 'Blair reins-in flawed Brown' with a pointed reference to the strength of the briefing and Downing Street's assault on the Treasury. The suggestion that Brown had 'psychological flaws' was attributed to a senior source in Downing Street. There was nothing subtle, it seemed, about this message. It was beginning to look like internecine war.

As the *Observer* was being digested over Sunday breakfast in political households, and the phrase 'psychological flaws' was entering the lexicon of Westmister insiders, Charlie Whelan was preparing for a trip to Brussels. His hopes of a quiet Sunday morning before a lunchtime taxi to the airport were shattered by the warbling of his pager and the shrill ringing of his mobile phone. Although the Routledge storm had been blowing over, he had anticipated a Blairite salvo in the Sunday press but nothing on the scale of the briefing to the *Observer*. He told reporters the stories were 'garbage' and a 'pathetic attempt to undermine Gordon'. Then he hurried to Heathrow to meet Brown and Balls *en route* to a meeting of European finance ministers the following morning. The Chancellor wondered aloud to his press spokesman whether the 'garbage' line had been too strong.

Campbell, meanwhile, was also taking calls. The *Express on Sunday* had come up with an exclusive angle on the Routledge row, alleging that Tony Blair had given Brown a dressing-down at the full Cabinet meeting that week. The

Prime Minister, it was said, had urged colleagues to pull together and avoid internal divisions. No names were mentioned, but the newspaper's political editor Simon Walters quoted one minister present claiming the words contained a warning to Brown. It was a story on which Alistair Campbell threw cold water with relish. No such thing was said, he told journalists, the report was nonsense. His reaction to the *Observer* story was noticeably more muted and there was no attempt to disown it. He repeatedly described the Prime Minster's relationship with the Chancellor as strong and very productive. The Government would not be judged on this issue anyway, he argued, but on issues like schools and the Welfare State. He later denied that he was the source of Rawnsley's story. Some Westminster insiders believed his fingerprints were all over it.

With Sunday evening television bulletins giving way to Monday morning's headlines, the supposed falling-out of Blair and Brown was back on the news agenda. The idea of a 'psychologically flawed' Chancellor was given a thorough working-over as political correspondents noted that Downing Street had launched a retaliatory strike. It was inevitable, then, that the issue would surface in Brussels where the Chancellor was appearing before the cameras after his meeting. Sure enough, at the press conference he was asked whether he was caught in a row with the Prime Minister.

Giving his first public comment since the appearance of the Routledge book, Brown dismissed the question as 'tittle-tattle and gossip' and added that he wanted only to get on with his official duties in Brussels. But the story had been given 'new legs'. Back at Westminster, briefing and counter-briefing continued, with Downing Street sources turning their fire on Whelan. Look at the Scottish Television documentary, the single currency fiasco and now the Routledge book, and the same name keeps cropping up, they argued.

Among Labour MPs, bewildered by the pace of developments in a row that seemed to come from nowhere, there was resentment at the intervention of Downing Street. Some who were willing to criticize Brown's involvement with the Routledge book were just as prepared to question the judgement of the Prime Minister's associates. Describing a member of the Government as psychologically flawed seemed inexcusable, whatever the provocation.

Increasingly there was the view that, as one New Labour member put it, 'Tony's people were getting back at Gordon's people' to the detriment of the Labour Party. One senior source concluded that 'Blair and Brown have not fallen out . . . their rival courts have.' There was a determination that for the good of the Government the squabbling must end and that there were no rights and wrongs on either side of the argument.

As with many episodes in the ebb and flow of Westminister politics, the show moved on, but the Routledge row was not forgotten. Paul Routledge found himself in demand to appear on discussion programmes and even a game show. 'What's the difference between *Coronation Street* and Paul Routledge?' he quipped to friends in the Members' Lobby. '*Coronation Street* is only on five nights a week.' Publishers beat a path to his door and Routledge was quickly signed-up to do an unauthorized biography of Peter Mandelson. The political editorship of the *Express* was dangled in front of him, though the offer was mysteriously withdrawn. Routledge was convinced that it was the revenge of Number 10 and that the *Express* proprietor, Lord Hollick, a well-known New Labourite, had been leant on. Other journalists certainly believed that prominent Blairites intervened to block Routledge's career move.

To those outside the Westminster loop it seemed a fuss about nothing, political gossip for the chattering classes. But the storm over the biography left a trail of destruction in the corridors of power. Gordon Brown was said to be deeply shocked by the reaction to the book. Whelan was dazed and exasperated, having endured another round of 'Charlie must go' rumours. He could not believe that events had spiralled so wildly out of control. He and Brown's other allies pointed the finger at Seamus Milne and the *Guardian* for sensationalizing the book and at Blair's spin-doctors for distorting the contents. Downing Street in turn argued that the reaction to the book was predictable and only proof that the Chancellor should never have got involved. Labour was still miles ahead in the opinion polls and facing a divided and ineffective opposition. Yet less than a year into the new Government's life the fulcrum of New

Labour had been jolted. Here were a Chancellor and a Prime Minister apparently at odds over a four-year-old quarrel. It did not augur well for the real pressures that would arise if a dispute over policy developed.

Chapter Fourteen: Trio at the Top

In the wake of the biography row, it was clear to the Prime Minister that his colleagues could not delay mending bridges. So he instructed his two closest generals to meet and sort things out once and for all. One bleak afternoon in late January, the slick, dark-suited Minister without Portfolio passed quickly through the labyrinth of corridors linking the Cabinet Office with Number 10 Downing Street. Peter Mandelson was bound for a meeting with the Chancellor, but first he popped his head round the door of the office at Number 10 occupied by his sponsor and friend, the Prime Minister. 'What shall I say?' asked Mandelson of his boss. Tony Blair replied, 'If he's remotely friendly, grasp the opportunity.'

When Mandelson arrived at Number 11, Gordon Brown was waiting for him in his official study, a grand book-lined room overlooking the rose garden behind Number 10, which previous Chancellors had used for their Budget broadcasts. Dusty Treasury records were packed around the walls.

Mandelson's opening gambit was solicitous. 'Are you happy?' he ventured. Brown shook his head. 'What have I got to be happy about?' he mumbled, the biography still gnawing away at him. Mandelson persisted with the cordiality, showing a degree of genuine respect.

Brown struggled to come up with the right civil phrase

to address somebody whom he had so often disparaged. Nevertheless, it had to be done; it was his duty to the Prime Minister whom he knew was desperate for a happy Labour family, and it was his duty to the Party, which remained his first love and which had to regain its poise rapidly.

In the meeting that followed, the two would sue for peace. They straightaway resolved to draw a line under the perceived wounds and hurts which had been opened up by the recent fiasco over the biography. Then they set out ways in which they could co-operate. As one source put it, 'it was an agreement to let the past be the past and to work together for the good of the Government'. The meeting lasted a full hour. By the end, they had devised a form of pact that would ensure that both their interests would be secure. Brown willingly agreed to support the case for Peter Mandelson's promotion to the Cabinet. They would also hold a series of regular meetings to keep their lines of communication open. They knew that the very well-being of the Government depended on it. Before they parted, they both resolved that the meeting should remain confidential. They didn't want a highly publicized 'Munich-style agreement' according to one source close to the two men.

The following day, Brown went to Chequers, the official country home of the Prime Minister, to convey the results of the meeting to Tony Blair. It was a strained and difficult meeting but the two men agreed between themselves that there was less to the biography than the press fury would suggest. As Brown put it, 'There were no difficulties between Tony Blair and myself caused by the book.'

The relationship between Brown and Mandelson, now in such difficulty, had in fact been the rock on which New Labour was built. The two men together with Blair were an inseparable cadre driving the modernizing mission. An aide of Blair's in those years says: 'Tony has spent more hours in Gordon's company during his political career than with anyone else apart from Cherie.' According to another, Brown and Mandelson 'worked for six years together every day and night, including Christmas Day and Boxing Day, sharing every part of their political life'.

There was a fourth man in the close Labour team at this stage. This was Nick Brown, the MP for Newcastle East and a former union organizer who entered the Commons with Gordon Brown and Tony Blair in June 1993. Brown, who went on to become Chief Whip, was well-connected with the trades unions and he masterminded campaigns to get Gordon Brown and Blair elected to the Shadow Cabinet.

In the wilderness years following Labour's humiliating defeat in 1983, the quartet vowed that the Party must be transformed and reconnected with a public that had bought the Thatcher dream. Mandelson, not yet an MP, was then the Labour Party's communications director. He used his role to promote his modernizing friends in the media, in particular Blair and Brown, ensuring that the Party, the MPs and the unions realized they were the cutting-edge, the men to watch. When in the late eighties Mandelson was asked by the journalist Anthony Howard to propose for a television interview the MP of the younger generation most likely to lead the Party, he put forward Gordon Brown. But some felt the respect was not wholly reciprocated. One of Gordon Brown's former aides remembered, 'Although Gordon worked with Peter, he never trusted him. I remember him saying early on, "Watch Peter, he'll do us in."'

The quartet would discuss policy and tactics for much of their waking hours, and in April 1992, only hours after the shock of another general election defeat, they met secretly in Newcastle. Neil Kinnock was about to step down as leader, and the four wondered whether this was their opportunity to go for the main chance. Gordon Brown was assumed to be the senior partner, and this might have been his moment. But the natural successor to Kinnock was John Smith, who had become a good friend of Brown during the period when they had worked together in the opposition Treasury team. Brown felt that closeness prohibited a race and Smith was duly elected. The four came to an understanding that Gordon Brown was the natural heir in the event that something happened to John Smith, but as events turned out they were never to meet again to discuss the matter.

Over the next two years, the four's fortunes changed greatly. Gordon Brown, by now Shadow Chancellor, took up the difficult but necessary task of revolutionizing Labour's economic policy.

'It was doing John Smith's dirty work in an ideological sense,' said one observer. Hitched closely to the fortunes of the leader, Brown was exposed to internal Party sniping. His stock fell as he stamped out traditional spending pledges and defended membership of the European Exchange Rate Mechanism, right up until sterling's humiliating exit. But as Brown was ground down by the experience, Tony Blair was exploring new political pastures. He had toughened Labour's stance towards the unions, and then used the Home Affairs brief to develop Labour's boundaries on crime policy. People began to talk about him as a future leader – even Brown himself, who told a close colleague: 'I will make the Labour Party safe for Tony Blair.'

On 12 May 1994 the unthinkable happened: John Smith died, and in the extraordinary aftermath there was no time for rational discussion among the four. Any understanding from two years ago went by the board. Outside forces took over, with many Labour MPs and commentators saying openly the leadership had to go to Blair. A series of apparently well-informed newspaper stories pushed the case for Blair, and Gordon Brown and his allies suspected that Mandelson was behind it. In turn, Blair's camp resented the way they saw Charlie Whelan pushing the case for Brown. With Nick Brown siding with Gordon and serving as his tactician in his leadership bid, the quartet was rent asunder. The feud which was to reach its nadir with the biography had its origins here.

Gordon Brown was devastated by the leadership debacle. A lifetime's dedication to Labour politics had failed to deliver the glittering prize. A former friend of Brown from Edinburgh University days, Carol Craig, who is now a management psychologist, believes that up until then Brown would have expected all his friends to defer to him. 'He was always the cleverest and most important in the sense that he had a mission.' But the leadership episode changed everything. 'Tony was younger than Gordon but in the dominant position. That would never have happened to Gordon before, and to begin with Gordon would have found that very difficult.'

The stresses of the leadership episode did not surface again until the biography. Blair was shaken and longed for a reconciliation between his old allies. 'Tony has been begging

Peter and Gordon to patch it up for the last four years and they have ignored him; he does not understand the emotional depths and traumas,' is how one well-placed Labour MP who knows both men well put it. But this time he really put the pressure on both men for a rapprochement. It was a mark of Brown's desire to stay on good terms with Blair that he extended the hand of friendship to Mandelson.

Brown had the assurance of knowing that he was still Blair's closest confidant. There remained a mutual respect despite the fury over the book. A top civil servant who observed them at close quarters puts it thus: 'They are like siblings, very close, but that does not stop them having differences. Gordon is much closer to Tony than Nigel Lawson ever was to Margaret Thatcher.'

The Blair–Brown partnership is an enigma in a political world where dog is expected to eat dog. Close friends talk of the two having complementary skills but a single goal and determination. Whereas Brown has the ability to think through policy and political tactics, Blair has the talent to apply them. One Labour MP puts the working relationship in this way: 'Gordon works out the policy, while Tony tops and tails it for public consumption. Brown is the conscience of the Party, Blair the polished presenter. They are as close as the Nobel-winning scientists Crick and Watson.'

The balance of these two remarkably different and strong intellects has not changed since they shared a small Commons office in 1983, when they were elected as Members of Parliament. Political commentator Anthony Howard says of the Blair–Brown relationship. 'My guess is that they are closer than any pair since God knows when; normally the PM is senior to the Chancellor and it is highly unusual to have them from the same Commons intake.' The Chief Secretary to the Treasury, Alastair Darling, says: 'Gordon and Tony between them are the lynchpin of the whole Government.'

Commentators impressed by the close bonding between the two are quite prepared to concede that there are tensions beneath the surface, as in any close relationship when it is subject to daily and immensely powerful pressures. Brown's economic adviser Ed Balls says the greatest pressure on the relationship is a media with a political axe to grind, and he points to their attempt to find alleged differences in their attitudes to EMU. 'Some newspapers want a split between the two, so that they can be nice to Tony and attack Gordon as the "great EMU-fanatic crusader". But there was never any difference between them.'

The possibility that outsiders may think they see differences where none actually exist is increased because Brown and Blair do have different emphases in their political philosophy. Economist Gavyn Davies says: 'Gordon has a slightly stronger belief in the importance of equality of outcome. He is more active in ensuring that the opportunities are actually realized. Gordon believes the basic bedrock of the economy should be the free market, but he shows a bit more willingness to intervene with the outcomes of the free market . . . What has really struck me over the years is how much Gordon and Tony agree.'

Will Hutton emphasises the differences: 'Gordon is a social democrat and a man with deep Party roots who believes in redistribution. Tony, on the other hand, wants to bind the Party to the Liberal Democrats. There is a range of difference.'

But while rank and the status of office might have conspired to fill Blair with a sense of his own importance and make him look down on the man who failed to win the job he so desperately wanted, all the evidence suggests that his respect for Brown, and his view that Brown is the intellectual powerhouse, continue unchanged. The veteran Labour backbencher Tam Dalyell believes that 'psychologically Tony still sees him as senior partner and gives him a free hand to run the economy and domestic policy, as part of the unspoken deal between them'. After all, no Prime Minister can do everything and Blair has been preoccupied with foreign policy and Northern Ireland. During the Gulf crisis, when Dalyell was leading Labour opposition to the use of force against Iraq, he was invited to meet Blair in Downing Street. Blair, just back from his visit to the White House, was 'giddy with fatigue', according to Dalyell. He argues that with these pressures it is quite healthy for the Prime Minister to leave the Chancellor 'effectively running the country'.

The relationship between Prime Minister and Chancellor may have survived out of political contingency, but the feuding of the factions continued. One lot referred disparagingly to

Blair's 'Praetorian guard', the other to Brown's close-knit clique of advisers. Much attention focused on Whelan, and it was thought that Blair had pushed Brown to fire him on at least three occasions but he had been rebuffed. Blair was also thought to be worried about the aggressive tone of Ed Balls. Senior Downing Street aides complain that their counterparts, even the Chancellor himself, withhold information from them. Westminster's social world reflects this divide. 'You don't see Blair people at a Brown party or Brown people at a Blair party,' said one insider.

Ministers and MPs around Westminster tut-tut at the dissension. One man who has seen it all before is the Treasury's former Permanent Secretary Sir Terence Burns. He had sat at the heart of Whitehall through the rifts and rows of the Conservative years, the most notable being Thatcher's falling out with Lawson and Clarke's differences with Major. Prophetically he had said earlier: 'In government the greater risk is often not the principals falling out with colleagues – but the tension between the supporters. You may be more at risk from your own armies than through the personal relationship.' Some Labour insiders wondered privately what it would be like by the end of a five-year Parliament if the armies were coming to blows after less than twelve months in office. Worse still, few were in serious doubt that the armies were doing no more than responding to orders of the principals to whom they were loyal.

In public, Brown has never ceased to emphasize his closeness to the Prime Minister, and has said that many of his ideas were developed in the course of their long plane journeys to Australia and the United States when he and Brown were in opposition. For example, much of their policy on Europe was devised together in the eighties, and expounded on a platform they both shared at the USA/EC Association in 1991: 'Since then we have very much agreed views on the way forward.' Brown's wide-ranging role in Government has taken him out of strictly Treasury areas and into every corner of policy-making. Brown declares: 'All the ideas, such as constitutional reform, European policy and Welfare, were not something that happened after six months in Government, they happened through an evolutionary process over a long period of time. This process involved conversations with Tony Blair.'

Brown's closeness to Blair looks even stranger to foreign observers than it does to Britons who know the history and personalities involved. Standing in a bar having a chat between sessions of a conference where they were speaking, Blair and Brown heard one American businessman asking another, 'Who are those two standing over there?' 'Oh, they're a couple of Commies, up to no good,' came the reply, to the amusement of the British social democrats.

While the friendship has survived, friends have encouraged Brown to look after his patch and they have arranged meetings with supporters to build up his political exposure. The Westminster gossip mill was running at full tilt over a series of parties and receptions Brown and his friends have organized at Number 11 Downing Street. Backbench MPs, Party activists and trades union officials have been invited in by the Chancellor. Friends say Brown simply wants to bring the Party with him on the difficult economic policy decisions he has taken. Enemies claim the Chancellor is already running a leadership campaign.

Sources close to Blair say the Prime Minister is relaxed about Brown's socializing and understands the Chancellor's need to lay down markers for the day when the top job may become available. 'As long as it doesn't get in the way of the job,' they say, while admitting to the occasional smirk when 'A stream of stocky trades union types come waddling up Downing Street to one of Gordon's dos.'

Brown's grasp of political strategy, honed after a lifetime's dedication to the art, will have taught him to take nothing for granted. For now he must concentrate on the long-term economic reforms and drive for stability which he preaches with evangelical zeal. His fortunes are bound up with Blair's. As one of Brown's closest confidants in the Commons puts it, 'There's no row with Tony, he would never mount a coup against him; of course one day Tony may say to Gordon: it's your turn now, but that's the only way Gordon would take over from Tony.' Brown himself hedged at the suggestion that he might be the century's longest-serving Chancellor, while recognizing that some are doubtful of the Government achieving its objectives: 'We have to prove our case because we are dealing with entrenched interests. We have to succeed in appealing to the people. That's why a two-term Government is what Tony Blair's aiming at, as a first step.'

As Brown and Mandelson seek to build their new alliance, and as Blair surveys what he sees as his reunited Cabinet family, all will recall that this is not the first time the warring brothers have sought to patch things up. In 1996 they tried to bury the hatchet, but the rivalry surfaced again during the election campaign. And after the news of this rapprochement leaked, there was a renewed spat as each side accused the other of mud-slinging.

All this would suggest that Labour's trio at the top have yet to convince themselves that they are in power for the long term, where vanity counts for less, and lasting fame is the prize.

Chapter Fifteen:
Welfare to Work for Labour

There was no stopping the great Welfare crusader on the January morning when he was due to launch the first pilot schemes for his New Deal Programme. After running seven miles on his treadmill at his Scottish house (in what he implausibly claimed was forty minutes), he showered and snatched some breakfast. Still glowing from the exercise, his usually tousled black mane dampened, he tackled papers from one of the red boxes that had been couriered up from London.

It was the first working day of the New Year and Brown, relaxed and rested after his break from Westminster, was brimming with vigour. The Government was still sore from the battering it had taken from its own back-benchers over cuts in Benefit spending. Brown, however, was not depressed; indeed, he looked forward to the challenges of proselytizing the party and converting them to the doctrine of Welfare reform. The New Deal programme for the young unemployed was the rock on which New Labour hoped to build a new working Britain, and the only significant spending package launched by the Government.

A call had already come through from Charlie Whelan, to say that Brown would have the lead slot on the *World at One* and that other media were baying for his attention. They were one by one put in touch with the Chancellor on the phone in his study, the message was always the same, endlessly repeated, convincingly articulated: 'If you want employment opportunities for all, if you want the goal of full employment established for a modern era, it has to be done in a new way – not by assuming that you guarantee people the jobs they have forever, but by actually helping people get new jobs and helping make new jobs more available.' The questions asked in the *World at One* interview betrayed scepticism: 'Did the figures not suggest, Chancellor, that the number of young unemployed had fallen significantly and that the New Deal might be pushing resources the wrong way.' Brown's exasperation crackled through the airwaves. Unemployment was a dynamic phenomenon, constantly changing, he argued, and no less a challenge for that.

The interview over, Brown was collected by a ministerial car and chauffeured north from his home in North Queensferry. His route took him through his Dunfermline East constituency and past many former pit communities. The Fife coalfield was once the heartbeat of this region; now much of it was desolate. In Cowdenbeath Brown stopped off at his constituency office to pick up a copy of his speech, faxed up from the Treasury. For more than fifteen years, during hundreds of Friday surgeries here, Brown had heard the pitiful stories of long-term unemployment. His observation of households with two generations permanently out-of-work had steeled his determination to push forward the New Deal programme.

In Dundee Brown's first stop was a job centre. He could not wait to see the people, take the temperature and test their response. There was no lift, so all his jogging and training paid off as the Chancellor bounded up the three grey and dreary storeys. He was perfectly in breath to smile at the trainees selected as guinea pigs for the scheme – shake their hands, move from one to the next with a look that seemed to say, 'this is my creation'. These were the first participants in a scheme which offered four options, the most important being a six-month work placement with £60 per week paid by the Government to employers to subsidize wages.

During his time in opposition Brown had studied in minute detail the theory of Welfare to Work, but for the Chancellor this was the joy of Government. After so much pragmatism and curtailing his enthusiasm for action, he now has a chance to put the theory into practice, to apply his idealism to the daily lives of the downtrodden and the unemployed, for whom he reserves his deepest affections.

Brown's next task was to address a large meeting of Dundee employers, who received a different spin on the New Deal theme. For them the focus was on the structure and costs of the scheme, the fact that the young people who would join their companies would have been sifted out to ensure they were qualified and appropriate. They were a more quizzical audience, but numbers were large and Brown's enthusiasm appreciated. Later, one weighed up the package: 'You have employers who have seen the evil of unemployment, but I do think the Government has a lot of marketing to do as the jury is still out on the employers' commitment.' Another called for the scheme to be strictly controlled: 'Too many employers bring young people in and misuse them outside the system as general labourers without giving them proper training experience.'

Brown was the champion of the policy and he had pushed its theory for the last four years. Back in 1993 when the windfall tax on privatized utilities was conceived the intended use of the proceeds had been vague, with talk of measures to combat 'unemployment'. A year later this term had been refined to 'youth unemployment', and by the autumn of 1995 the New Deal was beginning to take shape. Shortly before the Labour Party Conference that year Brown was bouncing ideas around with Balls and Whelan in a car on the way out to Heathrow. 'We've got to spell out what the young people will be required to do,' said the Shadow Chancellor. As Brown darted into the terminal to catch the Edinburgh flight his two advisers got to work. Heading back into central London, they toyed with ideas on the back of an envelope. Thus the four options – a subsidized job, an environmental taskforce, the voluntary sector, or full-time training or education – were born. As one of them put it, 'It's amazing, the things you have to do in opposition.' From opposition into Government these ideas survived essentially intact.

Now, in June 1998, sitting hunched in his worn, green

armchair looking out on a panoramic view of the River Forth, Brown is absorbed in a subject which fascinates and challenges him . 'It is a new deal for young people, it's a new start in the war against poverty, and it is the beginning of the modernization of the Welfare State. Absolutely crucial to this modernization is the concept of work. If you look at what I call the "old deal", it left 3.5 million working-age households with no one earning a wage; and that clearly can't continue.' There was no golden age for the Welfare State, he says, it simply failed to address the problems of poverty from the 1960s onwards.

Brown explains that the rebuilding of the Welfare State must be based around opportunity and security for all: 'Firstly, getting more people into work, secondly, by making work pay so that work pays more than Benefits; thirdly, by giving people new opportunities in work the idea of a "ladder of opportunity"; and finally, by using public sector resources to help those who are incapable of working.' The Chancellor draws on the words of Sir William Beveridge, founder of the Welfare State, for inspiration, 'He said then that helping people out of poverty was not simply about insurance and national assistance – it was about education, employment opportunities and the Health Service.'

These thoughts, he says, encapsulate what he and Tony Blair mean by Welfare region. It is, along with the constitutional agenda and education, one of the three dominant themes of the Blair administration. All the more remarkable, then, that these two giants of New Labour with a radical vision for reform should apparently botch the project at the outset. Eyes were taken off the ball and a parliamentary revolt over a Benefit cut battered the self-confidence of the new Government.

It was Peter Lilley, the former Conservative Social Security Secretary, who paved the way for Labour's discomfort by instituting the reduction in Benefits for new single parent claimants. This was in November 1996, at the tail-end of the Major regime. Harriet Harman, Lilley's Shadow, made noises in protest and to one interviewer promised that a Labour Government would not implement the Tories proposed cut. Her remarks generated little publicity at the time, yet so close to a likely election victory they were perhaps tempting fate: in power after May she inherited Lilley's job – and his benefit cut.

For the first couple of months of office, ministers' boxes and diaries were brimming. The Chancellor's time was devoted to the Bank of England shake-up and the first Budget. No one, it seemed, had the energy or inclination to look seriously at the Benefit cut feeding through from the previous Government. Harriet Harman broached the subject with the Treasury. The feedback was, 'We have undertaken to abide by the Conservative spending limits so we cannot change their decisions on Benefits.' Treasury officials crawled all over her budget and Harman assumed she was pushing against a door that was firmly closed. Treasury sources later maintained, though, that if she had argued strongly then that the lone parent reduction was indefensible they would have looked again at the issue. To the relief of ministers and whips alike the measures went through parliament without significant opposition in late July. It seemed as though the matter was closed.

As autumn came the first squalls were breaking over the new Government. Labour MPs, some spoiling for a fight with their leaders, focussed on the Government's plans to impose student tuition fees and the lone parent Benefit issue. On fees, Education Secretary David Blunkett worked feverishly to sell the controversial policy to the Party rank and file. In and around the fringes of the Party Conference in Brighton he listened, cajoled and argued his case. By the time of the Conference debate on higher education a threatened revolt from the floor had melted away and Blunkett received a warm ovation. Government insiders contrasted this with Harriet Harman's approach – she did not prepare the ground in the same way on the Benefits decisions. Perhaps she felt it unnecessary as the vote in the Commons had come and gone.

Into November and a platform for rebellion had appeared. The Social Security Bill was due back in the Commons for its third reading and the Liberal Democrats saw an opportunity to revive the Benefits debate. They tabled amendments to the Government's Bill, calling again for the restoration of lone parent Benefits. A stream of Labour MPs began hinting they would side with the Lib Dems and oppose the Government.

But ministers, distracted by the embarrassing disclosures of the Formula One boss Bernie Ecclestone's links with Labour, seemed unconcerned by the threat.

Politically, there was no pre-arranged strategy for defending the policy. Harriet Harman argued that what resources were available were better targeted at the young unemployed rather than on Benefits. Other ministers would fall back on the line that the policy had been inherited by the Tories so could therefore not be changed. No attempt was made to justify the policy by suggesting that a two-parent family in poverty should feel entitled to the same state aid as a single parent family.

Brown's 'Green Budget' in November opened up the debate in a way which ultimately damaged the Government. The intention of the exercise was to flag-up themes for the main Budget the following March, setting out the Treasury's ideas and then leaving them open for a period of consultation. Aware of the escalating unrest over lone parent Benefits, the Chancellor opted to unveil a mini Budget. He announced what he called 'the biggest ever investment in childcare', designed to help lone parents move off Benefit and into work. £300 million was to be spent on developing a national network of after-school child care clubs. The cash was to come from the Exchequer and from proceeds of the National Lottery. The move had been foreshadowed in the July Budget but the Chancellor and his aides decided there was a political need to pump up the measure.

The child care strategy was not Brown's only gesture to the popular gallery. His other flourish was a £400 million 'winter warmer' for the elderly. All penioner households would be paid £20, those on income support £50, for help with heating bills. This was to be funded by an unexpected saving on Britain's contribution to the European Union Budget. Here, remarkably, was a populist measure which had not been leaked. Journalists accustomed to Charlie Whelan's ploys and briefings were astonished that this secret had held. The spin-doctor was delighted to have sprung a presentational surprise. The secret was so closely guarded, in fact, that there was subterfuge even within the Government.

When a civil servant from the Department of Social Security told Brown that the money for pensioners was being discussed around the office, the Chancellor barked back that he was scrapping the idea. It was later reinstated to the knowledge of only a handful of officials.

As Brown sat down at the end of his Green Budget speech on Tuesday 25 November, there was a pat on his shoulder from a beaming Prime Minister sitting alongside him. Labour back-benchers waved their order papers and the broadcast news bulletins gave full play to the measures for child care and pensioners. Many commentators concluded that the Government's largesse would soften the criticism over the lone parent Benefit issue.

However, that evening Labour MPs were lingering and gossiping in the lobbies and tearooms. If the Government could find £700 million for pensioners and child care clubs, they asked, why were they so rigidly refusing to restore the Benefit cuts for single parents? Far from facing down the rebels, Brown's Green Budget seemed to be stiffening their resolve. A Commons motion critical of Government policy was by then gathering significant numbers of Labour backers.

The Government whips then made a tactical error. They approached Labour MPs whom they believed to be compliant and suggested, in a way only Party whips could, that they removed their names from the Commons motion. The Chancellor would prefer – indeed welcome it they opined, if Labour members wrote to him with their concerns. The intervention backfired when MPs took it as a cue to launch a 'round robin' letter to Brown. Dozens of signatures were garnered in support of the demand for the lone parent Benefit cut to be restored. Because it seemed to have the tacit approval of the whips' office, conspiracy theories began to circulate. Some saw a machiavellian ploy by Brown to shift the blame for the policy onto Harman. He was using his allies amongst the whips, so the theory went, to direct their anger towards the beleaguered Social Security Secretary. Such claims were vehemently denied, yet they flourished on the Westminster rumour-mill.

By the first week in December no current affairs programme was going to air without a Labour rebel speaking out against the Government. Left-wing claims that New Labour was selling out on the dispossessed gained currency. The response from ministers remained confused. Some continued to use the argument that the problem was all the fault of the Tories, who had imposed the cuts, as if Labour administration was powerless to intervene. Harriet Harman ploughed on with her line that resources were scarce and that the Government was concentrating efforts on making it easier for lone parents to work. Emissaries were sent from the Chancellor's office to the Social Security Secretary. They suggested she might soften her tone and emphasize the Government's commitment to child care. Harman felt she was simply defending agreed Government policy and resented the intervention.

On the night of 10 December, Harriet Harman walked into the Chamber of the Commons with the Labour benches crowded behind her. As the requisite legislation came before the House and she appeared at the dispatch box there were constant interruptions from back-benchers on her own side. There was only one senior Cabinet minister alongside her, none of the heavy-hitters who usually supported her – like Brown and Blair. It looked as if she had been hung out to dry to take the blame for the policy. The night was a fiasco for Labour as forty-seven Labour MPs voted against the Government and another ten defied the orders of the whips and abstained. The Scottish Office minister, Malcolm Chisholm, became the first in the Blair administration to resign on an issue of principle. Four junior ministerial aides also quit.

With the press eagerly proclaiming the Blair honeymoon over, the confidence of the new Government was severely shaken. Masters of presentation and forward planning they may have been, yet one senior source was admitting 'We were caught flatfooted,' while another said 'We took our eyes off the ball.' Treasury sources argued that the Chancellor could not be expected to watch over every detail of Benefit policy. If Harriet Harman and her officials had felt so strongly about it, Brown's people continued, they could have shifted resources from other parts of their deparmental budget or at least drawn attention to the potential problems sooner. Harman's political obituaries began to appear after what looked like a steady trickle of well-informed briefings. Her friends retorted that she was simply implementing, albeit reluctantly, a policy agreed by the whole Cabinet, and one which had been nodded through in the summer.

As rumours spread about the Government's intention to curb Benefits for the disabled, the Prime Minister's concern was becoming clear. In a speech in his Sedgefield constituency setting out the arguments for reviewing Welfare spending, he revealed that he was setting up a Welfare Reform Committee. What was more, Tony Blair himself was to chair the committee. Sources close to Blair let it be known that he was seizing control of this important area of the Government's domestic agenda. It was easy to see this as a snub of Harman; some saw it as a blow to the prestige of Brown. The Chancellor's people diplomatically argued that they were delighted to have the Prime Minister's weight behind such a pivoted element of economic policy.

A series of Welfare roadshows were launched to sell the Government's thinking to a sceptical Labour grassroots. Brown was heckled and interrupted at one gathering in north London. Whelan later claimed that the Chancellor had enjoyed being back in the cut and thrust of a political meeting and that the troublemakers were 'All bloody Trots anyway.' David Blunkett was the focus of a robust grilling by Party members in Cardiff but, despite the presence of television crews scenting blood, Harriet Harman was given a polite hearing in Middlesbrough. Blair's flair for presentation and his ability to carry his party behind him settled nerves. As one senior Government source put it later 'The lone parent revolt became quite useful – it showed we were serious on tough decisions and got Welfare reform on the map.'

While the Government took knocks over lone parents and the disabled, the Chancellor's team and the Treasury machine quietly continued to piece together the second Budget. They knew they had a package of measures which would take the heat out of the Welfare debate overnight. They could only feel frustrated that the Budget was not timed earlier. Indeed one of Brown's aides later argued that the lone parent revolt might have been nipped in the bud if the child care and Benefit provisions of the Budget could have been announced four months sooner. Appropriately for a 'pro work' Budget, one Treasury official remembers never having been worked so hard before. Certainly

Brown and his familiar coven of assistants did not finally finish work till 2 a.m. on the morning of the Budget.

After the raft of stories about Blair's relationship with Brown a conscious effort was made to promote this March Budget as a joint effort. On the Saturday before Budget day Brown was up very early and driving through the Buckinghamshire countryside as dawn broke. He arrived at Chequers at 7.30 and was ushered by Blair through to the drawing room of his official country residence. As they had done since their days as young back-benchers they bounced ideas back and forward. There was no civil servant or official with them as Blair threw out thoughts on presentation and Brown furiously scribbled notes. Some commentators later sought to portray this meeting as Blair's last-minute reining-in of his Chancellor. The truth was that the important measures had been decided weeks earlier and the main point of discussion here was presentation.

Much of the Budget had been trailed as part of the consultation process introduced by the new Chancellor, but it nevertheless impressed MPs and media alike. The centrepiece was the Working Families Tax Credit (WFTC) which aimed to tackle the poverty trap. A Benefit called Family Credit was to be replaced by a tax credit, thus removing the punitive effect for certain households as people lost Benefits when they moved into low paid jobs. For example, a family on £200 per week would become £23 per week better off. Within the scheme there was to be a new child care tax credit and a similar credit to help the sick and disabled into work. Another boost to families was provided by a substantial (£2.50 per week) increase in Child Benefit. 'Making work pay' encapsulated the thinking behind the measures and the phrase recurred throughout Brown's speech.

Less noticed at the time but arguably more significant than the WTFC and the Child Benefit increases was the biggest reform of National Insurance Contributions in more than twenty years. The Chancellor raised the wage-level at which employers and employees started paying contributions. This was designed to encourage job creation at the lower-paid end of the market. But with that Brown raised the rate of employer contributions, so adding to the tax burden on the employment of higher-paid staff. It was a policy similar to that of by John Smith, then Shadow Chancellor, during the 1992 election campaign, and one which the Tories successfully highlighted in their campaign to brand Labour the Party of high taxation. Six years later here was a Labour Government implementing it without a murmur of protest.

Brown and his advisers had prepared the grounds carefully for the reform of National Insurance. Martin Taylor, the boss of Barclays Bank, had been invited to draw up an independent report on the workings of the tax and Benefit system. He recommended the key changes, including raising the employer contribution rate. With Taylor's weight behind the idea, Ed Balls and Treasury officials had little difficulty persuading the CBI and the Institute of Directors that the reform was sensible. Their support was sewn-up before the Budget and, in the words of one Brown aide, 'The Tories were never at the races.'

The respected economics writer Will Hutton argued that 'The second Brown Budget was a very skilful operation. The reshaping of the National Insurance system was not picked up at the time. The middle classes are congratulating themselves for getting off scot-free while beneath the waterline was a major redistribution.'

Labour MPs gradually came to the same conclusion: 'Gordon has squeezed Middle England without anyone realizing,' as one put it. With cuts in corporation tax even Tories were impressed – 'If only we'd done something like this before the election we might have won,' said one. Tony Benn, ever suspicious of Brownite economics, remarked acidly; 'Philip Snowden would have been proud of it' in reference to the ultra-orthodox Labour Chancellor of the Ramsay MacDonald era.

The Budget out of the way, Blair and Brown focussed on the next phase of Welfare reform. Here, there was a further source of friction in the shape of Frank Field, the Social Security minister and number two to Harriet Harman. Field's passion in opposition was the minutiae of the benefit system and spending. He was charged with producing a consultation paper setting out the Government's vision and aims. There were constant reports of bickering between Field and the Brown camp. These came to a head when the first draft of Field's consultation paper appeared on ministers' desks. Brown had wanted it published before the Budget but its spending suggestions were deemed too ambitious. Under pressure from Number 10 Downing Street, Field rewrote his paper, toning down the big ideas and the implied costs. It was published at the end of March, flagging-up discussion points but stopping short of concrete policy ideas.

As the Government's first year came to an end, Welfare reform was at the top of the agenda. As one insider put it, 'Tony Blair had made the Labour Party realize the Welfare State must be reformed.' Apart from Brown's Budget measures, though, little concrete had been achieved. Some took comfort from early favourable results from the New Deal programme, but others pointed to the massive hurdle still confronting the eager reformers: pension reform. The problems implementing that were coming to the surface when the Government had to postpone the publication of a consultation paper on the subject.

While the practicalities of this issue were facing close examination in the Treasury, the battlelines at Westminster were forming for the protracted and painful war. Welfare may be the test of Brown's resolve to change the face of Britain; it will also take him into the most bloody fights with senior and junior colleagues alike.

Chapter Sixteen: Treasury Tribulations

The 1997 election put into power a Chancellor with a large and dramatic programme promising political and social change. This immediately excited many of the civil servants, who could be expected to have a big role in the implementation – particularly as many had been forced to sit back and do nothing in the dying years of the Major administration. However, that enthusiasm turned to disillusion in some quarters as the Chancellor with a massive mandate for change in the country began to import change in the system.

In the process, the Treasury tree has been shaken – some have taken a hard fall and been bruised, others have flourished. Brown's inner circle has set up camp, and to an extent displaced the native civil servants. Officials watched Ed Balls, Ed Miliband and Charlie Whelan set up in their own offices. Some senior bureaucrats felt they were being supplanted and their well-established systems overturned.

But others have tried to respond to the new broom by reviewing their own systems in the light of the new Government's policy and style. These officials have warmed to an administration determined to make change quickly, even if implementing those changes required some short-cuts round traditional systems. Those who are less enthusiastic have pointed out the risks that can occur when speed and informality are of the essence. The fact that some of the Budget figures about family incomes were found to be incorrect at the last minute (panic-stricken Treasury officials had to stuff a 'corrigendum slip' into hundreds of envelopes containing the Budget press releases) was picked up as the price of the new relaxed style.

The role of the Chancellor's official Private Office has been one bone of contention for the men at the top of the Treasury tree. This office had always been the primary interface between the department and their political masters. Traditionally, it was a critical communications channel, a conduit for information and policy from the top of the Treasury to the bottom. Now, some feel its role has changed. According to one source, 'The Private Office has become subordinate. The principal Private Secretary's job used to be much coveted, but it is now less so and a more junior appointment.' The weakness of the new arrangement, says the same source, is that 'it is more difficult for officials to get a handle on what's going on.'

Civil servants beating a path to the Chancellor's door see Ed Balls as gatekeeper and sieve of the paperwork which reaches Brown. One well-placed Treasury insider has observed the changing style: 'Traditionally, the Treasury would write a submission and send it straight to the Chancellor. He would either tick it in the box and say go and do it or hold a meeting where it was thrashed out round the table. The method now is to start with the outline of an idea, try it out on Ed or Geoffrey; they advise changes, go back and reformulate the approach with the Chancellor.'

Such a radical departure was bound to unsettle the man at the top of the Treasury, the Permanent Secretary Sir Terry Burns. Throughout the eighties, he was one of the Treasury's most distinguished economists, a man whose clout with the Right-wing monetarist models had caused the Thatcherite crowds to cheer to the rafters. Shortly before he quit at the end of June 1998, Burns was described by one senior colleague as 'semi-detached' from the political masters to whom he was supposed to report. Sir Andrew Turnbull replaced the newly enobled Lord Burns.

Burns might have a felt a particularly personal problem with the new team, as they had a tendency to dismiss the monetarist economic models he had introduced over the eighties. Labour's men regarded the view implicit in these models (and publicly acknowledged by the Chancellor Norman Lamont) that unemployment was 'a price worth paying' for control of inflation as abhorrent, and they did not hold their tongue. It was Burns's turn to bridle, seeing his claim to fame denounced.

The new team's working style also perplexed the Permanent Secretary. To get decisions made he was having to deal not just with the Chancellor, but also with members of his coterie. Breaking through to the Chancellor was becoming increasingly difficult as the team exercised a strong control on crucial information. Burns was used to putting a word in a Chancellor's, or even Prime Minister's, ear, to guide a policy. Now he struggled to win time with one of the Chancellor's assistants. Said one colleague: 'Terry has found the change in working methods, and especially the team-based nature of it, quite difficult to adjust to. If you are a Permanent Secretary, you are used to regular one-on-one meetings with the Chancellor, dealing with everything up to high policy matters of the day. For discussions to be complete, and definitive (in terms of resolving issues), these are the only two people who count.

'Now, if you are in a situation where you count, but you are actually facing up to four guys, not just one – and only one happens to be in the room at the time – these meetings will seem neither complete nor definitive. You don't get the same interaction and that breeds frustration.'

There were rumours of a deterioration in relations between Burns and the Chancellor, and in February 1998 press articles appeared saying Burns was out of favour and might be on the verge of leaving. Friends say Burns was puzzled by the origins of these rumours; although at that stage Teflon's Tel's durability looked fool-proof, in retrospect they appear prophetic.

Burns had found his access to the Chancellor undercut by the thirty-one-year-old economics adviser Ed Balls. In the period before the 1997 election, all seemed well between the two economists. Burns and Balls met regularly so that Burns could explain to the younger man the practicalities of government and of administration. Burns had only limited access to the Shadow Chancellor at this point, but this was put down to

Brown's political commitments in the run-up to an election. However, Burns quickly discovered that he was getting a taste of the way the Chancellor liked to work. This was a shock to the system for the important mandarin.

Apart from anything else, Balls's youth must have been disconcerting to the much older Burns as he had to submit himself to inquisitions from the bright young economist adviser. But the irony here is that Burns himself was parachuted into the Treasury in 1980 at the age of thirty-five to head the Government's economic service. As Hugh Stephenson noted in his 1980 book *Mrs Thatcher's First Year*, 'the pill was bitter because an outsider (and one so young at that) was being made the titular head of the entire corps of over 380 professional economists.'

Whelan's proximity to the Chancellor and to Balls sounded the first alarm bells to the civil servants who were expected to work beside Brown and his team. One of these was the feisty Treasury press officer Jill Rutter. This blonde-haired fan of cricket and tennis had joined the Civil Service as a fast-stream recruit straight from university in 1979. She had met Brown at a dinner party when he was in opposition and she liked and admired him. However, Rutter had decided she did not want to continue working in the press office after the 1997 election and had asked for a transfer. This could not be arranged in the time available, and relations with Burns soured as a result.

When Brown came to power, the new Chancellor and his team soon posed problems for Rutter. The high-powered economist was expected to work beside a political press officer who came from a quite different tabloid school of PR. The relationship between the straight-laced Government official and the big-talking Charlie Whelan, who was expected to serve the public relations requirements of his political master, was inevitably tricky.

Rutter made her initial disquiet known to Burns, but friends say Burns was anxious to avoid rocking the boat for the new administration and reassured Rutter that the storm would blow over. Rutter's fears about the power of the Chancellor's press-men were confirmed early on, when Burns refused to broach with the Chancellor the wisdom of giving wide access to the Scottish Television crew filming the documentary *We Are the Treasury*.

Rutter's first row with the new men was not with Whelan himself, but with Whelan's colleague Ed Balls. This followed a media rumour that the Government planned to join the Exchange Rate Mechanism. The rumour had hit the currency and there were confused signals from the Treasury. Balls felt Rutter and her colleagues had not made adequate denials. The Treasury press officers in turn took umbrage when they were forced to deny rumours that appeared over a weekend that the first Budget was due on 10 June – they thought the rumours had been put about by Whelan himself. Rutter joked to Balls in the presence of a few journalists that the department was not paid overtime for making these sorts of denials. Balls went ballistic, telling Rutter that relations between she and Whelan had broken down. Rutter's card was now marked and she was frozen out of the inner media circle.

Ordinarily, civil servants in Rutter's position would be shuffled quietly out of the hot-spot to create minimum political disturbance and embarrassment, but in this instance everything seemed to go wrong. Burns proposed Rutter attend a course at Harvard to expand her qualifications, but by the time he gave her the application form she had missed the date for admission by six days. She was then given the opportunity to apply for a job as Policy Director for Women's Issues at the Department of Social Security, but she refused, fearing the position might eventually draw her into a new conflict with the Treasury (and in particular Ed Balls).

While Rutter feels some bitterness towards Balls, whose enmity friends say she still cannot understand, her greater animus is towards Burns, whom she feels could have done more to secure her a position. Observers say Rutter did not help her chances of finding a new job by making her desire to move so clear, and it is understood that a number of attempts were made to relocate her.

Rutter felt that she had no alternative but to leave the Civil Service – a prospect which was devastating, following a highly successful career lasting eighteen years. Friends and colleagues were moved to tears at her leaving-do, which was attended by her former boss Kenneth Clarke as well as the new Chancellor. Press reports suggested relationships had broken down with the new administration because Rutter was a Tory. In fact, it is understood Rutter has voted Labour on a number of occasions in recent years. She felt her superiors made no attempt to defend her professional integrity. This reluctant refugee from the usually so dependable Government service trod the well-worn path to the private sector, joining BP's economics department. But first she went on an extended African safari to erase the bitter memory of her exit from the press office.

The Rutter problem was only one issue besetting Burns as he struggled to understand and accommodate to the new administration. Brown's determination to stick to a cliquish, closely controlled power-base established in opposition was breeding some disquiet in the ranks of officials. Top officials put this down to a continuation of working practices learnt and successfully applied in opposition. They comforted themselves with the hope that the politicians would adjust themselves to the systems of government and the department's need for efficient systems.

In the atmosphere of upheaval, personalities were bound to jar. The former Treasury senior economic adviser and eminent academic Sir Alan Budd had decided before the election that he would help the new regime get established and then move on. Even so, he expected to brief the press on the economic technicalities of the first Budget. When he realized Brown himself would be doing that instead, he took himself and a gang of friends off to the races. Budd found Brown's hectic pace and style uncongenial and later told friends that he found the Chancellor quick to anger. Other officials learnt to deal with Brown's fury by 'quietly sidling out of the room'.

While some of the immediate judgements of the Chancellor's style have clearly been excessive, there seems little doubt that there have been problems in relations with the civil servants. One commented, 'His area of greatest trouble is in handling people, he likes to have his own way with colleagues. As time goes on, and others grow in strength, he will find it increasingly difficult to retain control. As things go wrong, they will find it harder to give the appearance of invincibility. At the moment, it's amazing how compliant his colleagues are.' The civil servant added, 'It is a very controlled style or method. There are all kinds of friendships and tensions. There is a battle for the ascendancy of ideas and who takes the credit – and who the blame. It has certainly been worked out in a more black-and-white way than is normal for an opposition moving into Government. This adds to the controlled nature of things to a high degree.' A well-placed Government source believes that 'Gordon has not harnessed the machine well – there are very talented people in the Treasury who could be better used.'

Will Hutton, author of the influential economic study *The State We're In*, gives his own assessment of Brown's style. 'People close to the Treasury are infuriated by the way they cannot pin him down, the way he breaks off a meeting with seconds to go, to go to another meeting without any prior warning. They do not like the way he has not mobilized the full intellectual resource of the Treasury behind him; the way he tends not to delegate; his narrow coterie of people through whom he operates. They find all that very frustrating.'

The frustrations have sometimes been felt by Cabinet colleagues as well. In opposition some found Brown domineering and at times insensitive; in Government, they see his Treasury pushing itself around. The most frequently quoted example is Cabinet ministers' pay. The Cabinet had agreed to forgo a payrise for their first year in office, but during the second year many wanted to accept an increase. Brown was away in Mauritius for a Commonwealth Finance Ministers' Meeting and many Cabinet ministers were shocked when he let it be known that he would be refusing the rise. They felt bounced into doing the same, and their resentment emerged at a Cabinet meeting in Brown's absence. It was all very well, they quipped, for Brown the ascetic bachelor, but they had family and other financial commitments to consider.

Brown later defended his position. 'On a salary of £86,000, I think people can manage. I don't think you can ask for pay restraint without there being equality of sacrifice. I think they did appreciate it – it was just reported in a way that was rather different – but I've never had a problem talking to my colleagues about it.'

The disillusion and dismay experienced by some politicians and civil servants are matched by the unashamed enthusiasm of others who are clearly thriving in the new, more informal and competitive atmosphere pervading the department. The most frequently mentioned rising star is Steve Robson, who has been at the Treasury as a man and a boy, and now seems destined for a leading role in implementing Labour's programme.

Robson, who made his mark during the Thatcher years as one of the key privatizers in the department, saw the mistakes made in 1979 by civil servants who thought they could twist the former Prime Minister and Chancellor Geoffrey Howe round their little fingers. The department lost prestige, and a number were cast out into the wilderness. A similar sea-change seemed imminent with the new Labour regiment – after so many years in opposition – and Robson was determined to be ready this time. His staff were encouraged to study and employ the language and approach of the New Labour men and it won him early approval from the new Government. Here was a man they felt they could do business with.

Robson also understood he and his colleagues would have to be flexible to adjust to their keenness to work and play as a team. There could be no question of expecting the new men to fall in with the old ways, he realized, as they were out to make dramatic changes in the country and the economy and these changes would be reflected in their approach to power and Government.

There was clue to Robson's rise to stardom other than his superior presentational skills. His understanding of the roles of Government and private enterprise appeared to chime with that of Brown and Balls. Robson was skilled at seeing opportunities for partnerships between the private sector and the state where the state could reap some benefit for itself. This was 'Third-Wayism' as understood by the Brown and Blair teams (without yet having the tag) and was a subtle adaptation of the approach he had successfully implemented for the former Government of privatizing everything that moved by contracting out all the risk and reward to the private sector.

Robson drew on his private sector experience – he had been seconded to the Government's venture capital organization 3i back in the seventies – to analyse the style of the new Government team, and the service they expected from their permanent staff. The emphasis was now on informality, something that came naturally to a man who placed minimal importance on status symbols and made a point of cycling to the office. Robson talked the sort of brash, macho language enjoyed by Brown and his team and his ability to switch easily between the company boardroom and job centres contrasted with the more hidebound style of many of his fellow mandarins. Robson's role and enthusiasm for the New Labour project was quickly acknowledged by the new team when they promoted him to the top echelon, immediately under Burns.

Another man who found himself moving rapidly up the Treasury escalator under Brown was Gus O'Donnell, a career civil servant who had served as John Major's press secretary at Number 10. As the Treasury's man in Washington he impressed the new Chancellor with his work for the G7 summit in Denver, Colorado. Brown summoned O'Donnell to return to the Treasury immediately, an inconvenience for the genial civil servant who wanted more time to move his family back across the Atlantic. O'Donnell, like Robson, was now part of the Chancellor's coterie.

The beauty of the team-oriented approach is that it enables civil servants, ministers and officials to pick up ideas from a great range of sources and then to put them into action with maximum efficiency. Brown has said that he wants to make the Treasury a catalyst of change throughout the Government, and the team he is creating will be the agents of the change. 'The Treasury is no longer the agent of monetary policy. The role of the Treasury is to help individual departments, like Education and Health, to get the benefit of public and private finance, so that the money that is invested both goes further and is invested to better effect.' No longer will the Treasury be seen in Whitehall as 'the bank that likes to say no'.

To achieve this, he wants to change the tradition that the good civil servant is the one who can find ten reasons for saying no to a proposal and not one to replace or amend it to make it feasible. One senior civil servant described Brown's style, in typically colloquial manner: 'He will take it if you say,

"This is a crummy idea and you are barmy!" but only as long as you give him a follow-on, a right way to do it. There are too many people in Whitehall who are brilliant can't-do men while Washington is full of brilliant can-do men. Ministers want people who tell you how you can do things.' Others see this as unwelcome interference in the long-standing Civil Service practice of giving dispassionate comment. 'Officials who don't give positive advice don't get called back.' One observer likened its patronage culture to that of an Elizabethan court.

The new Treasury's successful man will want to champion schemes and not be afraid of taking a risk, even if his ideas fail. In turn, he will also be rewarded if the scheme succeeds. Brown's top officials are being encouraged to put ideas forward to ministers and their officials on a single sheet of paper, rather than spend years researching and writing a proposal that does not correspond with the Government's approach. The single sheet should almost be regarded as a promotional vehicle to win the encouragement of a minister who will then have a document to take round to colleagues. With the support of the team, research by officials will be given the go-ahead.

The informality that Brown has introduced to hidebound civil servants flows right through to mundane matters such as working hours. Brown observes no strict schedule and when he is immersed in a project or a paper these go by the board. This has led civil servants of the old school to complain that decisions get made late at night, when nobody is present to take a minute or record the outcome of a meeting. The younger school are quite happy to let Brown and his team work in their own way, trusting that they will receive relevant information at the right time. Said one official, 'He is very easy to work with, as he is not very demanding; he just gets on with it. As long as his computer is working, he is reasonably happy. Some ministers need to be spoon-fed, but he is quite adaptable. He is quite happy to go on his own to the Treasury canteen and fetch his own coffee and sandwiches.'

Gordon Brown has set himself a massive policy mission and his chances of success will depend on his ability to harness all the talents of the Civil Service. While he and Balls may be forced to be more inclusive, some say it is their very single-mindedness and passion that will sustain them. Says Will Hutton, 'His admirers say Gordon Brown has a capacity to focus which is rare. He has an agenda, like Welfare to Work, which he is determined to push through – to the last ounce. He is obsessive about it, he is intellectually very able, and when he makes decisions, he pushes them forward. Many people say that he has the capacity to be one of the best post-war chancellors if he can only learn to delegate and manage the Treasury better.'

Chapter Seventeen:
The Verdict from Jim and Denis

Tony Blair and Gordon Brown came to Government inexperienced. But the last Labour incumbents of their positions are still watching them from a distance. James Callaghan and Denis Healey were Labour Prime Minister and Chancellor respectively eighteen years before. They were buffeted by economic turbulence and industrial strife in the late 1970s and took Labour to defeat at the hands of Thatcher. Now they are watching with eager expectation how their younger comrades will shape up.

The two old socialist generals grace the House of Lords but rarely enter the hurly-burly of daily politics. Here, they pass judgement on New Labour and Gordon Brown's first year in power. Callaghan, who presided over the Treasury in the 1960s, and Healey were two of Labour's last three Chancellors (Roy Jenkins, in between, defected to the Social Democrat Party).

First impressions are favourable. Says Lord Healey, 'I think he has done very well indeed so far. He is wise to keep a bit in hand against some big international upset. Anyone near the top knows that to change things properly you need to have at least two terms. You must spend a lot of time in the first term making sure you get a second. Politics is about winning and using power; you cannot use power unless you win it.'

Callaghan comments: 'I give him very high marks – as much

for his political as for his economic judgements; the Treasury is partly about politics, although that is frequently concealed because most Chancellors like to be looked at through economic spectacles. But handling the economy *is* political and I think he's handled it extremely well. It's all very well asking governments to be bold in their first year or two, but in fact it is far better to establish who you are and what you're like as an administration. Then perhaps you can be a little more bold once you are firmly established – people, especially foreign markets, then know how you are going to behave later on.'

On the decision to stick for two years to the spending limits laid down by the Conservatives there is general approval. Healey (a former Secretary of State for Defence as well as Chancellor) says, 'He was wise to say from the word go that he would stick to the departmental totals. I think he is going to shift money from defence into schools and Health – there is no reason on earth why we should spend a higher percentage of GDP on defence than the Germans.' Callaghan puts it thus: 'I support strongly his decision to limit public expenditure to the Tory limits in the first two years, and he should certainly resist any pressure to break that now. Having a period with a buoyant economy with unemployment going down has given him margin for when the economy slows down.'

On taxation, though, Healey and Callaghan's views are mixed. Healey says, 'It would be sensible to have a higher top rate-band. I don't think it would have damaged anything in the economy. It would have produced some benefits.' Callaghan is more circumspect. 'When he gave the pledge before the election not to raise taxes it was helpful in creating a climate of opinion that Labour would not, as the myth goes, raise every tax, frighten every taxpayer. Of course, as we got nearer the election it wasn't so necessary, but he wasn't to know that when he gave it. We shouldn't put up taxes for the sake of it. But, on the other hand, when services could be saved by putting a small additional burden on people who can afford to pay, then there's a case for it.'

On granting the Bank of England the power to set interest rates, Healey makes plain his disapproval. 'He made a great mistake by giving independence to the Bank. Eddie George is a good plain cook – a safe pair of hands – but he is not a subtle man and takes his traditional responsibility very seriously, and that is purely related to controlling inflation. You can afford to give independence to a fellow like Alan Greenspan, who knows that growth is as important as prices. You don't need an independent central bank if both the Chancellor and the Governor are sensible.' Callaghan concurs: 'The Governor and I used to work it out between us. I don't think the public distinguish between the Committee and the Governor and the Government – people blame the Government anyway. Politically, though, it was obviously a good decision for him.'

Healey believes that Brown has wrongly accepted the conventional wisdom which suggests that control of inflation is a function solely of interest rates. 'Using interest rates means hitting growth very savagely in the manufacturing sector. That is where I would quarrel with his policy.' However, the man whose time at the Treasury was punctuated by sterling crises, roaring inflation and, ultimately, the winter of discontent cannot disguise his envy of Brown's good fortune so far. 'He was very lucky compared to me because I inherited a lousy situation from a lousy Chancellor and he inherited a very good situation from a good Chancellor,' says Healey.

'Gordon has come in at a stable time on both sides of the Atlantic, with Britain doing better than anyone across the Channel,' he continues. 'He has been very fortunate, but he has used that fortune sensibly. The real test for Gordon will come when there is big international change. There is an even chance that before the next election there will be a stock market crash on Wall Street; the most worrying thing is a war in the Middle East; the impact of the troubles in Asia has gone much further than anyone could have imagined. So Gordon could find himself facing problems as difficult as I did in the foreign field.'

Healey points out how dramatically the political landscape has changed since the 1970s: 'We had the disadvantage of very powerful unions with strong political clout in the Party. Now unions are half the size they were in my time, when I spent half my time on wages policy.' And the Labour Party, he argues, is in an unparalleled state of harmony. 'There is no alternative to Blairism or Blair. It was never so with Attlee, Wilson or Callaghan, there is no force like Benn.'

European Monetary Union does not thrill the two old grand masters as it does Brown. Healey argues strongly that EMU will not work: 'You cannot have single interest rates unless you have a single fiscal policy; and you cannot have central exchange rates unless you have central control of fiscal policy. That means a central Government, a federal Europe – and I don't think a federal Europe will work.' Callaghan proclaims himself agnostic: 'It's a political decision. A single monetary policy may work but the impact on fiscal centres is debatable; there could be social unrest if the golden triangle exerts a pull on the rest of Europe – France, Germany and the Netherlands.'

Before the election Healey created a row by claiming that the single currency project would lead to rioting in the streets of Europe. He has not changed his mind one jot. 'Well, there *are* riots in the streets of Paris and Brussels right now! Economies do not operate the same way. South of the "olive line" people do not pay taxes, they tell the Government to sodd off and they live happily in the sun and drink wine. In North Europe, the miserable buggers pay their taxes, obey the Government and commit suicide!' While generally pessimistic, Healey concedes that the Government is right to make preparations for joining sometime in the future – just in case EMU works. 'Brown says wait and see if it is set up, and if it is working and in Britain's interest – that is a very sensible policy.'

On Brown's relationship with Blair, Callaghan says, 'I think the Chancellor and Prime Minister in any government tend to be the two that really matter, and here there seems to be a good relationship: Brown has established an authority in Government because the PM hasn't pulled any strings behind his back. I used to say to Denis, "If you want to do something come and see me beforehand – if we can agree, you can be sure we will get it through and I will do what I can, if we can't agree, I may not support you in Cabinet."'

Denis speaks from the perspective of a former Chancellor. 'They are equally able. Blair has charisma, especially on TV which is very important now. That is a disadvantage to Gordon. Gordon has a very good brain – as you can see from his writing

THE VERDICT FROM JIM AND DENIS 219

– but he is not as good as Tony at presenting. Blair doesn't have Brown's brain but he has his intelligence. You could argue that you have a 'get-the-voter' leader and a chap who runs the country as Chancellor.'

As to whether Brown is the heir apparent to Blair, Lord Healey is equivocal. 'There is no such thing in politics, it is so much a matter of chance. I don't say he won't be Prime Minister – it is possible – but it is a mistake to think he is certain to be. If Tony decides Gordon is the successor that will still not necessarily happen, except that I do not see an alternative to Brown.'

Westminster bar-talk has it that Blair may quit while he is ahead and stand down after two terms of office. In this respect, Lord Callaghan sees parallels with his own unexpected succession to Number 10 following Harold Wilson's resignation in 1976: 'Brown will make a good leader in dues course. Patience is a great virtue in politics – I think he will do himself harm if he shows himself too eager. I remember the temptations of ambition. I have already told him that I was older than Harold Wilson and didn't think I would become PM, but it happened – he's got years to go.

'Harold Wilson said to me "I've seen it all before – I've done it twice, I don't want to go on doing it. That could happen to Blair, too – you never know what's going to happen in politics. It's part of the charm of the whole business that the unexpected occurs. So Gordon should just sit quietly, go on doing his job. He shouldn't stay Chancellor forever – he should do Foreign Secretary, Home Secretary and get a good all-round approach, and then he's there if the Party and the country want him.'

Epilogue: Summer Surprise

A dispatch rider pulled up outside the Treasury on Thursday 11 June 1998. He delivered a small package containing a tie, with penguin motifs, and a simple message: 'Good Luck, Love Sarah.' But the gift arrived too late for the Chancellor to don, as he was immersed in final preparations for the statement he was to deliver to the Commons. Moments later, his ministerial car was speeding down Whitehall. There was no stopping a Chancellor determined to rewrite the rule-book on public finances.

Brown told MPs that he had set spending targets for the next three years. The annual spending carve-ups between rival departments were being replaced by what he called 'prudence and stability in public finance'. In another break from his Party's tradition, he announced he would be selling off a host of State assets, including the Royal Mint, the Tote and the Air Traffic Control network. The proceeds of the sales, along with billions he hoped to raise from the sale of other Government properties (including motorway service stations), would be ploughed into investment in hospitals, schools and infrastructure.

There was a warm glow around Brown as he moved on that June evening from his Commons statement on public spending to deliver his Mansion House speech to the City's financiers. This second audience were prepared to give the socialist Scot two cheers after his first year. However, they of all people knew that he was riding on the wave of a healthy economy: how he performed when the economic going got rough – and people such as Ken Livingstone crowed at his discomfort – would really determine whether he was the complete Chancellor.

The following day, the press lionized the Chancellor. Since taking power, Gordon Brown had not been far from the media front pages, but now once again he was the lead story. His speech was hailed as a 'mini-Budget', 'bold' and 'brave'. The language was redolent of Thatcherite days as the papers talked of £12 billion of sell-offs, 'shares for the workers' and so on. The Conservative opposition in the Commons, led by the newly appointed Shadow Chancellor, Francis Maude, was wrongfooted.

Brown had surprised his Government colleagues as much as the opposition. But that was part of his plan, as he was still negotiating the departmental budgets: here again was his spot-on sense of timing and surprise. The Chancellor was Conjurer once more. What ever would he bring out of his sleeve next?

Brown saw these changes as crucial to the success of his economic strategy and to the eventual re-election of a Labour Government. He told the authors of this book that previous governments have been bedevilled by the annual spending cycle, 'There's departmentalism, a series of rivalries, bargaining rather than justification of moneys by result and focus on muddling through the consumption figures and not taking a long-term view of what the investment needs of the economy are.

'I want a comprehensive approach to spending,' he continued, 'which is based on long-term planning and investment; public and private working together and with co-ordination between departments.' The focus, he said, would be on outcomes, and targets would be set. 'We want more money to go to Education and Health but for modernization, with cash in return for change, investment for reform.' Government will play the role of enabler as well as that of owner and employer. 'It is not just figures, it is a new approach.'

Sweeping onto a wider canvass as he looked further afield, Brown touched on the subject of Third World debt. A new passion entered his voice as he described recent visits to

Indonesia, Korea and Malaysia: 'To visit communities where there are open sewers and clear, unremitting poverty, and yet to see hope on the faces of the children, requires you to take action.' There had been action in the shape of the Mauritius mandate, a new commitment on debt-relief undertaken by Commonwealth finance ministers and brokered by Brown. But he wanted to go much further, 'How is it that there is all the technology for sanitation, all the medical expertise necessary to avoid a whole series of unnecessary diseases? That is a problem of political will.'

Was there one thing Brown would like to be remembered for from his first term as Chancellor? 'Bringing out the potential in Britain, helping people to see that they can make more of themselves and that we can do more as a country.' The Scot drew inspiration from his roots, 'The miners of Scotland, which is the constituency where I come from, and the farmers of Scotland, which is where my family come from – I think of them as people with great ambitions. They always believed that a dream to be successful is one that is shared and for all.'

And speaking of ambitions, what about his own – leading the Labour party? 'The potential of Britain,' he said, without hesitation and with a broad smile on his face.

Appendix One: Chronology

1 May 1997:	General Election held. Labour are swept to power with a 179-seat landslide majority. In his home constituency of Dunfermline East, Gordon Brown increases his majority to 18,751.
6 May 1997:	Gordon Brown announces that the Bank of England are to have sole responsibility for interest rates as of June 1997; he raises interest rates himself for the first and last time.
12 May 1997:	Brown attends his first EU finance ministers meeting. He makes it clear that Britain, should it wish to do so, would not be prevented from taking part in the single European currency simply because sterling had not already rejoined ERM. He has not yet decided whether it would be in the country's interest to join the first wave in January 1999.
14 May 1997:	The Queen's speech.
19 May 1997:	The Government announce that

Martin Taylor, Chief Executive of Barclays Bank, is to head a Whitehall task-force on reform of the tax and Benefits system. The task-force will consider options for modernizing the system to improve work incentives and reduce Welfare dependency. Taylor will devote about two days per month (unpaid) to the post. The task-force will operate for one year.

20 May 1997:   Gordon Brown announces a radical change to the financial services regulation bodies. The Bank of England will surrender responsibility for banking supervision to the Securities and Investments Board. Self-regulatory bodies are to merge with the SIB in the second phase of change. The 'new' SIB will become a single statutory authority with sweeping powers over banks, financial services, companies and markets. Howard Davies is appointed Chairman.

Eddie George, Governor of the Bank of England, causes a stir when he reveals he had contemplated quitting over recent changes.

1 June 1997:   George Bain, Head of the London Business School, is appointed Chairman of the Low Pay Commission. The Commission will report on a minimum wage.

2 June 1997:   Four economists are chosen as members of the Bank of England's Monetary Policy Committee: Sir Alan Budd, Charles Goodhart, Deanne Julius and Willem Buiter.

Tony Blair launches his Welfare crusade, designed to ease the

	unemployed off Benefits and into jobs, issuing a bold challenge to single mothers to seek work or training. It is launched from a south London housing estate.
6 June 1997:	The Monetary Policy Committee of the newly independent Bank of England implements its first increase to interest rates.
12 June 1997:	The Mansion House speech.
16 June 1997:	The Amsterdam Summit.
19 June 1997:	A Treasury-commissioned report reveals Kenneth Clarke's last Budget to be responsible for a £20 billion black-hole. Gordon Brown increases the forecast for Government borrowing by the same amount for the next five years.
23 June 1997:	The Government revive the flagging Private Finance Initiative with a Treasury task-force and a raft of incentives to pour private cash into hospital and schools. The task-force will replace the Private Finance Panel of Advisors by 30 September 1997.
24 June 1997:	Eddie George admits to being 'nervous' about launching the single currency during a period of high unemployment.
2 July 1997:	The first Budget.
10 July 1997:	Interest rates are increased for the third time since the election – this time by 0.25 per cent.
17 July 1997:	Gordon Brown clarifies the Government's five conditions, or 'tests', for British entry into the European Economic and Monetary Union. They virtually preclude entry in 1999, the scheduled starting date for

	the single currency, but pave the way for membership at a later date.
21 July 1997:	The start of the 'New Deal' for lone parents. The first eight pilot schemes involve an investment of £37 million over a two-year period.
22 July 1997:	The International Monetary Fund praises the British Government for establishing tight monetary and fiscal policies. CBI backs single currency.
24 July 1997:	Publication of the Dearing Report, wherein the charging of student fees is recommended.
29 July 1997:	David Clementi is appointed Deputy Governor of the Bank of England, responsible for financial regulation.
31 July 1997:	Mervyn King is appointed Deputy Governor of the Bank of England, responsible for monetary policy.
7 August 1997:	A fourth rise in interest rates.
11 September 1997:	Gordon Brown promotes Steve Robson, the Treasury's privatization specialist, to Second Permanent Secretary.
23 September 1997:	The Government appoints eight young City high-flyers to its new Private Finance Initiative task-force. A £165 million boost for higher education is proposed.
29 September 1997:	The Labour Party Conference begins in Brighton.
1 October 1997:	Moira Wallace, a private secretary to the Prime Minister, is chosen to head the Government's new social exclusion unit.
7 October 1997:	The Government announce a £100 million investment programme to equip schools with IT.

10 October 1997:   The new unified financial regulator
                     fills its top jobs, under Chairman
                     Howard Davies: Richard Farrant
                     becomes Chief Operating Officer;
                     Michael Foot is made Head of
                     Supervision of Financial Institutions;
                     Philip Thorpe is put in charge of
                     Authorization and Enforcement.
13 October 1997:   Tony Blair orders ministers to seek
                     immediate departmental savings of
                     £250 million to fund the National
                     Health Service during winter 1997.
14 October 1997:   Suggestions appear in the media of
                     a rift between Gordon Brown and
                     Tony Blair over the single European
                     currency.
15 October 1997:   Gordon Brown reveals plans for a
                     radical shake-up of the Treasury at a
                     meeting of all 900 members of its staff
                     held in Westminster Central Hall.
18 October 1997:   Press leaks suggest that the Government
                     has ruled-out joining the EMU before
                     the next general election.
20 October 1997:   Gordon Brown launches the Stock
                     Exchange's new electronic-trading
                     system.
27 October 1997:   Gordon Brown makes a Commons
                     EMU statement to clarify the
                     Government's position.
28 October 1997:   Brown launches a new super-watchdog
                     – the Financial Services Authority –
                     designed to boost consumer protection.
4 November 1997:   Labour and Liberal Democrats launch
                     a national campaign in favour of
                     joining the single European currency.
6 November 1997:   Interest rates rise to 7.25 per cent, this
                     is the fifth rise since May 1997.
11 November 1997:   Brown tells the City to prepare
                     for EMU.

18 November 1997:   Gus O'Donnell, former press secretary to John Major, becomes the Government's top economist.

19 November 1997:   John Denham, pensions minister, hints of an end to Serps.

25 November 1997:   The Green Budget statement.

26 November 1997:   Harriet Harman unveils plans for 30,000 out-of-school clubs as part of the Government's child care strategy.

29 November 1997:   The Geoffrey Robinson trust revelations break in the press.

2 December 1997:   Labour announces the introduction of Individual Savings Accounts. To replace Peps and Tessas.

5 December 1997:   The symbolic launch of Britain's presidency of the European Union.

8 December 1997:   The Government launches a twelve-strong 'Social Exclusion Unit'.

10 December 1997:   The Parliamentary vote on the Government's proposal to impose cuts on lone parent Benefit provokes Labour's first back-bench revolt.

13 December 1997:   In a move to head-off another Benefit revolt in the Houses of Parliament, Gordon Brown promises that the disabled will not lose their Benefits or be forced out to work.

28 December 1997:   Christian Aid attacks Brown over Third World debt.

5 January 1998:   The Government's flagship Welfare to Work scheme is launched in twelve trial areas, prior to national launch in April.

15 January 1998:   Tony Blair starts a nation-wide campaign to sell the Government's Welfare reforms to grassroots.

20 January 1998:   Geoffrey Robinson is cleared by the Parliamentary Standards watchdog of breaking House of Commons rules

for not declaring his family interest in a multi-million pound offshore trust. Robinson is rebuked for failure to consult on requirement to register interests.

11 February 1998: The launch of a national £8 million television campaign promoting Welfare to Work, aimed at persuading employers to offer work to people aged between eighteen and twenty-four.

16 February 1998: The right-wing Adam Smith Institute applauds the Government on the Welfare to Work policy.

17 February 1998: Labour peer, Lord Ashley, Head of the All-Party Disablement Parliamentary Group, accuses the Government of turning the disabled into militants by pushing ahead with plans to overhaul the Welfare State.

18 February 1998: Eddie George is re-appointed Governor of the Bank of England. Five new non-executives are announced: Bill Morris, the General Secretary of the Transport and General Workers Union; Roy Bailie, Chairman of W. & Gordon Baird Holdings; Graham Hawker, Chief Executive of Hyder; Sheila McKechnie, Director of the Consumers Association; Jim Stretton, Chief Executive of UK operations for Standard Life assurances company.

25 February 1998: The *Guardian* newspaper publishes a Budget leak that suggests that the Treasury will compensate for tax cuts for lone parents.

28 February 1998: Eleven EU Governments publish figures showing they meet the set criteria for economic convergence for

	EMU. Greece failed to qualify; UK, Sweden, Denmark chose to opt out.
2 March 1998:	The Government suffer two Lords' defeats over its Higher Education legislation in the House of Lords.
7 March 1998:	The Scottish Labour Conference in Perth vote to oppose the lone parent Benefit cuts. The carried motion describes the cuts as 'economically inept, morally repugnant and spiritually bereft.'
16 March 1998:	The Government publish a legally-binding fiscal code of conduct.
17 March 1998:	The second Budget of the Labour Government.
26 March 1998:	The Welfare reform Green Paper is published.
6 April 1998:	The nation-wide launch of the Government's flagship Welfare to Work programme.
2 May 1998:	The birth of the European Central Bank. EU members vote for Dutchman Wim Dulsenberg to head the new Bank following a Franco–German split. The first anniversary of the first Labour Government for eighteen years.

Appendix Two: First Labour Budget

Budget summary, July 1997

Welfare to Work Employers to get £75 per week to provide work for the long-term unemployed and £60 per week for young jobless in a £3.5 billion programme using funds from the windfall tax receipts. Up to £200 million allocated for advice, training and after-school support for single parents.

Dividends Tax credits paid to pension funds and companies to be abolished immediately, raising £5 billion – most of which would previously have gone to private pension funds. Charities to have special provision, with continuing tax credits until April 1999 and then a five-year transition funded by the Government.

Individual Savings Account To be set up in 1999.

Inflation 2.5 per cent this year, 2.75 per cent next year.

Company Tax Corporation tax for large firms cut by 2 per cent to 31 per cent and for small firms by 2 per cent to 21 per cent, backdated from April 1997. Advance corporation tax rate unchanged, but foreign income dividends scheme axed from April 1999.

Film Industry British films with budgets of less than £15 million will be able to write off 100 per cent of production and acquisition costs. The measure is expected to cost £30 million over three years.

Income Tax Remains unchanged. A 10p rate of income tax will be introduced as soon as it is prudent.

Health and Education Gordon Brown pulls a surprise by releasing funds from contingency reserve to boost Health and schools. With surplus funds from the windfall tax this amounts to £3.5 billion: £1.2 billion of this will go to the NHS; £2.3 billion will go to schools – of which £1 billion is to fund education and the remaining £1.3 billion is for capital investment.

Tax relief on private health insurance for over-60s scrapped.

Housing Mortgage interest tax relief (MIRAS) cut from 15 per cent to 10 per cent, adding an extra £10 to monthly payments from April 1998. Stamp duty increased from 1 per cent to 1.5 per cent for property sales above £250,000 and to 2 per cent for sales above £500,000.

VAT To be cut on fuel and power from 8 per cent to 5 per cent as of September.

Domestic Fuel Gas levy reduced to zero from April 1998, cutting average bills by 2 per cent. Fuel bills will fall by £90 compared with 1996.

Cigarette and Alcohol The cost of a packet of twenty cigarettes up 19p from 1 December. Alcohol duties to be reviewed; meanwhile, duties will rise in line with inflation, adding 19p to a bottle of spirits, 1p to a pint of beer, 4p to a bottle of table-wine and 1p to higher strength alcohol, including alcopops, from January.

Motoring Petrol and diesel up 4p a litre. Annual car tax to be an extra £5 from November, making it £150.

Windfall Tax Windfall tax on private utilities will raise a net £5.2 billion to go towards funding the Welfare to Work programme, payable in two instalments in December 1997 and December 1998. Excess funds to go to schools. The [estimated] tax will be levied as follows:

Regional Electricity Companies East Midlands – £96 million
London – £140 million
Manweb – £97 million
Midlands – £134 million
Northern – £118 million
Norweb – £155 million
Seeboard – £110 million
South Wales – £90 million
South Western – £97 million
Southern Electric – £170 million
The Energy Group – £112 million
Yorkshire – £134 million

Generators National Power – £261 million
PowerGen – £203 million
British Energy – probably nothing

Others Scottish Power Core – £92 million
Scottish Hydro-Electric – £44 million
Northern Ireland – £44 million

Water Companies Anglian – £132 million
North West – £259 million
Northumbrian – £79 million
Severn Trent – £315 million
South West – £104 million
Southern – £127 million
Thames – £231 million
Welsh – £192 million
Wessex – £99 million
Yorkshire Water – £140 million

Multi Utilities   Hyder – £282 million
                       Scottish Power – £316 million
                       United Utilities – £415 million

Others   BT – £513 million
              BAA – £62 million
              RailTrack – £156 million
              British Gas – £515 million
              Centrica – £190 million

Budget newspaper headlines

The *Independent*

'A BUDGET FOR THE PEOPLE. It was not an exotically radical Budget. It was prudent, managerial, responsible. And that made it a brilliant opening Budget, because it describes exactly what this Government intends to be about. It looked and felt like they [Tony Blair and Gordon Brown] utterly meant it, and it left the opposition with nowhere to go.'

The *Times*

'BROWN IN BUSINESS: A COMMON SENSE BUDGET THAT DESERVES SUPPORT. We have a Government that seems to have no ideological pre-conceptions and tries to make tax changes that are appropriate to the needs of the economy. In his first Budget, Gordon Brown put himself forward not so much as the Iron Chancellor as the Commonsense Chancellor.'

The *Daily Telegraph*

'BROWN'S GIVE AND TAKEAWAY. An unexpected £3.5 billion extra for schools and hospitals sweetened Gordon Brown's "People's Budget", but pension funds and the privatized utilities will bear the brunt of Labour's first tax rises, totalling £12 billion over the next two years.'

The *Sunday Times*

'CITY EXPECTS RATE INCREASE DESPITE BUDGET TAX RISES. Research by Carma International (an agency which specializes in analysing the flavour and impact of media coverage for companies and other clients), proved that 53 per cent of all tabloid press coverage was favourable to the Budget and 15 per cent unfavourable – the *Sun* changed allegiance to Labour prior to election. The study also showed that the tone of Budget coverage became increasingly sceptical post-Budget in the *Guardian*, the *Times*, the *Independent* and the *Daily Telegraph*.'

Appendix Three:
Second Labour Budget

Budget summary, March 1998

Working Family Tax Credit Paid directly or through pay packet as of October 1999. When fully operational, it should provide £5 billion to help about 1.5 million working families, providing on average around £70 a week per family. In his March Budget speech Gordon Brown stated: 'For families where someone works full-time, there is now a guaranteed income of at least £180 a week . . . and to the same working family a second guarantee – that no income tax at all will be paid on earnings below £220 a week.'

Child Care Tax Credit For the low paid. The full 70 per cent of child care costs can be recovered for one child by families earning less than £14,000, and for two or more children in households earning less than £17,000. Assistance will be tapered so that help will be given for child care costs for one child in families with incomes up to £22,000 and for two or more children in households up to £30,000 – higher up the income scale than previously anticipated.

Child Benefit Raised An extra £2.50 from April 1999 for the first child.

Welfare to Work An extra £50 million to help homeless young people into jobs plus £100 million to help tackle skills shortage.

National Insurance Minimum start-rate for paying National Insurance raised to £81 a week, to take effect from April 1999.

Transport Extra £500 million investment in public transport, including a £50 million rural transport fund. Drivers of small 'clean cars' to have their licence fees cut by £50 as of 1999. Licence fees for buses and lorries to be cut by £500. Unleaded petrol up by 4.4p a litre, leaded by 4.9p, diesel by 5.5p.

Housing. Stamp duty increased from 1.5 to 2 per cent for property sales above £250,000 and 3 per cent for sales above £500,000.

Health and Education an extra £220 million for education and £500 million for the NHS.

Corporation Tax A 1p cut in corporation tax to 33p. Small companies tax rate reduced to 20p. First year capital allowances for small and medium-sized firms increased to 40 per cent.

ACT Abolished.

Cigarettes A 21p increase on a packet of twenty cigarettes as of 1 December 1998.

Alcohol 1p on a pint and 4p on a bottle of wine as of 1 January 1999.

Inflation 3 per cent this year, 2.5 per cent in 1999. Plans brought forward to close tax avoiding loopholes including off-shore trusts.

March Budget newspaper headlines

The *Guardian*

'BROWN'S GRAND COALITION: CHANCELLOR OFFERS RELIEF TO WORKING POOR WITHOUT PUNISHING MIDDLE ENGLAND. PRUDENCE WITH A PURPOSE IS BUDGET KEYNOTE. The Chancellor, Gordon Brown, offered a helping hand to the working poor while reassuring Middle England when Labour's first full Budget in twenty years heralded radical reform of the Welfare State and a concerted attack on poverty.'

The *Financial Times*

'BROWN UNVEILS TAX OVERHAUL TO BOOST JOBS. CITY BELIEVE RADICAL BUDGET HAS LEFT BANK TO SLOW ECONOMY AND WARD OFF INFLATION. In a radical Budget that still largely spared middle-income voters, the Chancellor confirmed that he would replace Family Credit with a more generous tax credit paid through wage packets.'

The *Daily Telegraph*

'BROWN SPARES MIDDLE-CLASS. BUDGET BOOM FOR FAMILIES, SAVERS AND THE LOW-PAID. Gordon Brown sought to keep faith with Middle Britain with a Budget that benefited families and boosted spending on Health and Education. He unveiled a series of measures to reward work and promote enterprise without hurting middle-income groups with higher taxes. It could have been so much worse both for Middle Britain and for the Prime Minister. Before the election, Tony Blair never missed a chance to pose as the champion of the middle-class interests and sensibilities that many feared Gordon Brown would savage yesterday. In the event, Mr Brown could not have been nicer.'

The *Evening Standard*

'A VICTIMLESS BUDGET. If Gordon Brown's Budget has been given the thumbs-up in the City as well as by Labour back-benchers, it is for a good reason: his measures appear as economically sound as they are politically astute. The overwhelming feeling in Middle England will be one of relief.'

The *Economist*

'HOLD ON A MINUTE. Gordon Brown must be thrilled by his

Budget's reception: congratulations all round, and hardly a word of dissent. Tory papers praised the Chancellor for not being old Labour – for not raising taxes much, for not increasing public spending much, for lauding enterprise and so forth, and for doing almost nothing that was outright crass. The Left-leaning papers praised him even more for not being just a Conservative with a red tie – for easing the tax burden on the lowest paid, for giving poor working families money to spend on child care, for emphasizing (and how he did emphasize) the fine ambitions of New Labour's modernizing project. The City was a little cooler (it wanted more fiscal restraint, then lower interest rates and a cheaper pound), but the complaints were muted. The City's newspaper, the *FT*, was entranced: "A prudent hand to those in need," it cooed.'

Index